D0886579

LITERARY PRESENTATIONS
OF DIVIDED GERMANY

ANGLICA GERMANICA SERIES 2

Editors: LEONARD FORSTER, S. S. PRAWER, AND
A. T. HATTO

Other books in the series

D. Prohaska: Raimund and Vienna: A Critical Study of Raimund's plays in their Viennese Setting

D. G. Mowatt: Friedrich von Hûsen: Introduction, Text, Commentary and Glossary

C. Lofmark: Rennewart in Wolfram's 'Willehalm': A Study of Wolfram von Eschenbach and his Sources

A. Stephens: Rainer Maria Rilke's 'Gedichte an die Nacht'

M. Garland: Hebbel's Prose Tragedies: An Investigation of the Aesthetic Aspects of Hebbel's Dramatic Language

H. W. Cohn: Else Lasker-Schüler: The Broken World

J. M. Ellis: Narration in the German Novelle: Theory and Interpretation

M. B. Benn: The Drama of Revolt: A Critical Study of Georg Büchner

J. Hibberd: Salomon Gessner: His Creative Achievement and Influence

LITERARY PRESENTATIONS OF DIVIDED GERMANY

THE DEVELOPMENT OF A CENTRAL THEME IN EAST GERMAN FICTION

1945–1970

PETER HUTCHINSON

*Assistant Lecturer in German in the
University of Cambridge
and Fellow of Selwyn College*

CAMBRIDGE UNIVERSITY PRESS

CAMBRIDGE

LONDON · NEW YORK · MELBOURNE

Published by the Syndics of the Cambridge University Press
The Pitt Building, Trumpington Street, Cambridge CB2 1RP
Bentley House, 200 Euston Road, London NW1 2DB
32 East 57th Street, New York, NY 10022, USA
296 Beaconsfield Parade, Middle Park, Melbourne 3206, Australia

© Cambridge University Press 1977

First published 1977

Printed in Great Britain by
Western Printing Services Ltd, Bristol

Library of Congress Cataloguing in Publication Data

Hutchinson, Peter, 1944–
    Literary presentations of divided Germany
    (Anglica Germanica: Series 2)
    Bibliography: p.
    Includes index.
    1. German literature – Germany, East – History and
criticism. I. Title. II. Series.
PT3707.H8   833'.9'1409   76–51414
ISBN 0-521-21609-5

CONTENTS

PREFACE

This study is a slightly modified version of a doctoral dissertation submitted in 1974 to the University of London. I should again like to express my warmest thanks to my research supervisor, Dr John White, who gave so freely of his time, encouragement, and highly constructive criticism at all stages of my work. It is also a pleasure to record my debt to Professor Siegbert Prawer, under whose guidance my research plans were initially conceived and who read the final manuscript in his capacity as Editor of the *Anglica Germanica* Series. His thorough scrutiny and his apt suggestions have considerably benefited the present volume, and the same holds true of the work done by my internal examiner for the Ph.D. examination, Dr Philip Brady. All three of the above have gone far beyond normal expectations in their advice and in their extension of scholarly friendship.

The Editors of *Forum for Modern Language Studies* and *Modern Language Review* have kindly granted permission for me to use several pages of Chapter Four which first appeared in their journals.

Finally, my thanks are due to a number of scholars in the field of *Germanistik*, in Selwyn College, in the country as a whole, and also abroad, who have generously replied to my wide-ranging queries with both promptness and courtesy.

Selwyn College, Cambridge P. H.
September 1976

1. INTRODUCTION

The concept of 'Germany' may still have some geographical significance, but the word can no longer be used in a political context without further qualifications. Radically different states currently exist within the German territories as they stood in 1937, and the likelihood of these ever being reunited is now internationally recognised as highly remote. It is, however, only comparatively recently that this view has come to prevail in the West: for almost twenty-five years following the Second World War Western politicians stubbornly maintained that the various parts of the former *Reich* comprised a single nation which had been temporarily divided by the victorious Allies. For most of the fifties, in fact, there was a certain confidence that some of these parts would one day be reunited, and when in the sixties it became clear that areas to the East of the Oder–Neiße line would unquestionably remain as Russian or Polish territory, there was still a firm hope that the Federal and Democratic Republics would be able to re-establish the German nation. Such hope was based on considerable illusion, and it was not until the election of Chancellor Willy Brandt (in 1969) that the Federal Republic began to adopt a more realistic attitude towards a state it preferred not to recognise. As a consequence, it was only in the early seventies that the impossibility of any form of German reunification became fully apparent to Western Europe as a whole.[1]

[1] There is a large number of studies of German history between 1945 and 1970, many of which devote considerable space to inter-German relations. One of the best compilations of dates and documents is that edited by Paul Reichelt, *Deutsche Chronik 1945 bis 1970. Daten und Fakten aus beiden Teilen Deutschlands*. Two useful interpretative studies are those by Herbert Lilge (*Deutschland 1945–1963*) and Ernst Deuerlein (*Deutschland 1963–1970*), both of which contain extensive bibliographies. Perhaps the most readable of all histories is that by Alfred Grosser, *L'Allemagne de notre temps 1945–1970* (also available in English as *Germany in Our Time*). The most reliable and up-to-date study of political developments in East Germany is that by Kurt Sontheimer and Wilhelm Bleek, *Die DDR. Politik, Gesellschaft,*

Naturally, the division of the German nation into two increasingly incompatible states provided writers in both East and West with an important and highly controversial theme. In the Democratic Republic (GDR) 'division' was early recognised as crystallising certain crucial global issues. Writers were therefore officially exhorted to depict its social, economic, and moral effects upon both parts of the nation. In the Federal Republic such direct governmental pressure was obviously lacking, but the importance of the issue was nevertheless emphasised by both authors and critics alike. Innumerable West German reports of daring escapes from the East also served to give the subject a strong emotional appeal, and Western hostility was further intensified by regular reports of East German oppression, injustice, and poverty. A further factor which undoubtedly promoted interest in this theme, on both sides of the Iron Curtain, has considerably diminished in importance over the last decade; but during the fifties and early sixties there was a deep awareness that the division of Germany – and in particular that of Berlin – constituted a serious threat to world peace.

The response of German writers to the division of their nation was considerable – particularly in the Democratic Republic. In the years immediately after 1945 writers in East and West generally restricted themselves to simple attacks on their counterparts, and this tendency to deal with division mainly by denigrating the other part of the nation persisted throughout the fifties. In the early sixties, however, a number of authors began to explore more carefully the consequences of differing economic and social structures for the respective parts of the German nation, and it is in the sixties too that most of the best works on this subject were written. Most of these were novels, and it is with them that my main interest will lie in this volume. But fiction is not the only genre in which the subject has been treated: it has also appeared in poetry, in drama, in radio and in television plays.

Wirtschaft (this too is available in English as *The Government and Politics of East Germany*).

It is curious that despite the prominence of 'divided Germany' as a theme in post-war literature, literary critics have repeatedly failed to recognise its importance. Some have even maintained that it has been much neglected by prose writers, in spite of the obvious attraction it would hold for their readers. Helmut Winter, for example, confesses himself baffled by what he considers to be the relative scarcity of the topic: 'It is astonishing that the theme "divided Germany" has been so seldom used by writers in East and West.'[2] Even Walter Jens, one of the most widely read of West German critics, has lamented that so few have treated the most important issue for contemporary German literature. Applauding Uwe Johnson's *Das dritte Buch über Achim*, which offers one of the most perceptive investigations to date, Jens declared:

Fünfzehn Jahre lang haben die Kritiker nun darüber gegrübelt, warum ausgerechnet das Thema der Themen, das Kardinal-Problem jedes deutschen Schriftstellers: die Teilung des Landes, nicht gestaltet worden sei...Das Thema bedurfte eines großen Schriftstellers, und ich glaube, daß der Autor, der jetzt als erster das Kardinal-Problem auf der Ebene der Kunst analysiert hat, ein solcher Schriftsteller ist.[3]

Jens's point is that all previous works have been failures in terms of 'Gestalt', but he refers to only two of these.[4] This is, however, more creditable than Hans Magnus Enzensberger, whose review of the same book refers to only one other work, one in which he admits the theme is clearly peripheral! Enzensberger expresses indignation that writers have neglected this vital issue for so long:

Dieses Thema, das auf der Hand liegende, das zentrale, zum Himmel

---

[2] 'East German Literature', p. 268.
[3] 'Uwe Johnson auf der Schwelle der Meisterschaft', p. 18.
[4] I.e. 'Zwerenz' Reportagen über das Leben in der DDR, handfest und grimmig, oder Gaisers redliche Verschlüsselungen (Graubünden als Marmorklippen-Modell des zerspalteten Deutschland)', loc. cit., p. 18. Jens is presumably referring to Zwerenz's *Ärgernisse. Von der Maas bis an die Memel* and to Gaiser's *Am Paß Nascondo*. The link between Gaiser's fantasy world (influenced, as Jens points out, by Ernst Jünger's *Auf den Marmorklippen*) and the situation of divided Germany is rather slight.

schreiende Thema der deutschen Teilung hat zehn Jahre lang auf seinen Autor gewartet...Die Tatsache, daß es zwei Deutschland gibt, ist bisher nur in einem einzigen Buch unserer Literatur, dem *Steinernen Herz* von Arno Schmidt, und auch dort nur am Rande, in Erscheinung getreten.[5]

Such misconceptions may be mitigated by the date of their formulation (1961), but it is more difficult to understand those made between six and ten years later, during which period the corpus of fiction to deal with division had greatly increased. 'Wohl nur ein einziger Autor, Uwe Johnson, hat sich bis jetzt in Westdeutschland dem Thema des geteilten Landes gewidmet ...' writes Guy Stern.[6] Hans Popper has been more guarded: 'Uwe Johnson is *reputedly* the first novelist to choose the divided Germany as his theme.'[7]

It is unfortunate that this view should have prevailed so long, for many writers dealt with the problems of division several years before Johnson, in the East as well as in the West. The myth of its total absence may well have arisen from the decision of the leading writers – including Böll, Frisch, and Grass – not to treat it.

Peter Jokostra, an Eastern refugee, has displayed a better acquaintance with the literature in question. Reviewing Hans-Christian Kirsch's *Deutschlandlied*, he commented:

Eine ganze Reihe von Autoren – so Uwe Johnson, Gerhard Zwerenz, Jochen Ziem, Joachim Burkhardt – hat sich mit mehr oder weniger Erfolg dem Problem des 'geteilten Himmels' – wie Christa Wolf die gesamtdeutsche Misere apostrophierte – gestellt.[8]

Johnson, Zwerenz, Burkhardt and Christa Wolf have certainly made the divided nation a central theme of their work,

---

[5] 'Die große Ausnahme', p. 235.

[6] 'Prolegomena zu einer Studie der deutschen Nachkriegsliteratur', p. 248. Stern continues as follows: '...wenn man von den ganz jungen wie Margarete Narwick [sic] und G. de Bruyn absehen will'. Günter de Bruyn is, of course, an East German writer.

[7] Entry on Johnson in *Twentieth Century German Literature*, edited by August Closs, p. 290 [My italics].

[8] 'Außenseiter hüben wie drüben', p. 6.

but Ziem considers the East alone in his fiction. It is therefore hardly accurate to classify him as a writer concerned with *division*. Although it can be argued that any author who writes about the East for a Western audience is implicitly treating the subject, the main concern of this volume will lie with those who have depicted both East and West within a single work.

Several other commentators have not appreciated the true range of literature which has dealt with this subject. Ekkerhard Kloehn, for example, suggests his article on Christa Wolf's *Der geteilte Himmel* is intended for a study of 'Die Teilung Deutschlands im Blickwinkel der Literatur in Ost und West', but he only discusses two other novels apart from that which gives him his title.[9] Wilhelm Voßkamp considers the theme a key one in modern literature:

Überblickt man die Gegenwartsliteratur unter dem Aspekt der beiden zentralen zeitgeschichtlichen Motive ('Drittes Reich'; allgemeine und deutsche Ost-West-Situation), läßt sich insgesamt eine breite Skala von Darstellungsmöglichkeiten...beobachten,[10]

yet he nevertheless quotes only the familiar works by Johnson (*Mutmaßungen über Jakob*), Kant (*Die Aula*), Christa Wolf (*Der geteilte Himmel*), and Grass's play on 17 June 1953: *Die Plebejer proben den Aufstand*.

While these critics may not claim their approach is exhaustive, they do not, on the other hand, state that they are dealing with selected representative works. Indeed, the boldness of their titles and formulations leads one to expect considerably more illustrations than are actually advanced. The same can be said of Werner Brettschneider's section 'Das nationale Bewußtsein' in *Zwischen literarischer Autonomie und Staatsdienst. Die Literatur in der DDR*. Referring to the issue of 'Republikflucht' in East German novels, the author writes:

[9] I.e. Uwe Johnson's *Das dritte Buch über Achim* and Erwin Strittmatter's *Ole Bienkopp* – in 'Christa Wolf: *Der geteilte Himmel*. Roman zwischen sozialistischem Realismus und kritischem Sozialismus'.
[10] *Deutsche Zeitgeschichte in der Gegenwartsliteratur*, p. 7.

Eine Anzahl von Werken geringeren Ranges haben das Problem zu einem Schema simplifiziert, das der offiziellen Propaganda entsprach: A. Der nach Westen Gehende erfährt die westdeutsche Wirklichkeit und kehrt geheilt in den ostdeutschen Musterstaat zurück. (J. Kupsch *Gefährlicher Sommer* [1955], H. Hauptmann *Ivi* [1969], Ch. Johannsen *Flug nach Zypern* [1969], M. Meng *Eine Tüte Erdnüsse* [1969] B. Die Liebenden entscheiden sich, von Westdeutschland enttäuscht, nach einigem Hin und Her für den progressiven Osten (J. Brězan *Eine Liebesgeschichte* [1963], Inge von Wangenheim *Du bist nicht mehr allein* [1960]). (p. 273)

To select four examples of the first category and only two of the second hardly justifies Brettschneider's claim that there is 'eine Anzahl von Werken' on this subject. But the most surprising feature of the above is the author's actual choice, for neither Hauptmann's *Ivi* nor Christa Johannsen's *Flug nach Zypern* are concerned with escape to West Germany!

Hermann Boeschenstein's more recent survey has revealed a far better acquaintance with the material in question. In 'Zur Erzähl-Thematik in der Literatur der DDR' he first considers anti-Western elements of the 'Erziehungs- und Heimkehrer-romane' (such as Günter de Bruyn's *Der Hohlweg* and Dieter Noll's *Die Abenteuer des Werner Holt*) before moving on to authors whose works are more centrally concerned with the divided nation: Wolfgang Joho, Ruth Kraft, Hanna-Heide Kraze, Brigitte Reimann, and Christa Wolf. Boeschenstein is mainly concerned with indicating the content and general ideological tendencies of the books he discusses, and he restricts himself to works published in the mid-sixties. Given this limitation, his essay contains helpful and reliable analyses of several significant volumes, some of which have not been considered by any other commentators.[11]

---

[11] A number of other critics have failed to appreciate the prominence of this theme. Horst Bienek, for example, considers Johnson's *Mutmaßungen über Jakob* the first novel to treat division (*Werkstattgespräche mit Schriftstellern*, p. 102), as does W. G. Cunliffe ('Uwe Johnson's Anti-Liberalism', p. 19), who uncritically adopts the opinion of Herbert Ahl (*Literarische Portraits*, p. 7). Writing on *Der geteilte Himmel*, W. Meyer-Erlach states that the 'theme has been treated in many variations' ('The Cultural Scene

Not surprisingly, studies devoted specifically to the literary presentation of a divided Germany are rare. Apart from that by Kloehn mentioned above, there is Rudolf Walter Leonhardt's 'Die deutsche Teilung in Literatur und Kunst', a largely journalistic survey which is concerned more with the separate development of literature in East and West rather than with works actually portraying division. These are considered only briefly, and again it is only the well-known novels that are mentioned. Lothar von Balluseck's 'Die guten und die bösen Deutschen. Das Freund-Feind-Bild im Schrifttum der DDR' is devoted mainly to 'Kinder-, Jugend-, Unterhaltungs- und Trivialliteratur' and deals only peripherally with what the author terms 'die anspruchsvollere Belletristik'. More informative is Wilhelm Jacobs' 'Das zweigeteilte Deutschland' (in his *Moderne deutsche Literatur*). Besides analysing the work of Johnson, the author refers to 'Hörspiele' by Gerd Oelschlegel, Richard Hey, and Claus Hubalek; to Arno Schmidt's *Das steinerne Herz*, and to Gerhard Zwerenz's *Ärgernisse. Von der Maas bis an die Memel*. By far the best study to date, however, is that by Manfred Leier, 'Die deutsche Teilung – literarisch'. This makes reference to various prose writers (Strittmatter, Wolf, Anna Seghers, Johnson, Reimann, Fries), dramatists (Hammel, Meichsner, Gustav von Wangenheim, Zinner, Keller, Pfeiffer), and writers of radio plays (Hammel, Meichsner). There are, however, far more works dealing with division than Leier has here suggested.

Most of the fiction which depicts a divided Germany is to be found in the literature of the GDR. It is therefore hardly surprising that the majority of West German critics should be less familiar with this particular field. Yet the fact that East German critics too have named very few works in their discussions of

in Germany Today', p. 176), yet he names no other examples. Frank Trommler makes an identical claim with reference to the literature written between *Der geteilte Himmel* and Manfred [sic] Heiduczek's *Abschied von den Engeln* ('Der zögernde Nachwuchs. Entwicklungsprobleme der Nachkriegsliteratur in Ost und West', p. 82), but he too names no other work.

this theme is decidedly odd. Hans-Joachim Geisthardt, for example, entitles one of his studies 'Das Thema der Nation und zwei Literaturen', which clearly suggests that the author's interests are broad; but he in fact only considers two novels, Johnson's *Mutmaßungen über Jakob* and Christa Wolf's *Der geteilte Himmel*. The claims he makes for the representative value of these works are undercut by his not naming further examples or demonstrating in what way they are representative. Erika Hinckel's 'Zwei deutsche Staaten und die Perspektive der deutschen Nationalliteratur' concentrates more on the relationship between novels written in East and West and the respective societies in which they were written (the main reason for her study being published in the sociologically orientated periodical *Einheit*, an official organ of the 'ZK der SED'); but she too names only a few novelists, as does Klaus Hermsdorf in 'Die nationale Bedeutung der sozialistischen Nationalliteratur'. The Party's official history of GDR literature, 'Skizze zur Geschichte der deutschen Nationalliteratur von den Anfängen bis zur Gegenwart', quotes only the well-known works by Jurij Brězan, Brigitte Reimann, and Christa Wolf,[12] and even a critic like Heinz Plavius, writing as late as 1976, has claimed that:

---

[12] It should, in fairness, be added that the authors give considerably more titles of works written in the West. The plays by Oelschlegel (*Romeo und Julia in Berlin, Die tödliche Lüge*), Günter Rudorf (*Die Stunde der Unschuldigen*), Wolfgang Altendorf (*Die Schleuse*), and Dieter Meichsner (*Besuch aus der Zone*) are mentioned, as well as novels by Wolfdietrich Schnurre (*Das Los unserer Stadt*), Martin Gregor-Dellin (*Der Nullpunkt*), Eckart Kroneberg (*Der Grenzgänger*), Manfred Esser (*Das Duell* [*sic*]), and Hans-Christian Kirsch (*Die zweite Flucht*). This discrepancy between the number of works given for East and West may be seen in the fact that these sections of the 'Skizze' were actually written by two West Germans (Kurt Ludwig Tank and Wilhelm Jacobs), a point which has come to light only through republication of the relevant passages in *Geschichte der deutschen Literatur aus Methoden*, edited by H. L. Arnold. (See in particular Vol. 1, pp. 82 and 88.) Esser's *Duell* is not, incidentally, concerned with divided Germany; nor is Gregor-Dellin's *Der Nullpunkt*.

A new official history of East German literature appeared while the present volume was in press: *Literatur der DDR*, edited by Horst Haase et al., an exhaustive survey of Eastern publications since 1945. Although

Ein erstaunliches und besorgniserregendes Phänomen ist. . .die Tatsache, daß in unserer Situation die Entwicklung zweier deutscher Staaten und die daraus entwachsenden Probleme und Auseinandersetzungen um die nationale Frage keinen oder zumindest einen immer geringer werdenden Raum einnimmt.[13]

Despite such widespread critical underestimation, 'divided Germany' functions as the central theme in a large number of contemporary novels and features as a peripheral motif in many more. It can, in fact, be argued that this is the most common specific theme in East German writing up to 1970. For although there are a number of broader themes, including the Third Reich, the war, the 'Aufbau', the 'worker', problems of adjustment to socialist life, and the individual and society in the GDR, no other topic has been treated over such a long period and in so many genres as that of the divided nation. In defence of the critics, it might be argued that not all of these works are of a high standard and that they are therefore unlikely to have come to the attention of most scholars. I hope to make it clear, however, that this topic has embraced far more works of distinction than has thus far been assumed.

It was inevitable that the problems of a divided Germany should soon preoccupy writers in the GDR. In socialist ideology literature is viewed primarily as a political weapon in the class struggle and the development towards a Communist utopia.[14] It is therefore expected to reflect current political problems as well as to indicate solutions to them. One of the first 'problems' of the new Eastern state was its Western neighbour, which, 'imperialist controlled' and 'restorationist' as it supposedly was, represented an immediate threat to peace. Political attacks

the authors cover a number of 'anti-imperialist' works which deal with the situation in West Germany (see in particular pp. 198–205; 328–93; 548–91), here too there is no discussion of literature which treats the presentation of a divided nation.

13 'Tendenzen und Probleme der Prosa', p. 36.
14 For further details, see Appendix.

on the Western Zones of Occupation (and later the Federal Republic) therefore began almost immediately after the division of Berlin in 1945.

If writers did not of their own accord choose 'the West' as a theme, then they were encouraged to do so by the political leadership. Not only did the politicians attack features of governmental policy in the West, but they also made repeated reference to West German culture. An early example of this is the Central Committee's famous resolution of 1951, the central document of the so-called 'Kampf gegen den Formalismus in Kunst und Literatur, für eine fortschrittliche deutsche Kultur'.[15] Here the immoral, 'formalist' art of the Federal Republic was vigorously denounced and writers were encouraged to support the exposure of imperialism and West German remilitarisation. The same approach was evident at the Third 'Deutscher Schriftstellerkongreß' of 1952, where the final manifesto was again directed principally against Western imperialism.

Walter Ulbricht's paper of the Fourth Writers' Conference (1956) once more stressed the importance of writers' work in the political struggle. Referring to tokens of friendship between Russia, China, and India, he commented:

Die Schriftsteller können sagen, daß sie einen bedeutenden Beitrag zu diesen Erfolgen der Friedensbewegung geleistet haben. Wir richten deshalb an Sie als Schriftsteller die Bitte, in Ihren Anstrengungen nicht nachzulassen, die Kraft des Wortes einzusetzen, um die Volksbewegung für die Sicherung des Friedens und gegen die NATO und die Remilitarisierung Westdeutschlands weiter tatkräftig zu fördern...*Es ist die gemeinsame Aufgabe der Schriftsteller in der Deutschen Demokratischen Republik und der friedliebenden Schriftsteller in Westdeutschland, die imperialistische Kriegspolitik der herrschenden Kreise in Bonn allseitig zu enthüllen, damit die Militaristen isoliert und die Kräfte des Friedens*

---

[15] This resolution, the 'Entschließung des Zentralkomitees der Sozialistischen Einheitspartei Deutschlands, angenommen auf der V. Tagung vom 15. bis 17. März 1951', is most readily available in Elimar Schubbe's collection of documents relating to SED policy, *Dokumente zur Kunst-, Literatur- und Kulturpolitik der SED, 1945–1971*, pp. 178–86.

und der Demokratie in Westdeutschland zur ausschlaggebenden Kraft werden.[16]

The final proclamation of this Conference re-emphasised the point:

...Jeder Roman, jedes Schauspiel, jedes Gedicht und jedes andere literarische Werk, in dem ein beliebiges Thema künstlerisch so gestaltet wird, daß es zu einer Waffe gegen die westdeutsche Restauration des Militarismus und für die friedliche Wiedervereinigung Deutschlands wird, hat Anspruch auf unsere besondere Förderung...[17]

Some ten years later the attitude towards the West was basically unchanged. At the '11. Plenum der ZK der SED' (1965) Ulbricht again drew attention to the role of the writer in the struggle against West Germany:

Der Schriftsteller, der Künstler und der Publizist stehen vor der Aufgabe, Kunstwerke von nationaler Bedeutung zu schaffen unter den Bedingungen des umfassenden Aufbaus des Sozialismus in der DDR, mit all seinen komplizierten Erscheinungen, die mit der Spaltung Deutschlands und der allmählichen Entwicklung des sozialistischen Weltsystems zusammenhängen. Gleichzeitig steht er der imperialist- ischen Machtpolitik des westdeutschen Staates, dessen antagonistischen Widersprüchen und dessen Druck auf das geistige Leben in West- deutschland gegenüber. Und wenn ein westdeutscher Schriftsteller fragt: 'Was ist die nationale Wahrheit?', so antworten wir: Die nationale Wahrheit ist, daß der Sozialismus in der Deutschen Demokratischen Republik siegt und die demokratischen Kräfte in Westdeutschland die Macht des Militarismus und der Konzernherrschaft überwinden werden, damit ein einheitliches, friedliches und fortschrittliches Deutschland erwächst.[18]

Encouragement to writers did not come from the politicians alone, however: *Neue Deutsche Literatur (NDL)*, the official organ of the East German 'Schriftstellerverband', also played a substantial role, particularly during the critical years 1959–1961. It was then that the Federal Republic was coming under increasing attack for its neo-Nazi policy, and it was also at this

---

[16] Quoted from Schubbe, op. cit., p. 422 [Italics in original].
[17] Schubbe, op. cit., p. 426.
[18] 'Zu einigen Fragen der Literatur und Kunst', p. 5.

point that its image reached a nadir in the press as that of the most despicable capitalist state in Europe. The attack was strongest in the regular, propagandist articles in *Neues Deutschland* (the official organ of the Socialist Unity Party), but *NDL* followed this lead by featuring a number of investigations into West German literature. During the eighteen months which preceded the erection of the Berlin Wall, *NDL* also gave clear prominence to articles, short stories, and extracts from larger works in which the West played a significant role. The Editor at this point, Wolfgang Joho (himself a writer), expressed a personal interest in the subject, and referred to it in 1959 in the following terms:

Die künstlerische und ideologische Auseinandersetzung mit Westdeutschland, die Darstellung des Verhältnisses zwischen Ost und West und der Konflikte, die sich aus der Zweiteilung unseres Vaterlandes ergeben, gehört zu den wichtigsten Aufgaben der Schriftsteller unserer Republik.[19]

The importance of national issues (i.e. those embracing East and West) was further emphasised in one of his lead articles of 1961, 'Unsere nationale Aufgabe'. Like West German critics at this time, Joho here bemoaned the fact that so few had turned to such a crucial theme:

Es ist eine bedauerliche Tatsache, daß eines der zentralen Themen unserer Gegenwartsliteratur, nämlich die Auseinandersetzung mit den hundertfältigen Problemen der geteilten Nation, noch immer unter 'ferner liefen' rangiert. (p. 11)

But possibly the most revealing example of how writers were encouraged to depict the West is to be found in the *Handbuch für schreibende Arbeiter* (edited by Ursula Steinhaußen, *et al.*), a manual for workers who indulge in writing as a serious hobby. In the section 'Worüber schreiben wir?' the authors suggest among other topics 'internationale Solidarität und Kampf gegen den westdeutschen Imperialismus' (p. 61), while in the section

---

[19] 'Blickpunkt Westen', p. 133.

on political cabaret the potential form of such attack is delimited:

Bedeutsam wäre beispielsweise die Enthüllung der Methoden, mit denen Bonn gegen das sozialistische Lager und besonders gegen unsere Republik arbeitet, oder auch der Methoden, mit denen der westdeutsche Bürger manipuliert wird. Dabei muß unser Publikum aber in seiner Erlebnissphäre angesprochen werden.

Die sogenannte West-Thematik wäre jedoch zu eng betrachtet, wollten wir darunter nur bestimmte Erscheinungen und Situationen in Westdeutschland sehen. Die Anfälligkeit mancher DDR-Bürger gegenüber der ideologischen Infiltration, die falsche Einschätzung des äußeren Bildes westdeutscher Städte, die Überbewertung von Einzelerscheinungen des westdeutschen Lebens und ähnliches gehören dazu. Besonders wirksam ist es, im Programm die Gestaltung solcher Erscheinungen bei DDR-Bürgern mit der Darstellung westdeutscher Probleme zu koppeln.

Für die Behandlung westdeutscher Probleme ist jedoch unerläßlich, daß sich der Textautor und auch die Gruppe ständig mit der Strategie und Taktik der Sozialistischen Einheitspartei Deutschlands und unserer Regierung vertraut machen, um diese Politik jederzeit wirksam unterstützen zu können. (pp. 249–50)

These recommendations, published as late as 1969, illustrate the firm continuity of East German policy in many matters concerning the West.

The encouragement of politicians and literary critics was not the only form of stimulus to East German authors. The recurrent politico-historical crises of the fifties must also have firmly drawn writers' attention to this theme. Most importantly, there was the uprising of 17 June 1953, which was denounced in the East as a West-inspired plot,[20] and the frequent 'Berlin crises' of that decade, particularly those of 1959 and 1960. Throughout this period relations between the two states were consistently strained, contact mainly taking the form of propagandist attack. One historical event, however, obviously stands out above all others in offering writers the greatest stimulus: the erection of the Berlin Wall on 13 August 1961. Although the

[20] See, for example, Arnulf Baring, *Uprising in East Germany June 17 1953*, pp. 102 ff.

thematic possibilities of a 'divided Germany' had long been evident (particularly since Anna Seghers' best-selling *Die Entscheidung* of 1959), it was not until division was total that the majority of writers began to deal with its significance for the German nation. For this reason it was around 1962–3 that the number of works on the subject reached a peak, although the topic continued to attract writers throughout the sixties. In 1968, for example, the three best-selling 'serious' books of the year were all centrally concerned with the theme of division: Werner Heiduczek's *Abschied von den Engeln*, Wolfgang Joho's *Das Klassentreffen*, and Anna Seghers' *Das Vertrauen*.

Such attention to the major national problem should certainly have satisfied Eastern politicians, who always showed a keen interest in the subject, but in one respect their concern was highly ironic. Although their aim (as well as that of West German politicians) was supposedly the reunification of Germany, the feasibility of reconciliation was never even hinted at by a single writer, either in East or West. On the contrary, the constant implicit conclusion was that reunification was totally impossible.[21]

The concept of 'division' itself requires some elaboration at this point, for it has always been considered in different ways by the different states, and particularly by certain factions within those states. For members of the West German 'Landsmann-schaften',[22] for example, 'Germany' is still divided into at least

---

[21] Cf. Leier, 'Hinweise auf die Wiedervereinigung finden sich freilich nirgends' (loc. cit. p. 182). Jürgen Rühle is the only other critic to comment similarly. Referring to novels by Eva Müthel, Gerhard Zwerenz and Uwe Johnson, he states:

> Alle drei Schriftsteller bringen Beispiele für die Entfremdung zwischen Ost und West. . .Daß alle drei Schriftsteller die Entfremdung konstatieren, ist ein ernstes und beunruhigendes Signal. ('Schwierigkeiten der Verständigung. Die Interpretation der ostzonalen Wirklichkeit', p. 74)

[22] The 'Landsmannschaften' are associations of refugees or displaced persons from regions to the east of the Oder–Neiße boundary, i.e. from what in 1937 constituted 'Eastern Germany'. These refugees – or 'Heimatvertriebene' as they were known in the West – had their own political party for several

three parts – the Federal Republic, the Democratic Republic (still known to some of them as the 'Soviet Zone of Occupation'), and the former German territories to the East of the Oder–Neiße border with Poland. The West German government now only acknowledges a division into two parts, of course, and so – yet in a more limited sense – does the Democratic Republic. But the question of 'division' has in recent years come to signify something far deeper than the question of frontiers and sovereignty – which was the essence of all earlier inter-German disputes over the so-called 'German Question': it is now rather a question of whether a German 'nation' actually exists (and if it does not, then one obviously cannot speak of a 'divided' nation).

The West unhesitatingly affirms the idea of a continuing nation, albeit split into two parts, and Willy Brandt's comments of 1970 exemplify the current view:

25 Jahre nach der bedingungslosen Kapitulation des Hitler-Reiches bildet der **Begriff der Nation** das Band um das gespaltene Deutschland. Im Begriff der Nation sind geschichtliche Wirklichkeit und politischer Wille vereint. Nation umfaßt und bedeutet mehr als gemeinsame Sprache und Kultur, als Staat und Gesellschaftsordnung. Die Nation gründet sich auf das fortdauernde Zusammengehörigkeitsgefühl der Menschen eines Volkes. Niemand kann leugnen, daß es in diesem Sinn e i n e deutsche Nation gibt und geben wird, soweit wir vorauszudenken vermögen.[23]

The East Germans, however, have modified their conception

years in the fifties and they pressed successive Western governments for firm political action to bring about a return to their homeland. Much of the writing on the situation of the 'Heimatvertriebenen' is emotionally flavoured; Alfred Grosser writes a very balanced account of their problems and activities in *L'Allemagne de notre temps 1945–1970*, pp. 333–41. The membership of the 'Landsmannschaften' has, of course, greatly declined since the late sixties.

[23] 'Bericht zur Lage der Nation', 14 January 1970. [Bold and spaced type as original.] Brandt clearly held these words to be crucial, since he repeats most of the above paragraph in his second 'Bericht zur Lage der Nation' of 28 January 1971. Both speeches are given in full in the *Verhandlungen des Deutschen Bundestages. 6. Wahlperiode. Stenographische Berichte*, Vols. 71 and 74. The passages are to be found on pp. 840 and 5045 respectively.

of the German 'nation' in the course of recent years, and it is rather ironic that they should have done so in response to West German overtures of diplomatic recognition, *détente*, and 'peaceful coexistence'. Although until around 1969 the GDR generally acknowledged the existence of a single nation which had been temporarily divided, it now tends to claim that there are *two* distinct German nations: one socialist, the other bourgeois. Further, the implication is that Germany has always been divided, and that the present border only substantiates a deeper, spiritual division, one which has existed since the beginnings of the class struggle.[24]

The premises of the East German writers I intend to discuss follow (and in many cases, anticipate) the attitude of their leaders, for they also see division as a product of different attitudes rather than simply historical decisions. For them too division was present before 1949, and any sense of unity prior to that date was only illusory. As Franz Fühmann puts it while musing on the period before the foundation of the GDR:

So hatten wir denn unser Bündel gepackt und waren über die Grenze [des Sudetenlandes] gegangen, in den einen Teil Deutschlands und in den anderen Teil Deutschlands, das damals noch eins war *und doch schon gespalten.*[25]

For Fühmann, as indeed for most East German writers, the roots of present division are evident as early as 1933: in the decision for or against fascism.[26] The problems surrounding the

---

24 For further details of inter-German views on the concept of the 'nation', See Wilhelm Bleek and Kurt Sontheimer, *Die DDR. Politik, Gesellschaft, Wirtschaft*, Chapter 10.

25 'Böhmen am Meer', *König Ödipus, p. 397.* [My italics.]

26 Although most East Germans seem to take 1933 as the turning point in German history, others are inclined to see the sense of spiritual division reaching back far further – to the 'Spartakus-Bund' of Rosa Luxemburg and Karl Liebknecht, for example, or even to the nineteenth century. Erich Brehm elaborates this latter idea in his poem 'Zweierlei Deutschland', the opening stanza of which uses a formulation comparable to that of Fühmann:

Was ist des Deutschen Vaterland?
Das Land, das Ost und West erfand?

divided nation are thus not considered as merely 'political' or 'German', but as spiritual and international, embracing the far wider issues of East and West – Communism and Capitalism, Soviet Russia and the USA – rather than those of an individual nation. Such a situation offers, as H. J. Geisthard has pointed out, an important thematic source to the Communist writer:

Dieses eigentümliche Verhältnis [daß die heute in zwei Staaten gespaltene deutsche Nation gegenwärtig auf zwei unterschiedlichen sozialen Entwicklungsstufen existiert], das zugleich mit dem Kampf der beiden Weltsysteme verflochten ist, bedeutet für die Literatur ein großes und erregendes Thema.[27]

In many East German novels the image of a divided Germany often bears little relationship to reality: the image of the West is almost inevitably presented with excessive harshness, while that of the East itself is often idealised. In Stefan Heym's *Schatten und Licht*, for example, the opulence, neo-Nazism and violence of the West is emphasised and exaggerated, and so, on the other hand, is the undeviating conformism and loyalty of East German citizens. The same degree of exaggeration is to be found in practically all the stories and 'Hörspiele' of Karl Heinz Brokerhoff's '*Wie sie uns sehen.' Schriftsteller der DDR über die Bundesrepublik*. Even if a number of pieces in this anthology are based on actual occurrences in the Federal Republic, the manner of their presentation – i.e. *exclusive* attention to negative aspects of Western society – is clearly tendentious. Few writers are prepared to give a total view of the West in which

Ach, Deutschland war ja längst gespalten,
als Ost und West für eins noch galten!
(*Deutsche Teilung*, pp. 121–2)
Gerhard Zwerenz (a refugee from the East) has made the same point with reference to literature: 'Die zweigeteilte deutsche Literatur von heute ist nicht die einfache Folge der geographischen Teilung von 1945: die Wurzeln reichen weiter zurück in die Geschichte'. ('Das gespaltene Wort', p. 82) Zwerenz is the only writer to have acknowledged this openly in the West. To my knowledge it is only East Germans who have made this claim.
27 'Das Thema der Nation. . .', p. 48.

there would be an opportunity to counter-balance weaknesses with positive qualities. The vast majority prefer to concentrate on criticising acknowledged failings, usually aspects of capitalism which have been eradicated in the East. And of those writers who have attempted an epic treatment (Anna Seghers, for example), the presentation is consistently far harsher than circumstances justify.

Although the image of the West presented in East German fiction has naturally been determined by a number of social and ideological factors, it is important to recognise that these factors are by no means as distinctive as might be supposed. A consideration of several examples from English literature will make this quite clear.

Christopher Campos' *The View of France*, Philipp D. Curtin's *The Image of Africa*, and Allen J. Greenberger's *The British Image of India* all investigate the image of another country in the British mind at different times in history. This image, the authors conclude, was only rarely determined by actual circumstances abroad: it was normally developed to conform with English preconceptions, irrational though these often were, and changes in reality were only rarely reflected in it. (Ironically, changes in the political climate of England normally determined the current image of nations abroad.) Greenberger, for example, generalises on the English image of India as follows:

It is events in England, and in the West in general, which determine the image held of India at any particular time. From this it follows that the images were not changed by the Indian reality. It is far more likely that the images have influenced the way in which the reality was seen. The changing images appear to have had little to do with developments in India. (pp. 6–7)

A similar pattern is evident in the East German view of the West and, *mutatis mutandis*, in the West German view of the East. The internal political climate has largely determined – and, more important, still controls – the manner in which events outside each country are interpreted.[28]

[28] This 'internal political climate' naturally embraces such diverse elements as

It might well be expected that the mutual images of East and West Germany could never be quite as inaccurate as, say, that of India and England. A common language and at least some sense of brotherhood would suggest that visitors from the West would detect discrepancies between Western image and Eastern reality. Yet, as Karl Franke's research into the subject has proved, this is far from being the case: travellers, presumably conditioned to expect a specific image of the country they are visiting, seem to be insensitive to aspects which they do not presume to find. The chief reason for this, suggests Franke, is prejudice: 'Vorurteil und Sentimentalität versperren oft die Sicht auf Tatsachen.'[29] All three social historians agree on this point too. Curtin, for example, assesses its significance for the European image of Africa:

[Reporters] were therefore sensitive to data that seemed to confirm their European preconceptions, and they were insensitive to contrary

the press, radio, and schoolbooks, and Horst Siebert's study of a particular aspect of the latter category (*Der andere Teil Deutschlands in Schulbüchern der BRD und der DDR*) provides corroborative evidence for many of the points made in this section. Siebert's exhaustive study of the schoolbook image of East and West also gives considerable insight into the manipulative methods of *both* German states. Charlotte Lütkens and Walther Karle provide further illustrations of the manner in which 'national images' are manipulated in schoolbooks in *Das Bild vom Ausland. Fremdsprachliche Lektüre an höheren Schulen in Deutschland, England und Frankreich*.

R. E. Spiller has discussed some important ways in which creative writing itself can reinforce a distorted image of other nations. He begins his remarks on international misunderstanding with two 'pessimistic premises':

The one is that the literature of national self-examination is more likely than not to become an agent of international misunderstanding; and the other is that nations often read the literature of other nations for self-interested and political rather than intellectual and literary reasons. They tend to choose those books which suit the social and political needs and backgrounds of their own culture at that particular time rather than those which might help them dispassionately to understand the culture of the other nation. Both reader and writer are victims of the oblique light of self-interest rather than the direct light of truth, and the two oblique lights rarely come from the same angle of vision. ('The magic mirror of American fiction. A study of the novel of national self-inquiry as an instrument of international (mis)understanding', pp. 23–4.)

[29] 'Berichte über die DDR – nachgelesen', p. 383.

data...Data that did not fit the existing image were most often simply ignored. (p. 479)

The principle is similar to that of the optical illusion. The eye sees not what it is presented with, but what it expects, or has been accustomed to see.

A far more serious consideration is that even travellers who *are* sensitive to discrepancies rarely find a sympathetic audience when they offer new facts to readers in the West. Uwe Johnson makes this particularly clear in 'Eine Reise wegwohin, 1960', an *Erzählung* which elaborates the attitude held by the unidentified Western questioner of *Das dritte Buch über Achim*. In the earlier work the author brings out West German lack of knowledge concerning the East by making the questioner's queries and comments quite inappropriate to the situation. True, Western ignorance is essentially a secondary theme of the novel and is manifested mainly in the sporadic entries of the questioner, but Johnson clearly held the motif to be an important one, for in the later works it is developed in some depth. Karsch, the West German journalist, returns from a protracted sojourn in the GDR with a new insight into the national problem and with far more tolerance towards the other German state. But no one will believe that the East is different from what they have been led to believe over the last fifteen years, and the final sections of the story are devoted to harsh satire of the obstinacy and hypocrisy which characterise Karsch's journalist colleagues. Their prejudice and fierce hostility to the East, as well as the suspicion of the authorities that he has become a spy, finally lead Karsch to emigrate out of disgust for the political situation. Not only does his newspaper reject his findings ('Sind Sie bei sich...?' – p. 68), but his home is searched ('die polizeiliche Haussuchung mit dem Verdachtstitel Landesverrat' – p. 76), and even the maid hands in her notice, a very neat touch to suggest that the disgust for Karsch spans all classes of society.

Johnson's story provides a literary illustration of Franke's point that new, accurate information is ignored in favour of existing prejudice:

Bei Vergleich der Reiseberichte von 1964 mit der sogenannten Volks-
meinung von 1966 ergibt sich, daß die guten, die wirklichkeitsgetreuen
Berichte offensichtlich beinahe ohne Wirkung geblieben sind, und daß
die mit weniger Gewissenhaftigkeit und Verantwortungsbewußtsein
geschriebenen genau dem Geschmack und dem Vorurteil des breiten
Publikums entsprechen.[30]

The issue here at stake is a general one: the reader's expectations, or, using the psychological term adopted by E. H. Gombrich, his 'mental set'[31] is being challenged. The image of the
East which has been developed in his mind over a number of
years is suddenly called into question by a contradictory image,
which he will naturally be reluctant to assimilate. A tendency
to reject this fresh material will be coupled with a reinforcement
of his extant views.

The concept of the 'mental set' seems to me an important
one, for deep-seated levels of expectation affect not only the
reader's reaction to a work, but above all the writer's method of
composition. Certain East German writers have never visited
the West, for example, and of those who have been able to do
so, few have spent any length of time there. These authors have
nevertheless been able to treat the Federal Republic in their
work (even if it is in many cases used purely as an evil backcloth), simply because there are well-known Western political
stereotypes in the GDR, as well as established literary conventions about depiction of the West. Not surprisingly, therefore,
changes in the official image of the Federal Republic have been
slow, they have reflected developments in the internal East
German climate rather than changes in Western reality, and
they have in general been pioneered in works by the younger
writers. Some of the more important of these changes are referred to in my Conclusion.

The determinants of Eastern and Western 'mental sets' of
the 'other' Germany are obviously wide-ranging, but those
operating in the GDR are more striking and are detailed in the
Appendix: the image of the West current in that country has

[30] Franke, loc. cit., p. 383.   [31] *Art and Illusion*, p. 53.

been largely determined by governmental control of mass media. Cut off from the Federal Republic by restrictions on travel, censorship of mail and a ban on listening to Western broadcasts, the East German populace was for many years obliged to rely on the information provided by a state-controlled radio, TV, newspapers and schoolbooks, all of which provided an image of the West as far removed from reality as was the British image of the Raj. In this respect the GDR citizen's image of other countries follows the established international pattern, whereby internal political circumstances largely determine the view of external events. The difference lies in the fact that whereas one country's image of another normally rests on the attitudes of a (relatively) free press, radio, etc., that of the GDR rests upon the decisions of an ideologically motivated government. A further point is that in the East there are no overt dissenters from the Party line (such as Franke and Johnson in the West) who might be seen to offer an alternative view to the official one. The few who do see the Federal Republic as anything other than hostile are not in a position to voice their views, and the Eastern image of the West therefore remains practically standard and nationally accepted.

In discussing contemporary East German literature it is important to recognise the factors which have determined the Eastern view of the Federal Republic and to appreciate that the particular strength of works on the theme of a 'divided Germany' does not lie in the image which they present. The aim of East German writers is not to propagate new ideas concerning their neighbour, but essentially to reinforce conventional ones. There is consequently little originality in this image: the main qualities – and weaknesses – of the works under discussion lie rather in the means by which it is presented.

This factor simplifies the question of whether emphasis should be placed on a purely literary study of East German fiction or whether a strictly descriptive analysis of the images in question should be undertaken. Since even a cursory reading in this literature reveals close correspondences between the image presented in literature and that propagated by the press and other mass media, the aim of a descriptive study could only be to demonstrate in detail the close connection between literature and political propaganda in a socialist state. This would, in effect, have restricted value, for it would in general only confirm what has long been suspected in the West. It might, of course, also illustrate that East German authors are satisfying the socialist aesthetic demand that literature reflect current political views, but I consider that this task would have only limited import. It can, I feel, be undertaken incidentally to a primarily literary study of these works. East German fiction is, after all, imaginative literature, and to analyse it solely in terms of its ideas, or even social history, would be to accept the narrowness of vulgar Marxist aesthetics and ignore its most distinctive value.

The number of works dealing with the theme of the divided German nation is so considerable that it has been necessary to impose certain practical limitations on the present investigation. This study is restricted mainly to works of East German fiction written between 1945 and 1970, and it can therefore draw only peripherally on the wide range of Eastern and Western dramas, poems, 'Hörspiele' and 'Fernsehspiele' which have also dealt with the subject.

In choosing to exclude dramatic works, I have been influenced partly by the relatively smaller number of plays on the subject, partly by their low quality, and partly, unfortunately, by the unavailability of many texts.[32] The same applies to radio plays and television plays.[33]

[32] A number of such plays are listed by Manfred Leier in 'Die deutsche Teilung – literarisch'. Hans-Dietrich Sander lists a number of 'anti-Western' plays in *Geschichte der Schönen Literatur in der DDR*; see pp. 127, 143, 163.

[33] Leier (loc. cit.) refers to several radio plays, as does Egbert Krispyn in 'The Radioplay in the German Democratic Republic' and Wilhelm Jacobs in 'Das zweigeteilte Deutschland'. Jörg Lingenberg refers to a number of relevant TV plays in *Das Fernsehspiel in der DDR*.

The poetry has been excluded on different grounds, for much of it is of a high standard and many relevant poems are readily available in the collection by Kurt Morawietz, *Deutsche Teilung*. The poets, however, have tended to concentrate on specific aspects of division, such as the border and the increasing lack of communication (in both literal and figurative senses). And although they have done this with insight and pathos, they are inevitably unable to present within a few lines the highly complex nature of the problems that division has brought with it. The formulations of the poets are often succinct and suggestive, and I have on occasion quoted them to convey in a more telling fashion some of the points made by the writers of fiction. On the whole, however, it is only novelists who have been able to investigate in breadth, as well as in depth, the manifold aspects of a divided country.

Finally, the decision to confine my attentions primarily to East German rather than to include West German fiction has been motivated by the much larger number of Eastern works on the subject under discussion, and also the fuller investigation which East Germans have carried out. This notwithstanding, periodic reference has been made to West German works in order to supply an element of contrast, and I have given a general survey of Western novels in the Conclusion. It is perhaps worth noting that no Austrian or Swiss writers seem to have treated this theme – from what might have proved a far more impartial perspective.

The three major means through which authors have investigated a divided Germany can be classified as follows:

(1) THE TRAVELLER

Within the European tradition the figure of the traveller has been employed repeatedly to probe and to criticise various aspects of an alien world. East Germans too have recognised the functional value of a character whose sensitivity is a natural means of unmasking the spiritual weaknesses of the Federal Republic, and the 'traveller' is consequently one of the most recurrent motifs in their writing on the divided nation. While many Europeans have used this figure merely to register impressions, East Germans usually endow their hero with a reflective mind, a high degree of self-consciousness, and a firm moral standpoint. His impressions of the West are always compared explicitly or implicitly with similar features of his own country, and a moral assessment of the other half of the nation is manifest in his observations.

(2) THE REPRESENTATIVE

The tendency to analyse and assess a particular society through a typical representative is yet another traditional technique of the novelist. Perhaps the best known work to attempt such an analysis is Thomas Mann's *Der Zauberberg*, in which a number of figures possess both ideological and national representative function.

GDR writers have frequently depicted characters who are meant to be typical of either East or West and who are involved in a conflict which has ideological implications. The interaction of these figures at this level is seen to have macrocosmic significance, and their individual decisions to reflect those of the society, or 'Weltanschauung' which they represent. Through analysis of character the author can thus warn, criticise or predict in terms of the larger society which is implicitly being presented.

It is important to appreciate that ideologically representative figures need not be citizens of East and West respectively; it is just as likely for them both to be members of the Democratic Republic. As is suggested in the above quotation from the *Handbuch für schreibende Arbeiter* (p. 13), symptoms of Western society can be diagnosed in the GDR, and so too can opponents of socialism. A man's political commitment is not determined by geographical factors. Many authors are thus concerned to bring out the *spiritual* allegiance of their characters, and the way in which the conflict of private individuals can be made to symbolise that of international points of view.

(3) THE RELATIONSHIP OF DIVIDED GERMANY TO THE THIRD REICH

A final method of presenting the two Germanies has been to contrast them in terms of their respective relationship with the Third Reich. This is linked with one of the most insistent points of propaganda: that the Federal Republic is the natural successor to the earlier historical period, while the GDR, on the other hand, is seen to have severed all connections with that shameful era. Writers have therefore sought to reinforce an attitude already established in their reader's mind by illustrating West German restoration and contrasting this (implicitly or explicitly) with the movement towards socialism in the East.

Since East Germans have claimed the roots of division are evident as early as 1933,[34] an important corollary of this view is that any presentation of the Third Reich can be seen as a metaphorical portrayal of the Federal Republic, or at any rate of the mentality which it supposedly vaunts. Further, since the East Germans claim that their state stands for 'anti-fascism' or 'humanism', any clash between fascism and its opponents in the earlier period is by implication related to the present clash between restored fascism in the Federal Republic and the new, humanist society of the GDR. For this reason many war novels are in essence concerned with the issues which now divide the German nation. I shall not be dealing with these in the following investigation, but they are nevertheless relevant to this classification and considerably enlarge the corpus of fiction to deal with my theme.

The following chapters attempt to differentiate some examples

[34] Cf. above, p. 16.

of these motifs and narrative devices by which GDR writers have presented the theme of a divided Germany. As will be clear from the titles which recur in various chapters, a writer does not necessarily restrict himself to a single approach. In *Die Aula*, for example, Kant uses a traveller to investigate the West as well as the clash of symbolic (representative) values to suggest the national conflict as it can be seen in East German society itself. Considering the Federal Republic in terms of the Third Reich is also not an exclusive category, as is obvious from such works as Fries's *Der Weg nach Oobliadooh* and Fühmann's *Böhmen am Meer* (the traveller motif occurs in both). Some novels even feature all three approaches – Seghers' *Die Entscheidung*, Reimann's *Die Geschwister*, and Heiduczek's *Abschied von den Engeln*, for example. In general I have avoided discussing an individual work in more than one chapter,[35] and I have restricted myself to its most prominent motif. Occasional references to this work in other chapters should suffice to illustrate that a number of GDR writers will resort to all means available in order to make their investigation of the Federal Republic as complete as possible.

Each of the above three approaches will be isolated in a separate chapter, where my aim will be to analyse, compare and contrast the varying methods by which individual authors have exploited the potential advantages of what are basically traditional devices. A second aim of the discussions will be to evaluate the rhetorical success of the individual works, which have been chosen in part to illustrate the wide range and quality of writing on this subject. Most of the writers in the GDR are intent upon persuading their readers of the validity of a certain point of view and upon communicating their conviction in an artistically satisfying manner. I should therefore like to consider how

---

[35] The only novel I have considered in depth in two separate chapters is Kant's *Die Aula*, and I have done so for two reasons. First, because it lends itself ideally to the discussion on both occasions, and second, because it has proved the most popular novel – in East and West – to be written on this theme.

successfully these writers have assimilated such potentially disparate aims into a literary achievement and, no less important, how often the failure to incorporate the didactic aim into a convincing narrative has resulted in writing which hardly rises above the level of propaganda.

2. THE TRAVELLER

The figure of the traveller has always been a commonplace of literature. Throughout his long history he has assumed innumerable guises and possessed varying degrees of sensitivity, extending from the ostensibly impartial observer, who is prepared to register his observations without commentary, to the querulous misanthrope, who finds fault with everything he sees. Yet into whichever category he may belong, the traditional itinerant has usually concerned himself with the *mores* of the country he is visiting, and – with the obvious exceptions of Mme de Staël and Heinrich Heine – has rarely devoted much time to politics.[1]

In the literature with which I am concerned, however, the above system of priorities has become inverted. For the East German traveller it is politics – as reflected in society – which command greatest attention. A second respect in which this traveller differs from his literary forbears is in his moral standpoint. He is usually an ordinary citizen but is endowed with a high degree of commonsense and a keen awareness of social responsibility. Such qualities lead to a sustained sense of conflict between him and the society he is visiting, a dialectic which is likely to be appreciated by the East German reader: not only does the traveller tend to be an ideological representative of East German society, but the point of view from which his investigations take place is very close to that of the GDR reading public. A final contrast with tradition lies in the fact that

[1] For the reaction of the German traveller to other nations, see, for example, C. V. Bock, *Deutsche erfahren Holland, 1725–1925. Eine Sammlung von hundert Berichten*, and W. D. Robson-Scott, *German Travellers in England, 1600–1800*. The preoccupations of French travellers seem to be equally unpolitical: Cf. Roy E. Palmer, *French Travellers in England (1600–1900)*. For a full study of the traveller in literature, see H.-J. Possin, *Reisen und Literatur. Das Thema des Reisens in der englischen Literatur des 18. Jahrhunderts*; and for a study of satirical possibilities in this field, see Donna Isaacs Dalnekoff, 'A Familiar Stranger: The Outsider of Eighteenth-Century Satire'.

the traveller's experiences rarely contribute a new element to the Eastern image of the Federal Republic, i.e. the foreign country. As was suggested in the previous chapter, East German writers normally aim to reinforce ideas that are already well-known.

During his period as Chief Editor of *Neue Deutsche Literatur*, Wolfgang Joho regularly pointed out to his colleagues that one of their duties was to depict the problems of the two German states.[2] He himself gave a lead in this respect with *Es gibt kein Erbarmen* (1961), an account of the decline and fall of a half-hearted socialist writer who escapes to the West, and also with his later novel *Das Klassentreffen* (1968), a far more detailed investigation of life in the West as seen through the perspective of a convinced Party member.

The later novel represents one extremity of the range of works which describe the sensations of the traveller and the reactions to him: it is typical of the simple, often crass methods employed by those who rely on discursive commentary rather than the suggestive power of the characters and situations they have depicted. Such commentary is, of course, usually rendered superfluous by the clear nature of the plot, and while it might be appropriate in a work of reportage, it is certainly not in a work of fiction. Joho's documentary *Zwischen Bonn und Bodensee* (1954) is more satisfactory in this respect, the aim here being to report a journey to the West undertaken in the early fifties. Drawing parallels with an earlier period, criticising West German injustice, and moralising in general is acceptable within such a work as this, in which there is no attempt to distance author and narrator. The same applies to Eduard Claudius's *Paradies ohne Seligkeit* (1955), which has much the same scope and employs a similar approach. But in imaginative writing the reader expects less overt methods, however much of an overlap there may be between the author's autobiography

[2] See Chapter 1, p. 12.

and his narrative. Writers who consistently supply their reader with 'assistance' of a direct nature will be denying the latter a sense of participation in the experiences of the narrator-traveller.

As the title of *Das Klassentreffen* suggests, the main event of this novel is a class reunion on the fortieth anniversary of their 'Abitur'. The first-person narrator, a writer who lives in the GDR, returns to his home town in the Federal Republic for the occasion. His aim, as he openly admits, is not really to enjoy himself or to reflect on happy memories of childhood, but to confirm his views about the spiritual nature of the other part of the country. Throughout the novel impressions are registered with precision, and the narrator is unable to refrain from drawing his reader's attention towards what he wishes to emphasise. This is most striking in his use of images, the most important being that of the mask. One of the narrator's immediate impressions of his colleagues is that they are all hiding behind some form of shield when they are in open society. He longs for a glimpse of their real faces and determines to try and discover these:

Ich wünschte, hinter die Masken vor ihren Gesichtern zu sehen, ich sehnte mich nach einem ehrlichen Gespräch...Ich war entschloßen, nicht nach Hause zu fahren, ohne es wenigstens versucht zu haben. (p. 44)

The structure of the novel is determined by this decision. The author visits a number of his schoolmates in personal, informal surroundings and soon finds that these masks have been donned as a form of self-protection. Moreover, they are evident at all levels of society, from that of humble librarian to wealthy managing director.

In addition to the above episode, this imagery is used on five further occasions, while that of the 'Schleier', a variant, occurs twice.[3] Corresponding imagery is that of military defences: citizens of the West are seen to have sought the refuge that various professions could offer them, such as the librarian

---

[3] References to the 'mask' on pp. 44, 47, 52, 87, 151, 165; to the 'veil' on pp. 49, 56.

Bastian, who has taken cover behind his books, a form of 'Schutzmauer' (p. 88), Jochberg, the former Nazi, who has 'unter die Fittiche des Staates gekrochen' (p. 261), the businessman Hägelin, whose desk is a 'Festungswall' (pp. 141, 151), and the cleric Reinacher, whose robes form a 'Schutzpanzer' (p. 49). In each case the author discovers that it is a sense of guilt which has driven these citizens into the defensive role they now play.

Another striking image is that of the confessor. On two occasions the narrator is under the impression he is being considered as a higher spiritual figure. First, as a judge of former conduct, particularly that during the Third Reich: 'Eher bemühten sie sich zu beweisen, wie sauber sie sich gehalten – als sähen sie in dem Mann von drüben so etwas wie einen Gewissensrichter, vor dem sie sich rechtfertigen zu müssen glaubten' (p. 47). And also as a father confessor, who will not only listen patiently to transgressions, but also maintain secrecy: 'Er hatte mir sein Herz ausgeschüttet, so wie sie fast alle mir, dem Fremden von "drüben" gegenüber beredt wurden, als sei ich der Beichtiger, der ihr Geheimnis bewahren würde und vor dem sie nicht ihr Gesicht zu verlieren fürchteten. . .' (p. 87). The extended use of the mask and related images firmly draws attention to the insecurity imputed to the members of West German society, yet although these images are fairly striking in their own right (they are, after all, traditional), the traveller nevertheless frequently draws attention to them, ensuring that the points which have struck him do not escape his reader.

It is in this determination to underline facts which should be self-evident that the chief failing of *Das Klassentreffen* lies. Consistency in imagery is not a common feature of East German prose, and it is therefore likely to be obvious to even the least sensitive of readers in such a context – not least when the images of mask and veil are introduced four times within nine pages, and on each occasion they are used in conjunction with the same verb – 'lüften'![4] By employing these images with such

[4] I.e. pp. 47, 49, 52, 56.

regularity and forcefulness Joho is undermining the suggestive value they would otherwise have possessed, and the same applies to two other motifs of the novel: the burden of the past (already prefigured in the motto – '*Die Vergangenheit ist niemals tot. Sie ist nicht einmal vergangen.* William Faulkner'), and the spiritual bankruptcy of West German citizens. Both are featured far more frequently and insistently than is artistically justifiable in a work of fiction, and their presence is all the more striking owing to the very fact that they are commonplaces of Eastern propaganda. Joho overdraws characters and situations simply, it seems, in order to bring out even further what are already recognised as undisputed moral weaknesses. Such faults as these are, unfortunately, common in works by the older generation as a whole, and in this respect *Das Klassentreffen* is typical. The later novels of Anna Seghers, for example, Inge von Wangenheim's *Du bist nicht mehr allein*, and Ernst Schuhmacher's 'Bundeswehrleutnant 1962' all suggest that the authors' depiction of the traveller's experiences is subordinate to their political intentions.

A more sophisticated technique is evident in Manfred Meng's *Eine Tüte Erdnüsse*. Meng too makes use of a first-person narrator, but he employs a completely different perspective: first, his hero is an immature adolescent; and second, he is a defector from the GDR. The latter's attitude to the West is consequently far different from that of the mature and politically committed narrator of *Das Klassentreffen*, although the function which he performs – in relation to the reader – is basically the same.

Like the traveller, the refugee can easily function as a critic of the country to which he has fled. Martin Berg, the hero of *Eine Tüte Erdnüsse*, begins as a defector but becomes so critical of life in the West that he eventually decides to return to the East. (The same applies to the hero of Klaus Steinhaußen's 'Kähling kehrt zurück'.) Yet far more important than his developing criticism is the defector's initial *suppression* of commentary. Defectors are constantly surprised by various aspects of the West which they find objectionable, which they had not expected, or which are present to a much greater degree than Eastern propaganda has led them to believe. (These are, incidentally, typical reactions of actual refugees.)[5] And although they try to make light of such disturbing features, their feelings and experiences may well be more cautionary than those of the socialist traveller himself. Unlike the latter, the defector is obviously loath to make comparisons that would be favourable to the land he has left; the reader, on the other hand, is likely to be very much alive to such suppressions.

Martin Berg's experiences in the West follow the standard pattern: apparently hearty reception, congratulations on escape, and then the reality of the first 'Flüchtlingslager'.[6] This is succeeded by interrogation, the transit camp, further interrogation, long periods of boredom and disappointment, and finally, the airlift to the Federal Republic. But once again there is a hated camp, and it is only several months after leaving the GDR that Martin actually begins work in the West. There is a strong sense of dramatic irony throughout these scenes, and Meng is relying on his reader appreciating the folly of Martin's naive hopes – his feeling that the Federal Republic is in all respects

---

[5] See, for example, *Ich bin Bürger der DDR und lebe in der Bundesrepublik. 12 Interviews*, edited by Barbara Grunert-Bronnen. Some of the more revealing of these interviews were featured in *Der Spiegel* under the title 'Sehnsucht nach dem Kollektiv. DDR-Flüchtlinge über ihre Erfahrungen in der Bundesrepublik'.

[6] The Spartan conditions of the transit and refugee camps are described in a number of novels, obviously as a further form of discouragement to potential defectors. Brigitte Reimann's *Die Geschwister*, for example, Hasso Laudon's *Semesterferien in Berlin*, and Fritz Rudolf Fries's *Der Weg nach Oobliadooh* all depict the grim nature of camp life and the unsympathetic attitude of the interrogators. The camp described briefly in Johnson's *Mutmaßungen über Jakob* is equally bleak, although novels by West Germans proper (rather than those who have fled there) suggest a different view. In Daniel Christoff's *Schaukelstühle*, for example, the only complaint against camp life is that it is boring, while Herbert Plate's *Das soll der Mensch nicht scheiden* refers to the friendly atmosphere in the camp and the speed with which the officials are able to deal with refugees.

superior to the East and that those in the West really care for him, despite all indications to the contrary. To the innocent Martin, all in West Berlin at first appear friendly and helpful; the reader, however, easily recognises their cynicism and contempt. By choosing an adolescent, who still has some belief in human goodness, Meng gives his satire a tragic note. Martin's disillusionment is a slow and slightly pathetic process, which culminates in the realisation he must be ruthless in his treatment of others if he is to succeed in West German society.

Martin describes and relates, but he rarely comments, and it is through this that Meng induces the reader to draw his own conclusions. The moral is illustrated in terms of plot and character and not, as in *Das Klassentreffen*, through direct statement or excessively pointed imagery.

Like most defectors, Martin escapes through West Berlin, a city which has always been a key target of East German propaganda. This section of the former capital was, of course, that part of 'the West' which GDR citizens were most likely to see until 1961, and there was therefore little point in suggesting it presented anything other than a sharp contrast to the drabness of East Berlin. For this reason the affluence of the 'besondere politische Einheit Westberlin' was made out to be even greater than was actually the case, but at the same time there were warnings that the city was a show-case erected solely to provoke the GDR, with its adverts and its exotic night-life functioning as a deliberate means of seducing East Germans into defection. This den of vice ('Sündenbabel' as it is referred to in Joachim Wohlgemuth's *Verlobung in Hullerbusch*, p. 181) was also constantly referred to as the centre for a large number of Western spies (again reflected in literature as an 'Agentenzentrale' in Heiduczek's *Abschied von den Engeln* (p. 304) and also, satirically, in the West German Herbert Plate's *Das soll der Mensch nicht scheiden* (p. 133)). Yet despite the warnings of propaganda, defectors are often initially overawed by the apparent splendour of much that they encounter here, and it is only gradually that they appreciate the brutality of the society which they have entered. Rather than subject the disappointed defector to open criticism, therefore, novelists often express pity for his folly and ignorance of true conditions. Even in such a comic novel as Fries's *Der Weg nach Oobliadooh* there is a slightly pathetic note in the description of the freezing refugees waiting at the transit camp gate, a note which is quite out of keeping with the satire in the rest of this section (pp. 217–18).

The progress of the defector is generally seen to be unenviable. Once a man has given up his Eastern papers the Federal Republic has little interest in him. He merely becomes one more of those who can be subjected to the exploitationary system – just as are all other citizens of the West – and, unaccustomed to the capitalist life, he may well experience initial difficulties which will cripple him. Defectors usually experience harsh treatment from this grossly materialistic society and are forced to capitulate to its demands. By slandering their former state and exploiting their position as refugees they are often able to earn a temporary and precarious living, but it is only through hard work and a heartless policy of exploitation that they can hope to succeed. This is a point which is made repeatedly in Meng's *Eine Tüte Erdnüsse* and also in such novels as Anna Seghers' *Das Vertrauen* and Joho's *Es gibt kein Erbarmen*. West Berlin may raise magnificent hopes in the defector, but the reality of the Federal Republic soon makes him long for a return to the East.

Another point in which Martin Berg resembles many other defectors lies in the fact that he has been 'seduced' into defection by a Western agency – in his case the RIAS.[7] This is considered part of the West German 'Abwehr' organisation, and a considerable number of East German writers have exposed the manner in which Western agents carry out their nefarious operation of encouraging (or blackmailing) Eastern citizens

---

[7] That is, the 'Rundfunk *im* *a*merikanischen Sektor' [von Berlin]. For brief details of this station, see the entry in *Berlin – ABC* edited by Walter Krumholz.

into coming to the West. Doctors and intellectuals are seen to be their key targets.

The prominence of this theme in literature can be explained in terms of the serious defection rate among the intelligentsia up to 1961. Despite the preferential treatment accorded them (which was totally at odds with the ideals of socialism), the professionally qualified continued to leave for the West at an alarming rate. Politicians could hardly admit that these were attracted by better living standards or, in many cases, a wish to escape to a more democratic political system, and so the fiction of a vast Western recruiting organisation – far out of proportion to that which actually existed – was invented.[8] This is mirrored in the frequency of the theme in literature, with the extremism of the politicians being reflected in the extremes to which certain writers have gone. In J. C. Schwarz's *Das gespaltene Herz*, for example, the West hopes to encourage (or blackmail) *all* East German doctors into 'Republikflucht' in order to precipitate a crisis and prepare the atmosphere for a revolution. And in Stefan Heym's 'Der Bazillus' scientists are brought to the West not for their research ability, but simply to prevent them from working for the East. In almost every case defectors are seen to be tricked into leaving the Democratic Republic. Few are seen to leave for reasons which could be termed 'genuine'.

Many novels which are set in both parts of the German nation reveal more careful composition in those episodes which take place in the Federal Republic. This is especially the case with novels in which a GDR citizen crosses the border from East to West, for here increased narrative sophistication almost invariably accompanies the geographical change. Two such works are Egon Richter's *Zeugnis zu dritt* and Herman Kant's *Die*

[8] It is naturally difficult to come by any reliable figures for any such organisation. For some details, see the entry on 'Abwerbung' in Krumholz's *Berlin – ABC*.

Aula, and I should therefore like to consider these in some depth. Both have proved extremely popular in the GDR, and both mark a qualitative advance on those works mentioned thus far.

The plot of *Zeugnis zu dritt* is in outline simple, but it is rendered complex through narration from three different perspectives. As Thomas Feitknecht puts it:

In den Ich-Erzählungen des Psychologen Dr. Lotz, den Reflexionen des Pädagogik-Professors Brünecke und den Episoden über den Schuldirektor Keller wird retrospektiv die Geschichte einer Lehrerin entwickelt, die aus mangelndem Mitgefühl und wegen ihrer Verstösse gegen die Schulordnung aus dem Lehramt entfernt worden ist.[9]

The heroine, Elisabeth Möbius, suffers the fate of a typical war-widow who is left with child; but despite severe psychological stress and bitterness towards the leaders of the Third Reich she manages to survive and, encouraged by friends, is able to recover by becoming a teacher in the new state of the GDR. In spite of an enthusiastic beginning, her development to full socialist conviction is a slow one. She has considerable misgivings about certain aspects of the new educational system and therefore decides to defend a brilliant but unscrupulous pupil, whom none of the other teachers will recommend for a university place. The others are soon justified in their appraisal of the character concerned by the defection of his family to the West, while, to Elisabeth's grave humiliation, her own son follows them shortly afterwards. From this point the theme of a divided nation – hitherto only peripheral – becomes a major one, reaching a climax in the heroine's decision to visit West Berlin in order to persuade her son to return.

Up to the point at which disagreement over the pupil begins, there has been little comment on the fact that Germany is divided. One of the teachers muses on his country and compares it with the West, but this is an exceptional occurrence:

[9] *Die sozialistische Heimat. Zum Selbstverständnis neuerer DDR-Romane,* p. 51.

Keller liebte das Land, in dem er lebte, und darum hatte er es oft schwer. Die anderen drüben hatten es leichter, die Herren, sie machten im Grunde dort weiter, wo sie aufgehört hatten, immer nach altem Muster und mit den gleichen Zielen. Aber hier geschah etwas, was es in Deutschland noch nicht gegeben hatte, hier baute man ein neues Bildungs- und Erziehungssystem auf, das. . .(p. 61)

This isolated remark offers a sudden reminder of the criterion against which present events should be measured, while it is also typical of most contemporary novels. Although the divided nation may not be as much as a minor theme in many of these, isolated comments similar to the above are to be found in almost all of them. The fact that these comments are often short or cryptic does not diminish their importance; in the context of a politically sensitive reading public, the smallest indication of division will serve to relate a work to the national situation.

The division of Germany becomes more prominent when the pupil's father is introduced. He is characterised in terms of his possessions, mainly his Mercedes, and appears as a proud, selfish materialist. To quote Feitknecht again:

Alles an ihm erhält, mehrfach wiederholt und mit deutlich negativem Vorzeichen, das Attribut 'fremd': sein Auto westdeutscher Herkunft, seine Kleidung, seine Brille. . .Weitere Attribute – der Arzt ist 'straff gespannt und ständig auf dem Sprung' (S. 86), sein Mercedes hat ein 'Haifischgesicht' (S. 106) – wecken Assoziationen zu einem Raubtier und stempeln den Arzt zum Repräsentanten des westdeutschen Revanchismus. (pp. 52–3)

It therefore appears a matter of course that such a character should defect when his plans for his son are thwarted.

In these two figures Richter has introduced an important question of the socialist society. The father is an 'ausgezeichneter Chirurg', the son a brilliant pupil, but both are egoists with little concern for their fellow men and the new society; so should their immoral and, above all, typically *Western* behaviour be tolerated in that society? Owing to the son's character none of the teachers can recommend him as a suitable university candidate, with the sole exception of Elisabeth, who is concerned with 'objektive Tatsachen' – a Western preoccupation. 'Es geht mir doch nur um die objektiven Zensuren des Schülers, und nicht um seinen Charakter' (p. 79), she maintains, finding no difficulty in considering these qualities independently and thus becoming guilty of 'Objektivismus'.[10]

The point of *Zeugnis zu dritt*, as of a large number of contemporary East German novels, is that such qualities *cannot* be considered independently.[11] While ability may rate above all else in the capitalist world, the socialist is bound also to take into account a man's political convictions. After the war, it is argued, the Western Allies were content to use men according to their ability and often turned a blind eye to their political record; such a procedure allegedly did not take place in the East. Elisabeth too comes to the realisation that all activity is, in the last resort, political, and that her previous attitudes were ill-founded. But this is a conclusion she reaches only after her experiences in West German society.

Elisabeth's visit to West Berlin centres on two categories of experience. First, impressions which are new to her, and second, suspicions about the West which are corroborated by what she observes. Most travellers' experiences follow a similar patttern.

---

[10] I.e. considering matters without reference to the Party line. 'Objektiv' therefore has negative connotations in contemporary East German usage.

[11] The decision to reject a man on account of his 'unsocialist' (and therefore 'Western') activities is never seen to be easy, however, and it figures as a central issue in such works as Karl-Heinz Jakobs' *Beschreibung eines Sommers* and Erik Neutsch's *Spur der Steine*. Jurij Brězan's *Eine Liebesgeschichte* offers a close parallel to *Zeugnis zu dritt*, charting as it does the spiritual development of the apolitical Dr Hartung – who initially considers that a doctor should be judged on his medical ability alone – from his 'Western' position to a socialist attitude. Hartung's progress bears a clear similarity to Elisabeth Möbius's: it is only after contact with the West that he realises a doctor's private and political life must be taken into account in any assessment of his ability. Dismissal for unsocialist activity, although at first sight unfair, is seen to be justified by the moral basis upon which the new regime is founded.

Whether or not such themes are set against the East–West background, the East German reader should have little difficulty in recognising that the issues here raised are closely related to those which now divide Germany.

The surprises are usually disturbing ones, the reinforced convictions inevitably of a political nature.

The first surprise of Elisabeth's trip is the ease with which she is able to travel first into East Berlin, and then from East to West. She becomes dissatisfied with the simplicity of the procedure as she recreates the mental experiences of her son, and gradually she comes to an indictment of the border control. The climax is carefully constructed, beginning with apparently neutral imagery; yet the very stress on innocence suggests its opposite:

> Sie stellte sich vor, daß er so offen und hell auch in diesem Zug gesessen hatte und daß die Blicke der Grenzpolizisten nichtsahnend und arglos über sein Gesicht hinweggeglitten waren. (p. 157)

The choice of adjectives is intentionally ironic, and the same technique is continued later in the page. Elisabeth buys a ticket for the S–Bahn:

> Für zweimal zehn Pfennige rutschte ihr die Karte in einer kleinen weißen Emaillewanne entegegen. Sie nahm sie heraus und spürte, wie einfach es war, den Weg des Sohnes nachzugehen. Sie beobachtete, oben an der Bahnsteigsperre, aufmerksam den fahrkartenknipsenden Beamten in seinem hölzernen Kasten. Sie achtete auf seine Hand und seine Augen um ihres Jungen willen. Aber die Hand knipste immer nur Karten, schnell und skrupellos, die Augen sahen den Fahrkarteninhaber nicht an, sie starrten gleichgültig auf die unablässig knipsende chromglitzernde Zange. Teilnahmslos, uninteressiert. Sie dachte, vor dem knipsenden Beamten: Sie haben es ihm leicht gemacht. (pp. 157–8)

By this point the critique has become far stronger. The deliberate simplicity of these sentences (contrasting with preceding complex structures) reflects the ease with which the operation can be undertaken, while the breaks between sentences (reinforced by the repetition of *Sie* nahm... *Sie* beobachtete... etc.) impede the flow and give emphasis to the individual actions. Yet the indictment of the above lies not only in the final sentence, which summarises the whole, but in the accumulation of synonyms which follow 'skrupellos': 'gleichgültig', 'teilnahmslos', 'uninteressiert'. The two latter, forming as they do a sentence on their own, stress that there is nothing to appeal to the conscience of those leaving the Republic, least of all this final control.

The long, and action-filled paragraph in which the above appears is concluded by a summary of Elisabeth's emotions of helplessness and anger. These are expressed through a succession of short, pregnant phrases, some of which have been previously employed. Their repetition at this point lends them force and allows them to crystallise Elisabeth's impressions of the journey from East to West:

Gevierteilte Stadt, zweigeteilte Stadt, Stadt mit zwei Welten, zwischen denen der Zug hin- und herpendelte, für zwanzig Pfennig und eine gelbe Karte, arglos, gleichgültig, ein Stück technische Automatik. (p. 158)

The indictment is once again implicit. Only at the end of the following paragraph (which marks the climax of the first part of the heroine's journey) is it expressed openly: 'und sie dachte noch einmal: Sie haben es ihm leicht gemacht' (p. 158).[12]

Elisabeth's visit takes place in 1961, but before the key date of 13 August, and the heroine's attitude towards the East–West crossing is such that it would justify erection of the wall. Similar views are expressed in Christa Wolf's *Der geteilte Himmel*, in which the heroine, Rita, also travels to the West on a brief visit, also shortly before 13 August. Rita is surprised by exactly the same inefficiency on the part of the 'Grenzpolizisten' and the ease with which one can buy a ticket for the journey to the West (which is occasionally taken on the over-head *S-Bahn*,

---

[12] The ease with which one could buy a ticket, as well as its symbolic nature, have been highlighted by two other writers besides Richter. In Christa Wolf's *Der geteilte Himmel*, for example, the heroine reflects:

Darin unterschied diese Stadt sich von allen anderen Städten der Welt: Für vierzig Pfennig hielt sie zwei verschiedene Leben in der Hand. (p. 242)

And in Heinduczek's *Abschied von den Engeln* the defection of a schoolteacher is commented on as follows:

Riedmann war nicht der erste und wird nicht der letzte gewesen sein, solange eine S-Bahn-Fahrkarte genügt, um den Sozialismus gegen den Kapitalismus auszuwechseln. (p. 309)

so that the passage between two worlds can be symbolised in terms of the actual landmarks). Christa Wolf's novel was written in 1963, still close to the time of the Wall's erection, and it may be for this reason that she allows Rita to rebuke directly the lamentable state of the controls: 'Nicht sehr wirksam, diese Kontrolle, dachte sie fast enttäuscht' (p. 242). Elisabeth Möbius's criticism is less overt, a point which is hardly explicable in terms of character. The date of publication may well have been one of the main factors influencing Richter's reticence, for by 1967 the manifold advantages of a closed frontier were far more evident than they had been in 1963.[13]

As was suggested above, it is a common claim of East German propaganda that many refugees were seduced by the superficial glitter of West German life, and in particular by the 'Schaukasten' of West Berlin. It was, of course, never denied that life in the West was more comfortable, that food was better, more exotic and plentiful, and that luxury goods were to be obtained in abundance. But against this image of plenty was set a spiritual failure: material wealth was seen to be based on immorality and exploitation. A fragment by Anna Seghers, 'Eine Begegnung', is wholly devoted to substantiating these claims: a conversation between two old acquaintances, one now in the West, the other in the East, reveals the different moral standpoints of each part of the nation. The material wealth of

[13] Similar criticism is to be found in Strittmatter's *Ole Bienkopp* and in Heym's 'Im Netz' (collected in *Schatten und Licht*). The judgment is here implicit and relies to a far greater extent on propaganda, for in both cases a traditional manoeuvre of the divided city is being carried out: goods, bought cheaply in the East, are being taken over the border and sold for a higher price in Western currency; this is exchanged for an even greater number of Eastern Marks, which are illegally taken back into the Democratic Republic. One of the reasons for the erection of the Berlin Wall was to stop this illegal currency flow, which was severely damaging the economy of the GDR. The same activity is revealed in Eckart Kroneberg's *Der Grenzgänger*, Anna Seghers' *Das Vertrauen*, Arno Schmidt's *Das steinerne Herz*, Dieter Meichsner's *Die Studenten von Berlin*, and Ruth Kraft's *Menschen im Gegenwind*.

the West is seen to have resulted only from selfish and immoral proceedings; the progress of the East, although slow, has been based upon moral integrity. It is for this reason that the friends of defectors hope that the former have not fled for the luxuries of the West, for this would represent a moral failure: sacrifice of integrity for the material attractions of Western society.

Elisabeth Möbius too is naturally eager to deceive herself that her son has not defected in order to enjoy the luxuries with which he now begins to entertain her – but the process of self-deception proves difficult. The scene is an exclusive café on the Kurfürstendam:

Aber sie empfand gleichzeitig, als die weißbekleideten Kellner ihnen vornehm und diskret servierten, Eis in Silberbechern, Sahne in Silber-schalen, goldfarbenen Kognak in rauchfarbenen Schwenkern, silberne Löffel mit dem Wappen des Hauses, silberne Platten mit ziselierten Rändern, daß es dies nicht gewesen sein konnte, was ihn hergezogen hatte in diese Stadt. Dies nicht und nicht das andere: OSRAM, OSRAM, OSRAM – Hell wie der lichte Tag! REISEN auf Teilzahlung mit Severin & Co. Für 246 Mark mit der exklusiven DC. 3 der PAA auf das sonnenüberflutete Mallorca, *Vigoleis Thelen – die Insel des zweiten Gesichts.* Dies alles, fühlte sie, war es nicht gewesen, was ihren Jungen hierhergezogen hatte, obwohl es viele hierherzog. Dies war es nicht gewesen, was ihn verführt hatte, obwohl es viele verführte. (p. 161)

Richter handles this important psychological moment particularly well. In few other passages of the novel is there such care over narrative detail and sentence structure. The slightly archaic lexis of the opening sentences ('servierten'; 'Silberbecher'; 'Schwenker'; 'Platte', etc) emphasises that the world in which the present action occurs is anachronistic. The enumeration of aristocratic items – which begins in what we expect to be a short subordinate phrase, but which increases in length to become the dominant element of the sentence – emphasises the decadence of the Federal Republic. Against this quiet opulence is set the other aspect of the West, the brash commercialism best seen in the blatant advertisements. The interdependence of these apparently disparate elements is subtly exposed in the thought associations of the following paragraph, where the two are more firmly linked. Elisabeth, thinking dialectically, is unable to separate this splendour from the contemptible methods of the society that has produced it: 'Und sie nahm, zwischen silbernen Tellern und bernsteinfarbenen Kognak ASBACH URALT – DAS BESTE VOM BESTEN, von wohl parfümierten Rauchschwaden umflort, DER DUFT DER GROSSEN WEITEN WELT...'. The brashness of this world is reinforced typographically, as it is in most East German novels which attempt to show up the hollowness of this aspect of the West.[14]

Although Elisabeth desperately wants to see an exception in her son, her use of the emphatic ('nicht gewesen sein konnte') nevertheless betrays her anxious doubts. Her lack of conviction is also neatly reflected in the symmetry of the final sentences: she twice raises a point only to dismiss it, but the very act of raising it reveals her obvious unease. 'Fühlen' does not suggest confidence, while the use of 'verführen' is a tacit admission of guilt.

The host of advertising slogans and the splendour of the West disturbs Elisabeth, throwing her partly off-balance. Her sense of alienation is intensified by the ensuing conversation with her son, who is seen to be already too much at home in his new society to understand her. The suggestion of a spiritual chasm between them has many parallels in contemporary fiction; in contrast to West Germans, who have tended to overlook this aspect, Eastern writers have repeatedly illustrated the misunderstanding of motivation which has resulted from ideologically

---

[14] The use of adverts to characterise certain aspects of the West has figured elsewhere: in Harry Thürk's *Der Narr und das schwarzhaarige Mädchen*, for example (p. 6), in Christa Wolf's *Der geteilte Himmel* (p. 267), and in Erwin Strittmatter's *Ole Bienkopp*, where the journey from East to West Berlin is symbolised in terms of adverts. Ramsch, the capitalist, leaves behind the slogans of an East Berlin harbour:

Erst mehr arbeiten, dann besser leben!

and reads with pleasure those of the West Berlin side:

Leiste dir etwas; du hast es verdient, rauch Camel!

(pp. 166–7)

In Hasso Laudon's *Semesterferien in Berlin* the contrasting political slogans of the East and the brash advertisements of the West form a basic structural principle of the novel.

contrasting backgrounds. Elisabeth and her son talk at cross-purposes, neither able to understand the other's point of view. Richter emphasises the gap between them and between their new societies through a number of stylistic features. The sudden break between pages 160 and 161, for example, jolts the reader into an awareness of Western luxury, while the precious language in which that luxury is described suggests the author's disdain of it. Tension is created and sustained through a succession of short paragraphs (some of only one line), and through the sharp exchanges of speech. The elements of conflict and contrast are used throughout to hold the reader's interest and to increase identification with Elisabeth. This section as a whole is in fact built on the juxtaposition of opposites, from sentence construction – long sentences frequently being followed by short, incisive ones, which take full resultant emphasis – to the level of ideas and the depiction of character. Added to this there is more detailed and penetrating psychological intrusion by the author than in any previous episode. These features combine to make pages 157–61 the highlight of the novel, a spiritual crisis through which Elisabeth is able to reach a deeper understanding of division and of its human consequences.

The second work I should like to discuss in depth is Hermann Kant's *Die Aula*, which undoubtedly represents one of the most subtle attempts to depict divided Germany by means of a sensitive traveller. Kant's judicious handling of this figure is to a certain extent surprising, however, for he has often expressed a violent aversion to the Federal Republic, in articles which occasionally degenerate into little more than diatribe. 'Vielfaches Unbehagen und ein Modell', for example, ostensibly a review-article of Wolfgang Weyrauch's *Ich lebe in der Bundesrepublik*, rapidly develops into a polemic against political aspects of the West, particularly neo-Nazism. Although the author begins in a factual tone, he soon reaches an emotional fervour, rejecting the neutral term 'Bundesrepublik' and substituting such polemic circumlocutions as 'Bonner Staat' and 'Adenauers Herrschaftsbereich'. Similar style and content are to be found in his other essays written around this period, such as 'Macht und Ohnmacht einer Literatur' and 'Darmstädter Dilemma', while his reviews of West German literature in *Neue Deutsche Literatur* are equally aggressive. It is difficult to believe that only a short while later (from 1963, in fact, when *Die Aula* began to appear in serial form in the young intellectuals' weekly *Forum*), Kant was engaged in the skilful understatement of many of the features he had vociferously attacked in these earlier studies. The perspective he now adopts clearly proves his ability to distinguish between literature and polemic essay, an ability which is lacking in many other East German writers.

Die Aula traces the life of journalist Robert Iswall from childhood in Hamburg to early middle age in the GDR. The action begins in 1962, as Robert receives an invitation to speak at the closure of his former 'Arbeiter-und-Bauern-Fakultät',[15] an assignment which he accepts and which then determines the structure of the whole work. From this point the individual episodes which Robert recalls, as well as his daily routine, are all in some way related to the task he sets himself: for his flashbacks – at first idle musings in a search for anecdotal material – rapidly develop into a serious investigation of his own life, and with it the history of Germany. His visit to Hamburg, undertaken to report on the (1962) floods, enables him to widen his perspective and to assess the situation in both parts of the nation.

It was suggested above that the border crossing from East to West frequently marked a climax in the novels to depict division. Kant too exploits the emotional tension aroused by such a moment, and by presenting a number of small yet significant details, he is able to evoke a sense of unease. In the following passage, for example, the traveller Robert crosses the border

[15] For details of this form of further education establishment, see the entry in *DDR Handbuch*, edited by Peter C. Ludz.

of the Federal Republic on his way to report the floods in Hamburg:

> Der Zug verließ Schwanheide, am Bahndamm rief ein Transparent: 'Die Deutsche Demokratische Republik grüßt alle Reisenden', unter einem Wachpilz stand ein Posten und winkte, dann kam das Niemandsland und dann ein Schilderhaus mit einem Adler daran, und dann kam Büchen.
> Auch hier war der Aufenthalt kurz; es stiegen nur wenige Leute aus.
> Die Uniformen der Kontrolleure waren von betont zivilem Zuschnitt, die Pistolen sah man nicht, und die breiten Schiffermützen erinnerten eher an Hafenrundfahrten denn an Grenz- und Verfassungsschutz. (p. 68)

Through occasional disquieting suggestions a certain fear of the Federal Republic has been raised by this stage of the novel, and at such a critical point as the border crossing, the parataxis of parts of the above conveys the mood of uncertainty that afflicts the traveller. The disjointed first paragraph, with its swift succession of clauses, represents a psychological rather than a purely visual experience of two worlds, although Kant suppresses the former and forces the reader to form his own impression of Robert's thoughts through the latter's images. As a consequence, the difference between the friendly attitude of the GDR and the neutral – but in contrast, cold – atmosphere of the Federal Republic emerges starkly through the juxtaposition of brief impressions.

The isolation of impressions is continued in the third paragraph, in which the undertones are obvious enough. Through the structure Kant is able to elicit a sense of danger and to warn that appearances are deceptive. The feeling of disquiet already aroused is reinforced by the abruptness of the movement from clothes to guns ('die Pistolen' gaining full emphasis by being the first words of this anastrophic clause), while the aura of innocence surrounding those clothes ('von betont zivilem Zuschnitt') is harshly exploded by the laconic reference to weapons. Such description is as significant for what it does *not* say as for what it actually does.

If the construction of this sentence elicits unease in the West European, then it will intensify the hostility of the East German, whose reactions to the Federal Republic have been predetermined by the propaganda to which he is exposed. Conditioned to react with suspicion to any aspect of the West, he will immediately recognise that in spite of the apparently casual dress of the guards, they are by no means the civilians or harmless 'trip around the bay' captains which they appear to be. Their civilian style uniforms will be seen as an attempt to disguise their true military role, and the fact that their guns are hidden makes them doubly untrustworthy. Kant's readers are, of course, well schooled in the view that the wolf in sheep's clothing is far more dangerous than the open enemy, while Robert cleverly makes even the sheep into wolves by his cynical attitude towards them. He also adds that these figures are not only concerned with 'Grenz-', but also with 'Verfassungsschutz'. The progress is thus from the concept of the 'Kontrolleur', with its harmless connotations, to the more ominous phenomenon of concealed weapons, and then from the light-hearted 'Schiffermützen' and 'Hafenrundfahrten' to the heavier and more serious 'Grenz- und Verfassungsschutz'. The latter words are normally employed only in dignified contexts, but here their comparison with the happy-go-lucky air of the holiday harbour has an element of the grotesque. The guards may be seen either as cunning and dangerous beneath their disguise, or as the ridiculous defendants of capitalism, the innermost essence of which is potentially threatened by the harmless visitor from the East.

Kant's tendentious aim becomes clear if the dress of the border guards is considered objectively: their uniforms are in fact of a more civilian cut than those of their GDR counterparts, but they are nevertheless unmistakably military. Furthermore, their guns, when worn, are usually clearly displayed. Kant's desire to arouse or confirm distrust in his reader is therefore unmistakable. This factual distortion is combined with deliberate understatement of psychological impressions for a tendentious effect.

The traveller's impression of Western hostility is intensified by another passage of understatement only two pages later. Robert is questioned by a border guard who – contrary to all expectations – proves surprisingly human. The unusualness of such an experience gives rise to a short passage of musing:

Robert sah ihm nach und dachte: Mein lieber Freund, dir möchte ich öfter begegnen, du scheinst ja nicht so scharf auf Kommsemit und Handschellen zu sein, und ich bin es auch nicht. (p. 70)

This is the second occasion (within half a page) that Robert implies that the guard is exceptional. But although the man is not ready to pounce on any innocent suspect, the implications of Robert's surprise are clear. Kant is not only insinuating that the potential visitor to the West is likely to have a hostile reception. He is also ensuring that if his reader is well received he will not be deluded by this but will recognise it, as does Robert, as an exception. The East German reader is, moreover, encouraged to do this within the ideological framework of life in the GDR. Schoolbooks in particular make use of this pattern of argument, which was common in the Third Reich and which is typical of propaganda in general. Horst Siebert, discussing the problem of why pupils are not disturbed by examples which seem to contradict what they have been taught, comments: 'Die Unterscheidung zwischen "Wessen" und "Erscheinung" erlaubt es, alle die Ideologie bestätigenden Beispiele als wesentlich und typisch zu verwenden, alle widersprechenden Fakten jedoch als sekundär und untypisch zu verwerfen.'[16] The occurrence of a contradictory example in real life is thus tantamount to an invitation to think dialectically. (One of Brecht's didactic plays of the thirties, *Die Ausnahme und die Regel*, offers an illustration of exactly the same idea.) But Kant's example is particularly effective, for it is by commending the individual – and therefore appearing to adopt a sincere approach – that he is able to denigrate the whole. Robert may not explicitly castigate all guards, but a condemnation is implicit

[16] *Der andere Teil Deutschlands in Schulbüchern der BRD und der DDR*, p. 71.

in his praise, which is elicited by the guard's surprising lack of the typical, negative characteristics.

In contrast to the obtrusive moralism of Joho's novels, that of *Die Aula* is rarely explicit. Kant keeps very much in the background and allows the traveller's descriptions and actions to carry their own suggestions, for these are usually implicit in the particular manner of expression, in the context of the novel, or in the context of East German propaganda. One feature acquires its forces from all three of these: Robert's article on the Hamburg floods, a masterpiece of tendentious understatement. 'Understatement' is, however, hardly the correct term, for the reader learns nothing of the contents of that article – he is forced to speculate on the implications of its omission. Whereas Joho (and of course, many of his fellow-writers) would have undoubtedly utilised such an opportunity to castigate severely the machinations of capitalist exploiters, Kant allows Robert to suppress his findings. And yet, through this very suppression, he forces the reader to become a detective himself; for it is in the absence of facts that the onus falls on the reader to form the small suggestions that have emerged into an overall picture. These hints are for the most part latent, but the reader has been carefully prepared for them. Robert's editor has warned him that there are 'Signale, daß die kleinen Leute wieder einmal betrogen werden, ernste Signale' (p. 50), and so the remarks of a flood victim may confirm the suspicion that big business – in the form of a margarine plant – was to some extent involved in the catastrophe:

'Wir kriegen alle eine piekfeine Wohnung, und das Gelände hier kriegt die Margarinequetsche dahinten. Seit zwanzig Jahren wollen sie hier baun, und nun klappt es endlich.' (p. 111)

And, in the absence of proof, there is an involuntary tendency to see in certain of Robert's cynical queries already proven facts. As he phrases his reply to the question 'Was willst du hier?':

'Nichts weiter, nur sehen, wie es hier steht, und wissen, wie es weitergeht: Ob der Deich aufgeschüttet wird, ob Entschädigungen gezahlt werden, wieviel und an wen, ob die Natur allein schuld war oder noch ein bißchen was anderes, ob sich andere das auch fragen und was für eine Antwort sie erhalten, ob hier jeder glaubt, daß alles ein Zufall war, ob man daraus lernt oder nicht; das will ich wissen, weiter nichts.' (p. 111)

A series of rhetorical questions is employed in a similar manner in Kant's 'Vielfaches Unbehagen und ein Modell'. The precise formulation of each question suggests that the hero is very much at home with the material and that he has a good idea of what the answers will be.

Although the above suggestions are the only ones to emerge, they would nonetheless be decisive for the East German reader. GDR propaganda frequently emphasises that capitalists will go to extreme and immoral limits to obtain what they require for personal enrichment, and there are two further factors which increase the likelihood of the disaster being seen as the work of a hungry capitalist. First, the fact that Robert's assignment is typical of many depicted in TV films: an actual event which has been reported in the Western press, but the background to which has remained obscure, is resolved by an honest reporter in search of truth.[17] And second, the fact that Robert is normally reluctant to expose scandals (although he has no pressing duties at the time, he lies to a film director who is eager to have him assist in an exposé of the 'Kringel–Konzern, diese widerliche Lügenfabrik' [a West German press]). This restraint is tendentious, however. It makes the reader all the more willing to accept the few suggestions that do emerge in the case of the Hamburg disaster.

Kant's intentional failure to draw conclusions leads the reader to more involvement in the psychology of the hero and forces

---

17 Cf. Jörg Lingenberg, *Das Fernsehspiel in der DDR*, p. 182. Robert is throughout characterised as the honest and objective reporter. One outburst in particular stresses his necessity to remain dispassionate in his profession. Stripping bare the glamour which supposedly attaches to the photographer-reporter's image, Robert emphasises at great length and with numerous examples: 'Reporter hören, sehen und berichten...' (p. 113) 'Sie lachen nicht, sie heulen nicht, sie berichten' (p. 114). The omission of the article on the floods is in keeping with this demand to avoid dramatisation, while it also acts as a further device in the indirect characterisation of the hero.

him to make from the understatement a less reticent image of the Federal Republic.[18] The narrative technique assists this

[18] There is another, even less striking way in which the reader is encouraged to form an adverse image of the Federal Republic. Part of Robert's trip to the West, in particular to Hamburg, is prefigured by Heine's similar journey in *Deutschland. Ein Wintermärchen*. The similarity between the two travellers is first raised on p. 51 of the novel, as Robert crosses the border into West Berlin and recites the second stanza of Heine's bitter masterpiece. There follows a succession of episodes which parallel Heine's movements: first, a humorous encounter with the border guards; the return to his native city of Hamburg; the reunion with his delighted but inquisitive mother; and finally, survey of the flood damage, which is compared with the fire of 1842, one of Heine's comments on it actually being quoted by Robert, together with some of his more biting comments on the citizens, which Robert considers metaphorically appropriate to those inhabiting Hamburg in 1962.

To the reader acquainted with Heine (and *Deutschland. Ein Wintermärchen* has often been 'Pflichtlektüre' in East German schools), such an introduction invites the reader to seek further parallels between the works. And in re-reading the poem it would be difficult not to see in those *Capita* following number xx (the return to Hamburg) a series of references to contemporary West Germany. Kant is very much at home with Heine, and he may well have selected this work for the added dimension it can contribute to his novel (which has the same satirical spirit and which bears as motto a quotation from Heine's *Französische Zustände – Artikel* vi, dated Paris, 19 April 1832). Heine's encounter with Hammonia, the embodiment of German philistinism, contains a number of lines which are particularly relevant to post-war West Germany as seen by the East: notably, the tendency to gloss over the past as by no means as black as has been made out, and to maintain that it was not without its positive features (Caput xxv, stanzas 8–14) – which represents, of course, a defence of the current *status quo*. More striking is the future of Germany, which Hammonia allows the poet to glimpse. Having sworn not to divulge what he has seen, Heine has to restrict himself to describing its insufferable stench, while the image of his sticking his head into the 'runde Öffnung' [her chamber-pot] in order to see it, is notorious.

Heine is Kant's favourite classical author, and it is difficult to believe that these allusions are not to be pursued. They enrich his satire of the Federal Republic by suggesting to the 'ideal' reader a number of further comic parallels, and they do so far more subtly than Wolf Biermann's comparable parody, *Deutschland. Ein Wintermärchen*, which relies on humour of a far cruder nature.

Other literary allusions in the novel, some of which serve a prefigurative function, include: Hagen and Siegfried; Tristan and Isolde; Thomas Mann; Fontane; Karl May; Margaret Mitchell; and a number of contemporary East

53

process. The almost total lack of third-person narration, with the consequent emphasis on direct speech and interior monologue, seduces the reader into a point of view very close to that of the hero. The reader therefore experiences the West as does the traveller himself. The following passage illustrates two important points concerning this process. First, that a high degree of empathy is demanded of the reader. And second, that the West European must possess some acquaintance with East German social conditions if he is to appreciate the implications of Kant's disguised rhetoric. Like *Zeugnis zu dritt*, *Die Aula* posits a reader who is as sensitive as its hero.

As Robert enters the Federal Republic an incredulous border guard enquires why he does not live in his native city of Hamburg:

> Der Kontrolleur sah in den Ausweis und sagte offensichtlich ehrlich verwundert: 'Wenn Sie aus Hamburg sind, warum sind Sie dann da drüben? Wie lange wohnen Sie schon dort?' 'Ich bin nach der Gefangenschaft nicht mehr zurückgekommen, und *dann habe ich dort studiert; das ging hier nicht.*' 'Sicher', sagte der Beamte, '*das ist wohl leichter bei euch.* Na, also, dann schreiben Sie mal nicht so schlecht über uns, als alter Hamburger.' (p. 70 [My italics])

There are two especially noteworthy features in this passage. First, the impact on the reader of the words 'offensichtlich ehrlich verwundert'. An appreciation of the implications of this phrase presupposes a knowledge of the East German's image of himself in the West, for the former is constantly led to believe that his West German counterpart has been conditioned to regard him as a victim of Russian oppression rather than a free individual. The guard is thus flabbergasted that anyone should wish to live in the 'Zone' of his own free will. Kant is here satirising the conditioning to which the West German is supposedly subjected with regard to the East, and there are several other satirical attacks on this aspect later in the novel.

German writers. Lothar Bornscheuer has examined allusions to Goethe's *Die Wahlverwandschaften* in 'Wahlverwandtes? Zu Kants *Aula* und Heißenbüttels *D'Alemberts Ende*'.

A second striking feature of this passage is the crystallisation in two brief comments (those italicised) of a major boast of GDR propaganda, namely, that it is practically impossible for the West German worker to send his children to university. (Another attack on this is to be found on page 84.) In spite of the simplicity of Robert's remark ('das ging hier nicht'), the guard is immediately convinced, thus ostensibly proving how profound a comment on East and West it really is. The guard's reply – which, in the eyes of East German readers, will appear as an understatement and in which 'wohl' may be seen as indicating either a face-saving effort or grudgingness and jealousy – will probably amuse the East German, and this category of reader, more critically aware than the West European, may well sense a note of embarrassment in the second sentence (a non-sequitur to the first), in which the guard hesitates slightly ('Na, also, dann...') as he extricates himself from an uncomfortable situation. The effect on the reader of a grudging acknowledgement is far greater than that of uncritical flattery, and by employing this indirect method of praising the East, Kant is able to disparage the West at the same time. The admission of GDR superiority is made even more effective by being placed in the mouth of an obvious opponent of the Republic.

Kant's aim again becomes clear through a more realistic consideration of West German border guards. To them a man who had chosen the East rather than his native town after the war would be immediately recognised as a hardened Communist – and this is, of course, a fair description of Robert Iswall. The possibility of a guard reacting in this manner (particularly in January 1962!) is therefore extremely unlikely. A more credible reaction is depicted in the author's 'Verschiedenes zum Gemeinsamen', an autobiographical sketch of a border crossing undertaken after *Die Aula* was published. As in so many of his other essays, Kant here adopts a moralistic tone and completely ruins the artistic effect. Fortunately, however, this is never the case in the novel: there Kant has relied on the power of suggestion alone.

A figure similar to the traveller, but usually far more critical, is that of the 'outsider'. Outsiders lack contact with their native society and therefore experience it as would a foreigner, yet while the latter may occasionally praise, the outsider's journey through everyday life inevitably amounts to a critique of it. Possibly owing to the cultural isolation of the GDR, there are few East German novels to exploit the advantages offered by this character, who is so well established in West European literature, particularly that written after 1945. Many Eastern writers have in fact preferred to use different figures when an outsider might have been more suitable for their purposes.[19] The few novels in which he does occur include *Das Klassentreffen* (where a number of minor characters are at odds with their society – but where the main means of exploring the other world is through the central figure of the traveller), Brězan's *Eine Liebesgeschichte* (Sabine), and Heiduczek's *Abschied von den Engeln* (Franz). Klaus Beuchler's *Aufenthalt vor Bornholm* is the only Eastern novel in which the hero himself is an outsider from West German society.

Whereas East German use of a Western outsider is limited, West German writers have used this figure far more frequently. He is, in fact, the most common means of probing Eastern society that is to be found in contemporary Western fiction. Although writers using this figure necessarily set their plot in the GDR, their perspective is anti-Communist: they tend to assess character and action from a Western point of view. Further, since their (Eastern) outsiders embody a number of qualities which are obviously derived from the ideals of the West, their novels contain an implicit – but nevertheless fairly conspicuous – clash of the two parts of the nation. Works falling into this category include Eva Müthel's *Für dich blüht kein*

---

[19] An outsider would have been far more effective than, say, the militarist ogres to be found in the books published by the 'Deutscher Militärverlag', particularly Heinz Kruschel's *Jeder Abschied ist ein kleines Sterben* or Werner Steinberg's *Wechsel auf die Zukunft*. In similar vein are Hans von Oettingen's *Rostiger Ruhm* and Eberhard Panitz's *In drei Teufels Namen*.

Baum, Martin Gregor-Dellin's *Der Kandelaber*, and Gerhard Zwerenz's *Aufs Rad geflochten* and *Die Liebe der toten Männer*. (These authors are all Eastern refugees now living in the Federal Republic.) The best of these, *Der Kandelaber*, is typical: a sensitive, conscientious intellectual who suffers mentally under the new socialist regime, becomes a victim of the complex and inhuman political machinery which protects the state from all hostile forces, however insignificant these might be. The book gains its indictive force from the fact that the hero was as much of an outsider in the Third Reich as he is in the GDR, while his experiences in the earlier period rapidly find modern parallels.

Similar parallels are revealed in Helmut Putz's *Die Abenteuer des braven Kommunisten Schwejk*, which is more representative of popular anti-Eastern writing in that its technique is less subtle and its targets more wide-ranging. The central figure, Josef Schwejk, possesses less interest as an outsider than as a foil to illustrate the evil features of the Democratic Republic. Putz utilises the same 'Schwejk' created by Hašek and later employed by Vaněk and Brecht (indeed, the hero actually mentions his lineage at one point), but the present figure can hardly stand comparison with his forerunners. The most enjoyable parts of the novel are those containing coarse humour, while the rest is a rather predictable series of highly improbable incidents which all throw into disrepute the government and ideology of the GDR. The image of Communism is totally black. There are attacks on the ludicrous nature of state planning, corruption and incompetence in the police force, national terror of the secret services, and the unpredictability of the Party line. The narrator does not attempt to conceal the fact that he is a West German and occasionally interjects derogatory comments. Many of his characters also frequently contrast their lot with the better material and ideological situation of the West.

Schwejk is a particular kind of outsider. His apparently naive innocence allows him to question even the most fundamental points of Marxist ideology and to react to the replies he receives in an unhypocritical manner (in contrast to practically every other citizen, who feigns Communist attitudes but often allows his true feelings to escape). It is in this that the book's main value as satire lies: criticism of the state is achieved not through the traditional, embittered misfit, but through a sincere innocent, who has much in common with the Fool of earlier centuries. The conception is good, but derivative, while the book's impact might have been far greater if the individual (and perhaps too numerous) episodes had been presented in less exaggerated form.

One writer who has used both 'traveller' and 'outsider' to investigate life in contemporary Germany is Uwe Johnson. His first two novels, *Mutmaßungen über Jakob* and *Das dritte Buch über Achim*, were, of course, published in the West alone, but there are nevertheless various reasons why they are worthy of brief consideration in this context. First, *Mutmaßungen über Jakob* was actually written while Johnson was still living in the Democratic Republic. (It was mainly on account of its theme that the book was unable to find a publisher in that country.) Second, it is worth bringing out that Johnson's work is not centrally concerned with the divided nation – as might superficially seem the case and has sometimes been claimed. And finally, the nature of Johnson's 'travellers' differs substantially from those of writers considered thus far. They are therefore useful for purposes of contrast.

Johnson has been described as belonging to neither East nor West but 'on top of the Berlin Wall',[20] and the fact he has used the characteristic figures of writers in both Germanies does suggest this statement is an appropriate one. So too does the fact that he has shown himself remarkably reluctant to take sides. Although East German writers inevitably criticise aspects of the

---

[20] See Horst Bienek's interview with Johnson in his *Werkstattgespräche mit Schriftstellern*, p. 98.

West, while West Germans reciprocate in the expected manner, Johnson's censure is indirect and exceptionally restrained. And whatever criticism there may be of one state, this is usually balanced by criticism of the other.

Despite the acclaim that Johnson received as the 'first' to treat the problem of divided Germany,[21] this theme is not the central preoccupation of his work. True, his early novels are all set against the background of the two Germanies, but their *theme*, as Mary Cock has pointed out, is that of 'personality',[22] with the difficulties of ever getting to know someone being made even more complex by the present situation of divided Germany. In *Mutmaßungen über Jakob* such difficulties are brought out in a stylistically striking manner: the loneliness and desperation of the outsider, Jakob Abs, as well as the practical impossibility of knowing exactly what sort of a person he was, are reinforced by sudden and erratic movements between conversation, monologue, interior monologue, and a strange form of narrative – quite apart from the unconventional use of punctuation and typography.[23]

If Jakob feels himself an outsider in his native East, then he is even less at home in the West. His journey there, undertaken to visit his childhood sweetheart Gesine, and his mother, who is now in a refugee camp, proves an uncomfortable and often disturbing experience. Even while waiting at the railway station Jakob betrays his inability to adapt to the different life style of the West. As Gesine recalls:

---

[21] Cf. Chapter 1, pp. 3–4.
[22] *The Presentation of Personality in the Novels of Max Frisch and Uwe Johnson*, particularly Part II. Some of the conclusions of this doctoral dissertation are contained in Miss Cock's 'Uwe Johnson: An Interpretation of Two Novels'. For a general survey of Johnson's treatment of the two Germanies in particular, see Alan D. Dunnett's short but perceptive dissertation *Die Schilderung des Lebens in den zwei deutschen Staaten im frühen Werk Uwe Johnsons*.
[23] For a lucid introduction to the difficulties presented by this style, see Colin H. Good, 'Uwe Johnson's Treatment of the Narrative in "Mutmaßungen über Jakob" '.

Ich sah ihn erst wieder abends auf den Plattforminseln vor dem Haupt-
bahnhof; es war nicht so dass er vor Warten nichts anzufangen wusste,
nur er stand eben nicht da wie ein junger Mann mit Geschäften und
Plänen hierzulande, der sich zehn Minuten zu vertreiben weiss nützlich
und elegant mit Zeitung und Zigarette, er sah verloren aus mit den
Händen auf dem Rücken reglos, es war so eine dauerhafte Art von
Dastehen. (p. 275)

This visit stands apart from those considered thus far mainly
because the character of the traveller himself is quite different.
Jakob is supremely honest with himself and with others, restrained, tolerant, and his attitudes, not blinkered by the ideologies of either side, allow a registering of impressions rather
than commentary on them. This is ensured through the indirect
means of presenting Jakob – never by means of discursive commentary (for even the narrator is attempting to understand and
to 'speculate' on his hero), but through the conversations and
monologues of others, both in East and West.

The problem of 'personality' is presented with almost equal
originality in *Das dritte Buch über Achim*, in which (as Miss
Cock has again pointed out) Johnson inverts the traditional
story-telling situation of the omniscient teller and the en-
thralled listener in order to bring out the teller's reluctance,
unease, and uncertainty concerning all matters relating to the
'hero' Achim and to East Germany as a whole. The problems
of a divided country emerge more forcefully in this novel, where
Johnson's particular use of the traveller (Karsch) represents a
strikingly successful means of suggesting the differences (and
rigidity) in each state's outlook. Karsch, a typically prejudiced
West German, visits the East at the request of his former
mistress and becomes involved in the attempt to write a biography of her present lover, the cyclist Achim. The story is
told in a question-and-answer form, in which an inquisitive
but politically biased questioner (we assume: a typical West
German) probes the traveller on his experiences in the East.
Throughout the novel Johnson emphasises the difficulty of
Karsch's giving a straight answer to any of the questions or of

drawing firm conclusions from his visit. And by allowing the questioner to attempt to seduce the traveller into an unambiguous reply, he indicates the gap between Western notions of reality, or of what is important, and the different ways of thinking, as well as the different criteria, of the GDR.

The disturbing nature of Karsch's findings, his increasing reluctance to reach any form of judgement, is masterfully summed up on one of the final pages of the novel – the description of Achim's reaction to the news of Karsch's departure:

Wie nahm Achim das auf?
Mit Bedauern. Er zeigte Bedauern. Er schien es zu bedauern. (p. 331)

This almost escapist progression crystallises the traveller's increasingly cautious reaction towards what he has seen in the East, and in particular to the character of Achim. His initial response is a purely subjective one, which is immediately corrected to an 'objective' statement. But the more Karsch saw of Achim, the less certain he became of his judgements, and so the final reply offers a compromise and consequently ambiguous position. Karsch now feels unable to reach any firm conclusions on human character – or on political institutions.[24]

Johnson's two novels which use the 'traveller' motif are distinctive chiefly because the author has refused to simplify any of the issues. His stylistic complexity is part of this attempt to force the reader into recognising complexity in life and political ideology, and he achieves this by using stylistic irregularities which make the reader participate more fully in the thought processes of his characters. The actual choice of traveller is related to this desire to bring out the discrepancies between points of view and ways of life. Neither Jakob nor Karsch possesses the firm political commitment which characterises

---

[24] Johnson's thoughts on this matter seem to have changed considerably by the time of 'Eine Reise wegwohin, 1960' (published in 1964, five years after he had come to the Federal Republic), for in this story the emphasis falls quite distinctly on Western intolerance towards all matters concerning the East, and particularly towards pro-Eastern sentiments. (The story is contained in the collection *Karsch, und andere Prosa*.)

such figures as the narrator of *Das Klassentreffen* or Robert Iswall, nor do they display the growth to political commitment that is seen in Martin Berg or Elisabeth Möbius. With Johnson's characters the development is almost a reverse one. Acquaintance with both Germanies serves only to bring them to a feeling of political uncertainty, for their final conclusions are that both German states are very far from ideal.

The fictional East German traveller is likely to arouse a variety of emotions in citizens of the Federal Republic. First, he may possess a curiosity value, as does Rita in Christa Wolf's *Der geteilte Himmel*. To the inquisitive West German the character from the East is an interesting phenomenon. As soon as her inhospitable hostess realises that she has come from the GDR, Rita is invited to have coffee:

Als ihr klar wurde, woher das Fräulein kam, war sie auf einmal bereit, Kaffee zu kochen. In ihre blassen Augen stieg etwas Farbe. Wer ließ sich die Gelegenheit entgehen, einen Gast aus dem Osten zu bewirten und auszufragen? (p. 248)

Another reaction to the traveller is one of sympathy. Many in the West react with pity to the 'Mann von drüben', whose material situation must be far inferior to their own. The narrator of *Das Klassentreffen*, for example, realises that he is being considered as one of the 'arme Brüder von drüben, denen man überheblich auf die Schulter klopft' (p. 22). A further reaction of the sympathetic is to offer food to the Eastern visitor, since East Germans like to suggest that many in the West still live under the delusion that this is scarce in the other part of the nation. There is, of course, little doubt that material conditions in the East were far inferior to those of the West during the fifties and that the food parcels sent to the GDR were gratefully appreciated; but present living standards allow writers to mock this outdated misconception. Although few West Germans can seriously believe that food is still scarce, Eastern writers nevertheless credit them with this illusion, which represents an easy satirical butt and which is commonly used in modern fiction.[25] In the following example Fritz Rudolf Fries makes his satire explicit by stressing that the speaker, who is addressing two Eastern refugees, has no first-hand knowledge of the Democratic Republic:

Was führt euch nur alle hierher, sagte der Fahrer, der nie drüben gewesen war. Habt ihr denn nischt zu fressen oder was? (p. 223)

But the most common reaction to the Eastern traveller is shown to be one of hostility. Pity is often displayed for 'victims' of the Communist system, such as defectors, but convinced socialists are regarded with a variety of emotions ranging from contempt to fear. This range is best seen in Stefan Heym's 'Der Präsentkorb', perhaps the most savage attack on the West to be included in his (tendentiously entitled) anti-Western collection of stories, *Schatten und Licht*. The reaction to Kant's Robert Iswall is also in the main a belligerent one, and the author stresses that this attitude has been carefully aroused in West German citizens by the actions of a malevolent Federal government. By suggesting that the reaction towards citizens of the East closely resembles a conditioned reflex, he hints at the considerable conditioning, in the form of political indoctrination, to which the West has been subjected. A number of other writers have suggested the same.[26]

Although it might be assumed that West and East Germans had more in common that their language alone,[27] the reception of the traveller, as well as his impressions of the West, suggest that this is by no means the case. Further, since the qualities travellers detect in the West are those which are lacking (or

---

[25] E.g. Uwe Johnson, *Das dritte Buch über Achim*, p. 316; Hermann Kant, *Die Aula*, p. 217; Ruth Kraft, *Menschen im Gegenwind*, p. 277.

[26] For further examples, see my ' "Conditioned against us..." The East German View of the Federal Republic'.

[27] Certain critics have, of course, claimed that the two Germanies do *not* share the same language. Details of the arguments are given by Colin Good in *The German Language and the Communist Ideology*, while some instances of this theme in literature are included in my Conclusion.

supposedly lacking) in the GDR, even the West European is able to gain some idea of those features which are different – or which are at least considered differently – in the two parts of the nation. The perspective of the traveller (or defector) alone, in other words, makes his observations an implicit commentary on divided Germany.

Works which employ these figures can be classified into two broad categories to which there is one exception: the work of Uwe Johnson. If Johnson's stance is taken as 'impartial', then the other positions can be classed as 'dogmatic' (as exemplified in the work of Joho) and 'persuasive' (as in that of Kant). In the former category travellers tend to be far less sensitive in their reactions to the other Germany, and far more convinced of its evil nature. Their attitudes and actions tend to be predictable in that they faithfully reflect the Party line, while the style of these novels also shows a surprising uniformity. Works by the older generation frequently fall into this category, such as Inge von Wangenheim's *Reise ins Gestern*, Ernst Schuhmacher's 'Bundeswehrleutnant 1962', Joho's *Es gibt kein Erbarmen*, and the later novels of Anna Seghers, particularly *Die Entscheidung* and *Das Vertrauen*. But works by the younger generation can also be included alongside these: Brigitte Reimann's *Die Geschwister*, for example.

Works with a more concealed rhetoric are generally superior in other respects, as can be seen from Fritz Rudolf Fries's *Der Weg nach Oobliadooh*, Dieter Noll's *Die Abenteuer des Werner Holt. Roman einer Heimkehr*, Christa Wolf's *Der geteilte Himmel*, and Joachim Wohlgemuth's *Verlobung in Hullerbusch*. Here the central character does not appear so much as a puppet being exploited solely to expose moral inadequacy, he is a rather more passive figure, and there is considerably more insight into his psychology. There is also far more attention to modifying the style to correspond to the differing situations in which the traveller finds himself. Writers in this category do not, however, consistently understate the issues or the traveller's attitude towards them to the extent pursued by Johnson. A major achievement of their works, particularly when contrasted with the more dogmatic, is the indirect, but nevertheless controlling guidance evident in their imaginative use of the traveller's situation.

3. THE REPRESENTATIVE

The depiction of divided Germany by means of ideologically representative figures has been another common feature of much contemporary East German writing. It is, in fact, more frequently employed than the motif of the 'traveller', one reason possibly being that writers need not use citizens of both Democratic and Federal Republic in order to bring out ideologically differing points of view. As Max Marula, one of the central characters of Heiduczek's *Abschied von den Engeln*, argues: 'Die innere Entscheidung eines Menschen allein hat Bedeutung, nicht die geographische' (p. 437). A man's spiritual allegiance is far more important than his place of residence, in other words, and a number of GDR writers have consequently shown how certain East Germans are politically closer to the Federal Republic than the GDR, just as many West Germans are shown to be closer to Communism than to the capitalist philosophy of their homeland. Writers can thus set their plot in either East or West Germany: what is important is that the reader recognises the representative function of certain typical characters.

For East German writers the present division of Germany reflects two ideologically differing attitudes towards life. The GDR represents socialism, or 'humanism' as it is often called; the Federal Republic, on the other hand, embodies capitalism and fascism. Because the conflict of these ideologies is seen as international, the interaction of any two characters who represent them has important metaphorical implications: it may suggest a clash not only of the two German states, but also of world powers. And although the West European is unlikely to see the conflict of two individuals in such terms, it is important to recognise that the situation is quite different for the East German, who is far more likely to have been trained in political thinking.

It is self-evident that in all East German novels the majority of GDR citizens will be representative of their country to the extent that they will reflect (positive) socialist qualities. There is, however, a more exclusive category of representative that can be distinguished: figures who have been consciously endowed with a particularly symbolic function. Whereas in any novel with a political purpose all characters are bound to assume an ideological role (and particularly in the context of a politically orientated audience), in certain cases this role is stressed to such a degree that the character must be regarded in the first instance as a mouthpiece for a political viewpoint. The most striking example of this is to be found in Uwe Johnson's *Zwei Ansichten*, in which symbolic nomenclature provides an unambiguous signal to the reader: the central male character is known only as 'B' (he lives in, and is in many respects typical of, the '*Bundes-republik*'), while the central female figure is named 'D' (her place of residence being the '*DDR*'). Few East German novels are as explicit as this, for there is, in general no need for the author to underline – or even point out – the particular way in which characters are representative of either East or West. Well informed by propaganda on the nature of each side, Eastern readers will recognise without hesitation those qualities which are normally associated with the respective states. Johnson's signals should be superfluous for those in the GDR: socialist readers will have little difficulty in perceiving with which characters their sympathies should lie.

There is a further reason why East German readers will easily recognise the representative function of such figures. In Marxist aesthetics the concept of the 'type' is not only a central critical category: it is actually a criterion of 'realist' literature, the only form of writing which the Marxist considers valid. Contrary to what has sometimes been assumed in Western Europe, the Marxist 'type' is not the 'average' or 'common' man, but an individual who stands for something larger and more important than himself, a man who embodies the general historical and social tendencies of a given period. Further, the author who manages to create a 'type' has also succeeded in recognising basic historical truths. As it is expressed by Hans Koch in an article for the forthcoming official *Wörterbuch der Kulturpolitik*:

immer lenkt das Typische den Blick auf eine tiefere, wahrheitsgemäße Erkenntnis und Wertung wirklicher Zusammenhänge und Beziehungen, auf eine wahrheitstreu verallgemeinerte Erkenntnis des Lebens, 'wie es wirklich ist'.[1]

The entry on 'Typ' for the same volume defines the concept more closely:

Gepräge, Eigenart; Grundform, Urbild, Vorbild. In der marxistisch-leninistischen Ästhetik bezeichnet der Begriff Typ (oder Typus) eine literarische oder künstlerische Gestalt unter dem Blickwinkel der in dieser Figur getroffenen Verallgemeinerung historisch und sozial bestimmter überindividueller Wesenszüge und Eigenschaften, die kennzeichnend sind für ganze Klassen, soziale Schichten und Gruppen, für die Mitwirkenden an bestimmten historischen Strömungen. Im künstlerischen Schaffen lenkt der Begriff innerhalb der Einheit der verschiedenen Momente der künstlerischen Verallgemeinerung (→*Typisierung*) gerade auf das historisch, sozial, politisch, ethisch und geistig für bestimmte Klassen, Schichten, Gruppen, historische Richtungen und Strömungen Repräsentative in den individuellen Gestalten und Figuren.[2]

In choosing to analyse what I have termed 'representatives' I am, in fact, dealing with what the East Germans would consider 'types'. I have avoided their concept owing to its evaluative connotations and also because I have tended to restrict myself to characters. For the Marxist, however, the 'type' also exists in situations and actions.

The earliest representative figures of GDR literature were created during the period of the 'Cold War', that post-war era of tense relations between the Soviet bloc and the West. This politico-historical concept is in one respect highly unsatisfactory,

---

[1] Quoted from Hans Koch's 'Stichworte zum sozialistischen Realismus' (p. 28), a series of definitions intended for inclusion in the *Wörterbuch der Kulturpolitik*, to be edited by Harald Bühl et al. The publication of this volume has been repeatedly postponed.

[2] Loc. cit., pp. 26–7.

however, for the Cold War, in the form that it existed, was not waged solely through the 'icy civilities' of formal diplomatic contact between East and West. It was conducted in the main through propaganda of a violent and inflammatory kind, which often approached the extremist vilification used in times of actual physical strife.[3] Not surprisingly, the tendencies of East German literature in this period were largely determined by such political warfare and by the appeals of the politicians; and although writers operated with more restraint than the latter, they nevertheless utilised a number of their methods. The most striking of these is their use of extremes in the presentation of character.

One of the political propagandist's most common ways of attacking his enemy is to present him as morally despicable. In order to achieve as unequivocal an effect as possible, the opponent is totally discredited in the mind of the reader, while reciprocal 'glorification of one's own' reinforces the natural human responses which this form of presentation is likely to elicit. This method of characterising one's opponent may be acceptable in political warfare, but there is a certain danger in striving to establish such a clear pattern of 'good' and 'evil' in works of literature. Extremism in the depiction of character results in the black/white distinction on which overt propaganda itself tends to rely and usually leads to an element of caricature and unreality. Even Bertolt Brecht falls a victim to this in *Schweyk im zweiten Weltkrieg*, and J. P. Stern has justifiably complained that the SS-men and 'Gestapo' are 'presented as gullible and stupid beyond the limits of our credence'.[4] If the writer is to convince his reader, then some

---

[3] There is no volume which deals with inter-German propaganda as a whole. For details and for further information on Communist propaganda as seen by the West, see Hans Schimanski, *Leitgedanken und Methoden der kommunistischen Indoktrination*; for Western propaganda (as seen by the East), see Heinz Heitzer, *Andere über uns. Das 'DDR-Bild' des westdeutschen Imperialismus und seine bürgerlichen Kritiker*. Both these volumes betray an obvious political bias.

[4] 'War and the Comic Muse', p. 200.

balance is necessary. Polarisation of characters may certainly illustrate to even the most undiscriminating of readers where the writer considers positive values to lie, yet the power of the work to persuade him of their importance may be undercut by his inability to accept the vehicles through which they are presented. The reader's reaction may consequently not be admiration or the desire to emulate, but simply a sense of amusement (or irritation) at the crassness of the writer's methods.

East German writers have naturally exploited the possibilities of this basic rhetorical technique – the rhetoric of 'sympathy' and 'antipathy' as Harvey Sucksmith has put it with reference to the method of Dickens.[5] In every work examined in this volume citizens of the GDR are presented as morally superior to their counterparts in the West; and if they are not, then it is inevitably suggested that their spiritual home lies in the other part of the German nation. Predictably, the clear, almost ridiculous, superiority of Communists above all other characters tends to dominate novels written in the early years of the Republic. Strongly influenced by the fervent mood of the Cold War, these works display a stark division of characters into the respective camps, Communist and Capitalist, East and West, sympathetic and antipathetic. Fortunately, however, the history of GDR literature shows a movement towards greater sophistication, particularly in the presentation of East German citizens and representatives of the Western ideology, and one of the aims of the present chapter will be to trace this development by concentrating on the changing methods of characterising those figures who are meant to act as representatives of the two different ideologies.

Developing modes of characterisation can be seen as part of a larger movement in GDR literary history, which, broadly speaking, can be seen as an evolution from 'telling' to 'showing'.[6]

[5] See in particular Chapter Seven of *The Narrative Art of Charles Dickens*.
[6] For the classical discussion of these terms in literary criticism, see Wayne C. Booth, *The Rhetoric of Fiction*.

Early East German novels, such as those by Eduard Claudius, Anna Seghers, and Hans-Jürgen Steinmann, betray an exposed form of rhetoric, particularly in the way that the reader is provided with information and opinions on characters and events. The angle of presentation is also almost invariably third-person omniscient. Later novels, however, especially those of the younger generation, reveal a marked advance towards 'dramatisation' and more indirect presentation of information and judgements. Works by Christa Wolf, Hermann Kant and Werner Heiduczek all provide good examples of this, and although certain writers have persisted with a simpler approach, these tend to be the second-rate (Renata Feyl, Hans von Oettingen and Kurt Steiniger, for example). The best have increasingly turned towards methods which have hitherto frequently been considered 'decadent' in the socialist countries, such as flashback, montage, interior monologue, and a shifting point of view. The present chapter will trace this evolution in so far as it relates to ideologically representative figures.

The first novel to use the divided nation as a central theme was Eduard Claudius's *Menschen an unserer Seite* (1951). This work is significant in two other respects: it was one of the first East German novels to take contemporary developments as its subject-matter (in contrast to the many others concerned with the Nazi era), and it was also one of the first works of stature to emerge from the GDR.[7] East German critics have long been

[7] John Flores' view that the book is 'entirely colourless and strictly functional propaganda' (*Poetry in East Germany*, p. 18) strikes me as an ill-founded judgement, as does that of Marcel Reich-Ranicki: 'Ein oberflächlicher Propagandaroman mit schematischen Gestalten, papiernen Dialogen und vielen langweiligen Beschreibungen' (*Deutsche Literatur in West und Ost*, pp. 452–3). Bernhard Greiner, who has written a perceptive analysis of the novel's faults, suggests that it 'gelangt über illustrierende Wirklichkeitsdarstellungen nicht hinaus' (*Von der Allegorie zur Idylle*, p. 70). Some Western commentators have reacted more favourably, however. Hans Peter Anderle, for example, finds that 'der Roman demonstriert die Möglichkeit, aktuelle mitteldeutsche Probleme optimistisch, aber ohne nennenswerten

united on Claudius's success in producing an outstanding early example of committed literature (although the hero's alcoholism did occasion some initial unease), and the novel has since come to be regarded as the archetype of the 'Betriebsroman'.

Menschen an unserer Seite centres on the struggles of the 'Aktivist' Hans Aehre,[8] a passionate but self-willed socialist, who is determined to undertake a new and dangerous method of masonry in order to avert the lay-off of many colleagues owing to blast-furnace difficulties in his steelworks. Aehre's plans are repeatedly sabotaged by Matschat, the production controller of the works, who is being paid secretly by the West German branch of the firm (the Eastern plant having been nationalised); but Aehre, with the help of his wife, is finally able to convince the progressive socialists among the management of the feasibility of his ideas. The novel concludes with the triumph of his project and the discovery of Matschat's treachery.

Claudius's presentation of division is mainly in terms of character. Two of the group of figures surrounding the hero visit the West, but their experiences there are limited; the image of the other part of the nation is evoked for the most part through the suggestions made by characters in the East. The main features of the Federal Republic are in fact the stock ones: there are machinations in progress between the Allies and Adenauer concerning arms production; submission of the workers persists, as in the previous capitalist era; and, inevitably, there is the continued existence of National Socialist elements. But far more important than the actual description of conditions in the West

Blutverlust darzustellen' (*Mitteldeutsche Erzähler*, p. 137), while Hans-Dietrich Sander, one of the most querulous of critics, considers the book superior to many others written at that time (*Geschichte der Schönen Literatur in der DDR*, pp. 119–20).

[8] 'Aktivist' was a title to honour those who showed exceptional efforts in increasing socialist production in the early years of the Republic. For further details, see the relevant entry in Hans H. Reich's *Sprache und Politik*.

As both Sander (op. cit., p. 120) and Greiner (op. cit., p. 69) have pointed out, Aehre is based on the figure of Hans Garbe, one of the GDR's very first activists. Claudius wrote an earlier story on Garbe's exploit, entitled 'Vom schweren Anfang'.

(which only amounts to a relatively small percentage of the novel) are the hints concerning that part of the nation. The most significant of these occurs early in the novel, when the reader is informed that the Western branch of the works is intent on disrupting production in the East to the extent of deliberately sabotaging it through the agency of Matschat. It is the latter who stands for the capitalist force still oppressing the GDR, and his struggle against Aehre acquires symbolic significance. Each becomes representative of the ideologies of the two German states.

Claudius manipulates the sympathies of his readers by the careful build-up of character. Although the reader's emotions are obviously likely to be gained by those who deserve them most as far as the plot (and, and in this case, political conviction) is concerned, the author indulges in a number of other methods specifically designed to promote sympathy. The first, although somewhat marginal, is nevertheless sufficiently striking to reveal the author's intentions in the book: 'Menschen an *unserer* Seite.' Claudius is here identifying himself, and, more importantly, his reader, with the central characters of the story. An equally direct method of asserting support for those whose actions he approves is characterisation through name. The technique is well established in German – as well as in most other literatures[9] – and it has been used particularly frequently by a contemporary of Claudius, Erwin Strittmatter. The latter's use verges on the ridiculous, however, owing to its excess and over-directness.[10] The stylisation is less strident in *Menschen an*

---

[9] Peter Demetz gives some examples from German and other literatures in 'Notes on Figurative Names in Theodor Fontane's Novels'. As René Wellek and Austin Warren have pointed out: 'The simplest form of characterisation is naming. Each "appelation" is a kind of vivifying, animizing, individuating'. (*Theory of Literature*, p. 208)

[10] The characters of *Ole Bienkopp*, for example, are named according to their professions or their dominant virtue or vice, with the result that the decadent capitalist is called 'Ramsch', the alcoholic ne'er-do-well 'Mampe Bitter', the 'Konsum' manageress 'Fräulein Danke', the undeviating Party Secretary 'Bleibtreu', etc. There is a sense of caricature and puppetry induced in these instances; it is difficult to take seriously characters with such names as these.

unserer Seite, where Strittmatter's equations are replaced by connotations. The name 'Aehre', for example, suggests both the ear of wheat (which in the Communist countries in particular is a symbol of successful growth and which is in fact featured on the GDR national flag), and the concept of 'Ehre', which is also applicable. The name of his opponent, Matschat, suggests rather different qualities: 'Matsch' (noun = 'slush') or 'matsch' (adjective referring either to the loser in a game or to something which is bad – both are relevant). Other examples include the pusillanimous technical director 'Wassermann', the feeble Party Secretary who is reputed to be a somewhat unsuccessful womaniser 'Bock' (nicknamed 'Böckchen'), and the new Party Secretary who effects a change in attitudes, 'Wende'. These names give a (sometimes ironic) reinforcement to the qualities of their owners; they are not, however – as are Strittmatter's – used as *initial* signals to the reader.

Claudius uses physiognomy in a similar manner – on certain occasions to arouse an antipathetic attitude towards a character, on others rather to reinforce sympathetic aspects. Using the features (particularly facial) as an index of character also has a long history in literature, and Claudius's methods are once again traditional. Those characters with positive traits have appealing features, such as the Works Manager Carlin, whose face is 'beherrscht, hager' (p. 35); Karin, Aehre's wife, has a 'gutes, breites Bauerngesicht mit den hellen aufgeweckten Augen' (p. 51). The villain of the piece, Matschat, is completely different. The first description presents a somewhat revolting figure: 'Matschats dickliches Gesicht mit den faltigen Wangen... Seine stets geschwollenen Augen' (p. 21), while his teeth later appear as 'ungepflegte Zähne' (p. 75). Kunzel, his coarse henchman, is equally repulsive: 'Sein ungefüges, grobes Gesicht...' (p. 350); Bock too is unattractive: 'Bocks Gesicht, nicht mehr gepflegt...' (p. 176).[11]

---

11 This process of character-introduction (with simultaneous analysis) through the features has a further extension in the use of animal imagery. Animals are used to describe actual events in the steelworks, for example, such as

The build-up of character is normally a slower process than the above examples might suggest, and Claudius does indeed operate with less direct means elsewhere. One of the most important ways in which he moulds the reader's attitudes is by giving depth motivation to the actions of all the central characters except Matschat and Bock. Through detailed investigation of their development up to the commencement of his story, he creates stature, in other words, for characters with whom our sympathies would normally lie. Their mistakes are consequently often seen to be motivated from good intentions. Other characters, however, are supplied with only a minimum of biographical data, with the result that no attenuating circumstances surround their (culpable) actions.

It is Aehre's motivation which is the most carefully presented. His determination to succeed against Matschat, as well as his stubbornness, are seen to spring from vivid childhood experiences of harsh oppression. His dominant memory is of his grandfather being whipped across the face by a 'Gutsbesitzer', who refused to allow him any more wood in the depths of a severe winter. Since that occasion Aehre has tended to see the ruling class as a whole in terms of the 'Gutsbesitzer-' or 'Hauptmannsgesicht', and even in the new socialist state he is able to detect examples of this category, chief among them being Matschat. The exploiting 'Gutsbesitzer' is an archetypal target of socialist attack (and not merely of propaganda in the GDR), which makes Claudius's choice of it all the more useful from an

the suction clearance of a furnace, in which the cleaner is like 'ein Elefantenkopf mit einem langen Rüssel' (p. 88), or other daily occurrences, such as Aehre's handwriting, which is 'krakelig wie Krähenspuren' (p. 45). But this imagery is most frequently used in the description of characters: a neutral image describes the mother of Andrytzki, a non-political figure ('in den Augen die bange Traurigkeit eines alten kranken Tiers' [p. 278]), but more revealing analogies are used in the case of Bock ('stockernd, gleich einem zu fett gewordenen Hahn', p. 21) and the characters working against Aehre, whom he calls 'Hyänen'. Yet it is the passionate and headstrong hero himself for whom the majority of animal references are employed. He is twice described as a 'Stier' (pp. 167, 364), twice as a 'Bär' (pp. 342, 366), and once as a rabid dog (p. 177).

ideological point of view. The successors to the former landlords are one of the main targets of the novel, for this type had not yet been totally eliminated from the East of 1950 (the date at which the action takes place). Andrytzki, a sympathetic figure who is forced into defection by Matschat, discovers that it is far more prominent in the West. His experiences there make it clear that the course of Western development is in fact being largely determined by such feudal figures.

The conflict between Matschat and Aehre acquires its symbolic function mainly through their respective biographies. The ideological differences between the two are reinforced through their class differences, and their fight can consequently be seen in terms of the class struggle. Aehre is presented as the oppressed, working-class victim of capitalist exploitation, who, like so many others, has been liberated through the 'socialist victory' and who is now prepared to sacrifice himself for the good of others. Matschat, on the other hand, does not appear as working-class or even to have a sense of sympathy with that group. As a 'Meister' of the old school he represents a willing lackey of the former rulers, a point which is underlined through his acts of sabotage. By allying himself secretly with the West, he complements this image of being spiritually a member of the Federal Republic and a supporter of the capitalist system which it embodies.

In Aehre and Matschat, then, Claudius has produced figures who are symbolic of Eastern and Western mentalities as seen by the GDR. Various aspects of their differing attitudes to life are brought out in the conflict between them, but it is fairly obvious from the start that the socialist point of view will not only appear superior, but that it will also triumph in the end. Bernhard Greiner has objected to this, maintaining that the schematisation deprives the novel of tension. Referring to methods of characterisation, he comments: 'Bei so eindeutiger Verteilung von Gut und Böse kann Spannung nur noch aus der Frage entstehen, wie das Böse entlarvt wird.'[12] Greiner is justified in sug-

[12] *Von der Allegorie zur Idylle*, p. 71.

gesting Claudius over-uses evil features, particularly in the case of Matschat, but it would be unfair to classify Aehre himself simply as 'gut'. Claudius is careful to show that his hero's character is far from perfect (a point which irritated a number of the first East German critics), and in this respect the author stands out against the majority of other writers of the Cold War period, whose 'positive heroes' are totally without fault.

There is a strong sense of moral purpose in *Menschen an unserer Seite*, but in order to achieve his ends the author does not rely solely on the ethical awareness of his East German reader. Like so many others who follow him, he uses qualities of a non-moral kind to characterise figures whom he nevertheless wishes to stand for moral entities. Apart from the typical actions which tend to promote sympathy for the hero and to alienate the villain, he reinforces the polarity between the two by such means as nomenclature, physiognomy, and tendentious imagery. In this way Claudius does not depend on a reader who shares his political beliefs and moral judgements. More recent novelists have been less explicit in this respect.

Menschen an unserer Seite contains several elements which recur in other novels to be examined in this section, but later writers naturally go beyond Claudius's pioneering, if elementary, presentation. As far as the novels' contents are concerned, there are two main developments. First, the actual interaction of representatives (rather than their depiction in isolation) acquires a more central position. And second, greater emphasis is laid on characterisation of the Western representatives. This development reaches a climax only in the mid-sixties, however, and many novels of the fifties reveal the clumsy propagandist techniques for which socialist writing in general is often criticised. The choice of extremes in character and situation, for example, idealisation and simplification of personality (especially of ideological representatives), and constant authorial interference in the narrative. These are all evident in such works as Erich Loest's *Die Westmark fällt weiter* (1952), Jan Petersen's *Der Fall Dr. Wagner* (1954), Eberhard Panitz's *Flucht* (1956), and Hasso Laudon's *Semesterferien in Berlin* (1959).

A typical product of the fifties was Anna Seghers' *Die Entscheidung* (1959), a work which unfortunately embodies most of the features listed above. Predictably, critical reaction to this book was sharply divided between East and West. Anna Seghers, President of the GDR 'Schriftstellerverband' and long-standing Communist, could hardly be attacked by East German critics who were desperately searching for great works of social-ist art, the absence of which was at that time causing Ulbricht some concern and which led to the Bitterfeld Conference of that year. Accordingly, *Die Entscheidung* was received in ecstatic terms in the East. In the West, on the other hand, the reception was decidedly hostile.[13]

The plot of this novel traces several years in the careers of a number of figures who are all in some way connected with the factories of the wealthy Bentheim family (as Robert Andrews has suggested, a disguised Krupp's or Thyssen's).[14] In the West there are the owners and managers of the firm, who are shown to be selfish and decadent. The characters of the East, on the other hand, are selfless and idealistic. They are grouped around the recently nationalised branch of the old Bentheim steelworks in 'Neustadt', and they are intent on building the factory up, almost literally, from the ruins of war. As in *Menschen an unserer Seite*, we are shown deliberate attempts by the West to sabotage the East German works and to tempt or blackmail the leading engineers into flight from the Republic. Although initially successful, the saboteurs fail to destroy the Communists'

[13] Grave reservations on the quality of the novel were expressed by a number of critics. Sabine Brandt, for example, concluded a devastating review with the following: 'Die Seghers nennt ihr Buch einen Roman. Es ist jedoch eher eine ideologische Heilslehre'. ('*Die Entscheidung* der Anna Seghers', p. 81.) The essence of all other Western objections is the same: it is the overtly programmatic nature of the book which is considered so disturbing.

[14] 'Anna Seghers' *Die Entscheidung*', p. 260.

enthusiasm, and the novel concludes with the triumph of the workers' labours.

One of the author's main aims is to demonstrate the difference between East and West in the years 1947–51, between emergent socialism on the one hand, and resurgent Nazism, capitalism and militarism on the other. (The second part of this projected trilogy, *Das Vertrauen*, traces the intensification of differences between 1951–3.)[15] The 'Entscheidung' of the title is the decision which each character in the novel is obliged to make against the background of this conflict, although many of them have already made a firm choice between the two sides – some as early as 1933.

Both the East (which in this case includes a number of representative figures from the USSR) and the West (the Federal Republic and also the USA, to which the action is occasionally extended) are presented mainly in terms of their respective ideological protagonists. Practically all the figures are introduced biographically, with the result that we are offered an immediate index to their character. The musings of Vogt (the Neustadt Party Secretary), for example, provide an unequivocal illustration of one of Anna Seghers' categories. Vogt knows he can rely on a colleague in East Berlin supplying his firm with what is required, simply because that colleague has never failed in the past:

Vogt baute auf Martin. Er wußte, daß der alles tat, was in seiner Macht stand, um diese Arbeit zu erledigen, so wie Martin vordem andere Aufgaben übernommen hatte – in illegalen Zeiten in Deutschland, im Spanischen Krieg oder im Konzentrationslager. (p. 330)

Within a subordinate clause the author has created a minor 'positive hero'; unfortunately, however, he is never developed beyond this basic outline. This example is more striking than most, but Andrews is right to complain: 'how often we hear

---

15 Anna Seghers now seems to have decided to make this the final volume of the trilogy, counting *Die Toten bleiben jung* as the first, and *Die Entscheidung* as the second. She may, nonetheless, complete another volume – in line with her original intentions.

recited the battle honours of the true comrade: Spartacus, the anti-Hitler underground, Spain, concentration camp, Soviet Union and the rest'.[16]

The battle honours of those in the West are equally predictable: the Condor Legion, SA or SS, 'Wehrmacht', shady business dealings in the new Federal Republic, and intense anti-Communism. Chapter Two provides several illustrations of this. Whereas the first chapter is set against the remains of the Eastern steelworks, Spartan living conditions in the 'SBZ', and warnings of resurgent Nazism in the West, the second takes place in the splendid villa of the wealthy 'Kommerzienrat' Castricius, who has drawn considerable profit from the Third Reich and the war. Castricius welcomes his daughter together with his son-in-law, Otto Bentheim, who has just gained release from a prisoner-of-war camp through the machinations of the eminent 'Justizrat' Spranger. Before the son-in-law is even described to the reader, Spranger talks at length on the dangers of Bentheim's remaining in the area, suggesting in the process the degree of his war crimes and also revealing the nature of his own corrupt procedures. Spranger's main concern is that his name is not in any way sullied by his present actions, since this might prejudice other financial negotiations in which he is engaged. In general, the representatives of the West are characterised by the two qualities which he displays here: first, their culpable actions during the Third Reich; and second, their wealth and strong capitalist urges.

It is impossible to speak of a single hero or single villain in the vast panorama presented in this novel (some 150 characters are introduced): both must be seen collectively, with the grouping of characters in the main – but not exclusively – one of East and West. The exceptions to this are the standard ones. There are a number of figures in the East who long for the prosperity and 'freedom' of the West or who are actually in the pay of some West German body: the engineer Büttner, for example, who encourages a number of waverers to defect, and the worker

[16] 'Anna Seghers' *Die Entscheidung*', p. 260.

Janausch, who has little sympathy for Communist ideals. But the West on the other hand, is not composed only of the capitalists. The Bentheim family's wealth is shown to be partly a result of inadequate pay to their workers, and when these go on strike, their march is violently halted by the police. Naturally, it is the East which is seen to be the true spiritual home of these suppressed figures.

Both Brettschneider and Reich-Ranicki have made fun of the strict grouping of the characters, and Ranicki's comments on *Das Vertrauen* serve equally well for the earlier novel:

Dennoch gibt es auch in der DDR böse Menschen. Nur daß sie nach dem Westen fliehen. Und auch im Westen gibt es neben den Industriellen und ihren verdummten Knechten auch gute Menschen. Nur daß sie sich nach der DDR sehnen.

Wer gut und wer böse ist, wird uns immer nachdrücklich mitgeteilt: '*Er sah vor sich Ulspergers schönes, hartes Gesicht, seine aufrechte Haltung.*' Einer, der ein schönes und hartes Gesicht hat und sich überdies aufrecht hält, ist natürlich ein vorbildlicher Kommunist.

Oder: '*Hell stach es aus Janauschs weißblauen Augen heraus in Webers ruhigen, noch jungen Blick, als berührten sich die Spitzen zweier elektrisch geladenen Drähte.*' Und selbst der Klassenletzte ahnt, daß sich derjenige, aus dessen Augen etwas heraussticht, als ein Verräter, der andere hingegen als ein treuer Sohn des Arbeiter-und-Bauern-Staates erweisen wird.

Reich-Ranicki then goes on to criticise the lengths to which Anna Seghers will go in order to reveal the loyalties of any particular character:

Aber mit einer derartigen Kennzeichnung ihrer Gestalten gibt sich Anna Seghers nicht zufrieden, sie hat neuerdings noch massivere Mittel in Reserve: Um die Abscheulichkeit jenes Janausch, aus dessen Augen etwas heraussticht, vollends zu verdeutlichen, läßt uns die Erzählerin wissen, daß er einen ekelerregenden Geruch verbreitet.[17]

Rather like Claudius, Anna Seghers is here using personal, non-moral qualities in order to reinforce a view which is essentially a moral one. The crassness to which Reich-Ranicki refers is explicable in terms of her strongly didactic intent, which has

[17] 'Bankrott einer Erzählerin. Anna Seghers' Roman "Das Vertrauen"', p. 28.

led to such basic, unambiguous methods throughout both novels.

This black/white method of presenting characters is rather primitive, and so too is the general manner in which Anna Seghers treats her reader, the way in which she *informs* him of characters' views and motivation rather than letting him adduce these for himself. As was suggested earlier, the difference is the traditional one between 'telling' and 'showing'. Anna Seghers 'tells' in this novel to the point of excess, and her analysis of characters' minds in particular is often clumsy and unnecessary. Another consequence of the good/evil classificatory scheme is that rather unconvincing figures have been produced. Characterisation of minor figures is, as both Andrews and Witold Tulasiewicz[18] have pointed out, perfunctory, and even in the case of major figures there is no adequate presentation of anyone's 'inner life' in which the earlier novels of Anna Seghers excelled. The same applies to *Das Vertrauen*, in which motivation is grossly oversimplified and characters tend to be analysed in political terms alone.

Anna Seghers' interest in this novel is in broad social and historical forces at all levels in two radically differing societies. She ranges from the lavish household of the wealthy Bentheims (with its grandiose meals and wines) to the basic simplicity of the restored bomb site in which the Enders family lives in the East. By switching rapidly from East to West as also from one end of the social stratum to the other (for here, as in *Menschen an unserer Seite*, ideological differences are reinforced by class ones), she reveals the changed economic and spiritual circumstances of the whole of post-war Germany. This epic perspective is widened further by the use of characters who have already appeared in a novel depicting another historical era: Castricius, Spranger, and von Klemm all feature in *Die Toten bleiben jung*, which deals with their activities during the Third Reich. Together with incessant allusions to the past in *Die Entscheidung* itself, this gives a further – explanatory – dimen-

18 See his introduction to Anna Seghers' *Hochzeit in Haiti*, pp. 28–9.

sion to the present situation. The USA too is introduced on occasions as a form of intensified Federal Republic. There the key feature of life may not be fascism, but it is certainly unscrupulous capitalism.

Both sides are repeatedly presented in terms of their political history, in which, as already suggested, moral decisions have had to be made: most importantly, for or against fascism. Associated with the anti-fascists are the themes of hope, trust, and humaneness, while the fascists live in a world of guilt, corruption and suspicion. There is a contrast too between the material standards of each side. There are constant problems in the Soviet Zone/GDR concerning building materials, food, and transport. Such problems seem non-existent in the Western Zones/Federal Republic, where Marshall Aid and a militarisation programme have apparently relieved all difficulties, at least for the rich. Although the splendour of the West is never denied, the immoral way in which it has been achieved is frequently suggested.

The sense of contrast between East and West is reinforced by the structure of the novel. This seems to owe something to Anna Seghers' acquaintance with Chinese literature, which she studied during her early career at the University of Cologne. Hans-Dietrich Sander is the only critic to have drawn attention to such influence, and he has done so solely with reference to the extremely wide range of characters, a typical feature of the Chinese novel.[19] Sander could, however, have gone further. There are two other characteristically Chinese features in the construction of *Die Entscheidung*. First, the tendency to move between characters (rather than events or situations); and second, to concentrate on one character (or set of characters) for a number of short chapters and then to return to him (or them) only considerably later in the plot. The main advantage of this technique is that it lends itself to regular counterpointing of the two states by means of their representatives. Contrasting life styles are juxtaposed and the differences between them (as also

[19] *Geschichte der Schönen Literatur in der DDR*, pp. 293–4.

between the ideologies on which they are based) are thrown into relief.

It is possible to consider almost every character of *Die Entscheidung* as a representative figure, for each one is seen in political terms and in relation to the philosophies of the two German states. Apart from the main characters, whose representative function is brought out mainly by their biographies, all the others are constantly having to make decisions of a moral or political nature. These naturally indicate the attitude towards life which these characters have decided to adopt. It was part of the author's professed aim to illustrate this process of decision-making at all levels of society, and to depict in particular the decisions which are raised by political division. As she explained in an interview with Christa Wolf:

CHRISTA WOLF: Was würden Sie als die Grundidee Ihres Buches bezeichnen?
ANNA SEGHERS: Das Buch heißt 'Die Entscheidung'. Mir war die Hauptsache zu zeigen, wie in unserer Zeit der Bruch, der die Welt in zwei Lager spaltet, auf alle, selbst die privatesten, selbst die intimsten Teile unseres Lebens einwirkt: Liebe, Ehe, Beruf sind sowenig von der großen Entscheidung ausgenommen wie Politik oder Wirtschaft. Keiner kann sich entziehen, jeder wird vor die Frage gestellt: Für wen, gegen wen bist du? – Das wollte ich an verschiedenen Menschenschicksalen zeigen.[20]

This overtly political aim has unfortunately led Anna Seghers into didactic techniques which are out of place in imaginative literature. In this novel, as well as in *Das Vertrauen*, she has sunk to the level of second- and third-rate writers, whose themes are in general conveyed in far bolder a manner than those of the more distinguished. In this respect *Die Entscheidung* is typical of the majority of novels written during the period of the Cold War.

Brigitte Reiman's *Die Geschwister* is frequently mentioned alongside Christa Wolf's *Der geteilte Himmel*, for the works

---

[20] 'Anna Seghers über ihre Schaffensmethode. Ein Gespräch', pp. 52–3.

have much in common. Apart from incidentals, such as both stories appearing within a few months of each other in 1963, and their authors being women of roughly the same age and historical experience, each work demonstrates a response to the Bitterfeld Conference of 1959. The theme of 'Republikflucht', combined with a love theme, raises the issue of the two German states in each work, while the main protagonists of both are the new, young, critical intellectuals of the GDR, those for whom the temptations of the West are not solely financial and who leave the East of their own accord – not on account of some West German 'Abwehr' organisation, as was usually the case in works of the fifties. Another motivating factor in their defection is the desire to escape an intolerable feature of GDR society: the Party dogmatists. Criticism of these figures combines with more general criticism of the socialist state, which was also rare during the preceding decade.

Die Geschwister centres on two days in the life of Elisabeth Arendt, an artist who is working in a factory under the Bitterfeld scheme.[21] Her brother's revelation that he is intending to leave the GDR (the date is 1960 or 1961) throws her into a state of indecision on the course of action she should adopt, into reminiscences on her student life and love affairs, and also into reflection on her constant struggles in GDR society. Although she has not yet joined the Socialist Unity Party, Elisabeth realises she must now do this; she also determines to persuade her brother to stay in the Democratic Republic, and together with her fiancé she finally succeeds in doing so.

---

21 At the famous conference of writers and Party leaders at Bitterfeld in 1959, writers and artists were encouraged to concentrate on depicting the working man in his industrial surroundings. Industry too was encouraged to assist this process by providing the necessary facilities for such creative artists, who were in turn expected to advise any workers who wished to attempt to write or to paint. An important sub-theme of *Die Geschwister* is that only in the GDR can the talents of the worker be discovered and fostered: in the West they will remain latent forever. Elisabeth's brother makes reference to this Eastern 'Kulturrevolution' at a climactic point of the story (cf. below, p. 88).

The potential defector, Uli, does not embody the qualities normally associated with the refugee. The main reason for his decision to leave is that he has been unfairly treated by the Party, and sections of the story concern his (justified) criticism of certain distressing aspects of day-to-day working problems. But the conflict in the story is not solely between him and his sister Elisabeth. It is the eldest brother of the family, Konrad, who provides a more definite counterpoint to the heroine and who comes to represent the key qualities of the other German state, in which he has now been living for several years.

In taking stock of her life and that of Uli, Elisabeth recalls the manner in which Konrad left for the Federal Republic, his initial difficulties in a transit camp,[22] his rise to power, and then his visit to West Berlin for a brief reunion with his sister and mother. This meeting is carefully anticipated and marks the first major climax of the story.

The depiction of Konrad begins well before the actual encounter as Elisabeth recalls the chief characteristics of her brother and prepares the reader for the expected conflict. Using the most primitive form of rhetoric first, she reveals that on the physiognomic level alone Konrad is unattractive: 'Er war ein dunkelhäutiger junger Mann mit einem Äthiopiergesicht, das seinen HJ-Führern ein Ärgernis gewesen sein muß, und mit aufgeworfenen Lippen' (p. 41). Elisabeth then moves to personal qualities: academic brilliance, yet also unscrupulousness, hypocrisy, sycophancy, a combination she sums up in the phrase 'Ellbogen-Mann' (p. 42). The immorality of his flight to the West is set into perspective by her musings on a former schoolfriend, 'Gregory', an engineer who also left the East and whom she occasionally used to meet when she travelled through Berlin. Although by no means the same ambitious type as Konrad, Gregory nevertheless resembles him in having no interest in what he designed, and it is in this disinterest that Elisabeth now recognises his chief failing. Her reproach is

22 Cf. above, p 34.

common in East German literature, and it is often levelled against Western scientists:[23]

[ich fragte mich] ob es für den exakten Mathematiker Gregory einen Unterschied machen würde, wenn er – statt Brückenbögen zu konstruieren – Spezialist für den Bau von Raketenabschußrampen geworden wäre. Ich dachte an unseren letzten Abend in Berlin und an diesen in meiner Erinnerung genau fixierten Augenblick, als ich stumm neben Gregory am Geländer lehnte.

Ich merkte auf einmal, daß ich den Fehler in seiner Rechnung jetzt gefunden hatte. (p. 57)

Moments of reflection such as this bring Elisabeth to a realisation of her political duty. Until Uli's sudden confession she has only been partially committed politically, but the present developments force her to recognise her obligations.

Only after some seventeen pages of flashback on Konrad and on his counterpart, Gregory, does the expected conflict take place. From the start, Konrad is seen to be unchanged. Frau Reimann again raises the motif of the 'Äthiopiergesicht', of which certain features seem to have hardened (her brother has been in the West for some time by this point): 'die scharfen, neuen Linien um Augen und Mund' (p. 59), and the view of Konrad as an 'Ellbogen-Mann' recurs for a third time. The point of view is that of Elisabeth, and so the reader is induced to share her reaction to the character of her brother and to life in West Berlin.

Elisabeth's antipathy is aroused in the main by the decadence of the West. Konrad takes great pleasure in inviting the Eastern visitors to the fashionable 'Kempinski's' and in boasting that his snobbish wife buys her shoes in an expensive shop where the film star Nadja Tiller is also a client and where she is treated as if she were a princess. The meeting progresses peaceably enough at first, with each character talking about his work, but the inevitable altercation occurs when Konrad is

---

[23] E.g. in Jurij Brězan's *Eine Liebesgeschichte*, Karl Heinz Jakobs' *Beschreibung eines Sommers*, J. C. Schwarz's *Das gespaltene Herz*, etc. Cf. above, p. 40.

roused to undisguised contempt by Elisabeth's story of the successful painting movement in her factory:

Aber mein Bruder Ellbogen-Mann gab nicht auf. Er wandte sich wieder an mich, er sagte: 'Wenn das wahr wäre, was du mir da erzählst, dann würde es bedeuten, daß die...*Kulturrevolution* in der Zone schon gesiegt hat. Und das willst du mir doch nicht weismachen, Lies, nicht wahr, das denn doch nicht?' (p. 69)

Whereas previously Konrad's letters had spoken of 'die sogenannte DDR', his shift to the use of 'Zone' reveals the extent to which he has identified himself with West German ways of thinking. Elisabeth's reaction, on the other hand, reveals the degree to which she has committed herself to the GDR: incited into its defence, she immediately forgets all her previous reservations and criticism.

One paragraph of this encounter is worth quoting in full. Elisabeth has just reprimanded her brother for reviling the state which financed his education:

Das Äthiopiergesicht schoß auf mich zu, mit roten Flecken auf den Backenknochen, zwischen den aufgeworfenen Lippen sah ich die Zähne, klein und sehr weiß. Ich kniff die Augen ein, mir war bang, ich hatte ihn getroffen, dieses einzige empfindliche Fleckchen auf der hornenen Haut des Tüchtigen, Ratenzahlenden, Rechnerischen, und hier nur war er verwundbar. Wir saßen noch an einem Tisch, Schwester und Bruder: Wir haßten uns schon. Meine Mutter, mit blassem, unglücklichem Gesicht, rührte sich nicht und sagte nichts, sie war unsere Grenze und unsere letzte Gemeinsamkeit. (p. 71)

Frau Reimann resorts to two older stereotypes in order to intensify Elisabeth's feelings: the (black) Ethiopian, ugly and horrific, as well as the 'hörnerne Siegfried', that figure of German legend who bathed in the blood of the dragon he had slain in order to have a horny, protective skin, which was impenetrable except in one spot. The rhetoric is again traditional: the repulsive facial features are made to seem part of the almost inhuman, automaton-like opponent. Details of Konrad which have been presented individually in previous scenes are here compressed into single sentences, while the actual structure of the sentences is paratactic. By presenting these tense moments directly, as the unfiltered, second-by-second experience of the frightened victim, Frau Reimann increases the reader's involvement and sense of identification with the latter. Another point is that the image of these three figures around the table is clearly intended to suggest the wider relevance of this conflict: the unusual use of the word 'Grenze' forces the reader's attention from the private quarrel to the national situation.[24] To present the division of the country in terms of this broken family relationship is highly appropriate, for it combines both the ideas of hatred for the other as well as that of a common origin.

The confrontation with Konrad sets Uli's choice into the appropriate political perspective, and although this is only part of a sub-plot, the episode in Berlin dominates the book as a whole. Its main function is monitory, and also to illustrate the nature of Uli's choice: between the way of life represented by his brother and that by his sister. Where Brigitte Reimann shows an advance on Anna Seghers is in providing a heroine who is by no means exemplary, and also by criticising certain features of GDR society. By avoiding idealisation (except, unfortunately, in the minor character Joachim, Elisabeth's fiancé), Frau Reimann makes Uli's final decision more credible: his choice is not between black and white, but between clearly distinguishable shades of grey. Stylistically, however, *Die Geschwister* marks little advance on Anna Seghers. The presentation of characters and societies is also simple, and at times

24 This point is made again on the following page, where Elisabeth feels that 'Die unselige Grenze zerschnitt das Weiße, damastenglänzende Tischtuch – der unsichtbare Schlagbaum, der mitten durch unsere Familie ging'. There is an aphoristic quality about this sentence, as well as that on the 'Grenze' quoted above. The same can be said of an earlier use of the word: 'Ich will nicht noch einmal hören, wie meine Mutter ihrem Sohn "auf Wiedersehen" sagt, der wenige Stunden später die Grenze überschreiten wird, die nicht nur Stadt von Stadt, Landschaft von Landschaft trennt' (p. 47).
   There is a tendency throughout the novel to use thought-provoking formulations of this sort.

over-simplified. It is not until Christa Wolf's *Der geteilte Himmel* that East German literature can boast of an artistically satisfying depiction of East and West.

Der geteilte Himmel has undoubtedly elicited more critical discussion than any other novel written in the Democratic Republic (although it will probably be overtaken in due course by Kant's *Die Aula* and Christa Wolf's later novel, *Nachdenken über Christa T.*). First, the work is something of a 'critic's novel'. As an analyst of literature herself, Christa Wolf is well acquainted with the various compositional means open to a writer, and she has exploited the majority of those that tend to be traditionally considered by the critics, whether or not they are well used. Second, the subject-matter of the book raised a considerable storm, with the criticism of GDR society causing particular anger to a large number of reviewers. Third, the novel was probably the first Eastern work of stature to have a substantial impact on the West German reading public. And finally, a reason close to the third, the novel's theme had a strong appeal to the reading public of both Germanies. In 1963 the final closing of the Berlin outlet was still a major conversational point on both sides of the Wall, and any novel set in that city had a strong topical interest.

The plot of *Der geteilte Himmel* is related mainly in the form of flashbacks. The heroine Rita, recovering in a sanatorium after a suicide attempt, recalls the events which led up to the decision to take her life. As a lonely, inexperienced village girl she had met Manfred Herrfurth, a brilliant young scientist whom she was able to follow to the city by enrolling for a teacher-training course. Through contact with others at her college and at a coachworks (where, like all other GDR teachers in training, she had to undergo industrial experience), she was able to develop her personality and to reflect on the quality of life in the Republic. The crisis of her life comes with the rejection of one of Manfred's inventions; disgusted by conditions in the

GDR he leaves for the West, leaving her broken-hearted. Although Rita follows him to Berlin, it is only in order to wish him goodbye. She returns to the Republic, but shortly afterwards throws herself on to the railway line at the coachworks.

Frau Wolf's presentation of division is mainly in terms of character, and the analysis of the novel by Ekkerhard Kloehn is therefore particularly convenient. Kloehn classifies the main figures under three separate headings: 'die Sozialisten', 'die Bürger', and Manfred and Rita.[25] This grouping is a useful one, although the headings have dimensions which Kloehn overlooks: the conflict between 'Bürger' and 'Sozialisten' has obvious international and historical implications, and it is also symbolic of a conflict at national level.

The 'Bürger' of *Der geteilte Himmel* all have distinct traits of the Western stereotype. Manfred's father, for example, is a political opportunist and was a member of the SA for the same reasons as he is now a member of the SED. He is selfish, without any sense of loyalty, and basically dishonest, with himself as well as his family. Manfred's mother is an equally distasteful person, whose blindness and vanity are even worse than those of her husband. Her clear spiritual allegiance to the West is evident in her listening to Federal radio stations, ironically referred to as her 'Evangelium' (p. 216), and her constant deprecating remarks on the Democratic Republic. Her snobbery and the general hollowness of her life with her husband, with whom she has no real communication, are further aspects of traditional Western decadence.

The decadence of the Herrfurth home is seen to be intensified in the professorial household to which Manfred and Rita are invited for dinner. Here the worst features of the 'Bürgerwelt' are revealed in the artificiality which surrounds every aspect of the evening – except, of course, the sincerely intended and vicious attack on a genuine socialist whose honesty will not allow him to sink to the level of the 'Assistenten', who vie

---

25 'Christa Wolf: *Der geteilte Himmel*. Roman zwischen sozialistischem Realismus und kritischem Sozialismus', particularly pp. 43–9.

against each other for the favour of their professor. Rita, the socialist convert, feels unsure of herself in these surroundings, which serve to bring out the worst in Manfred; his hypocrisy and vanity are well suited to occasions of this sort. The evening marks a turning point in their relationship, as Rita's newly-awakened political feelings lead her to fresh insight into the character of her lover and into bourgeois society.

The 'Bürger' are traditional targets of attack in GDR literature, and the author suggests there are many more of the types which are presented in the above figures. At one point reference is made to 'die vielen Herrfurths', and at others, as Kloehn has pointed out, she speaks of the 'Trägen' and the 'Spießer'.[26]

In contrast to the 'Bürger' stand the socialists, in particular Meternagel and Wendland.[27] Manfred Durzak has suggested that the opposition of these with the reactionaries is reminiscent of the all too familiar pattern on which many East German works rely:

In der Charakteristik von Wendland und Meternagel einerseits und der Eltern von Manfred Herrfurth andererseits läßt sich durchaus ein vertrautes Schwarz-Weiß-Schema erkennen.[28]

This judgment is rather harsh, since the colours are by no means as distinctive as those in the works discussed above. Meternagel is clearly a form of 'positive hero',[29] whose idealism

---

[26] Ibid., p. 45.

[27] The point is reinforced onomastically, although by no means to the same extent as in works by Claudius and Strittmatter. The socialists are Meter/ nagel, the honest and perfectly upright figure, and the new director of the factory who is able to effect a change, Wend/land. In contrast there are the domineering father and son Herr/furth. There is also the impetuous, immature Martin 'Jung'. Cf. Kloehn, loc. cit., p. 52.

[28] *Der deutsche Roman der Gegenwart*, p. 276.

[29] Durzak has suggested that Kloehn's comment on Meternagel ('Meternagel ... entspricht genau dem Typ des Helden im sozialistischen Realismus') is a 'vereinfachte Deutung' (op. cit., p. 407, fn. 7). I feel, however, that the quotation Durzak uses to make this point is not typical of the general attitude of socialist critics. Certainly, Kloehn overstates the case with his use of 'genau', but by 1963 the view that a 'positive hero' should be totally without fault had long since passed.

and self-sacrifice for the Party are exceptional, but he is a credible figure. So too are the other socialists: the new factory manager Wendland, the teacher Schwarzenbach, and Manfred's assistant Martin Jung. Together, these figures provide a counterbalance to all the less attractive features manifested by the 'Bürger'. The socialists' most striking qualities are their enthusiasm for life and for the construction of a new state, their optimism, selflessness, idealism and sincerity. It is their combined influence, not just that of Meternagel, which stimulates Rita into the desire to become a Party member.

The characteristics of Eastern and Western stereotype are not only *presented* in the above figures, but they are also revealed in conflict. The arguments between Manfred and Wendland, for example, take place not only on a personal plane: national issues – the pros and cons of capitalism and socialism – are at stake. The interaction of character reveals the East–West conflict in other areas too. The events of the coachworks, and even those of the brigade in which Rita works, are intended to epitomise the larger problems facing the GDR in the summer of 1961. Their microcosmic significance is stressed on two occasions. On p. 52, for example, Rita realises that the structure of her brigade can be seen in political terms:

Sie merkte: Die Brigade war ein kleiner Staat für sich. Meternagel zeigte ihr nun die, welche an den Fäden zogen und die, welche sich ziehen ließen; er zeigte ihr die Regierer und die Regierten, die Wortführer und die Opponenten, offene und versteckte Freundschaften, offene und versteckte Feindschaften. (p. 52)

The brigade comprises examples of various shades of political opinion, and through observing them Rita is able to broaden her acquaintance with the ways of the state as a whole. Shortly

---

Durzak is certainly correct in suggesting that Meternagel's unbridled enthusiasm is self-defeating, but what he overlooks is that this point of view is undoubtedly shared by Christa Wolf herself! Criticism of Meternagel's excesses is implicit in the story, while self-martyrdom in the interests of the Party has been criticised elsewhere. Notably in Erik Neutsch's *Spur der Steine* (Kati's father) and in Rolf Schneider's *Krankenbesuch* (the unnamed male speaker).

afterwards, the coach-works is made to stand for a larger unit, and on this occasion, specifically for the GDR:

Die Spannungen, schien es, denen das ganze Land seit Jahr und Tag ausgesetzt war, hatten sich nun gerade auf diesen einen Punkt zusammengezogen. (p. 72)

The sinking morale of the country as a whole (the year is 1961) is reflected in the decreasing production figures. The flight of the works director to the West makes matters even worse, but there is, of course, a way out of the disastrous situation: genuine socialist dedication to one's work, which Wendland proposes and which Meternagel is the first to adopt. It is the self-interest typical of the 'Bürger' which prevents many of the brigade from exerting themselves for no immediate gain (in fact, for temporary loss), but Meternagel's exhortations eventually bear fruit. The conversion of individuals to a new point of view marks a victory not merely for him, but for the ideology which he represents.

Aspects of the divided nation are presented on two levels in *Der geteilte Himmel*: first, through those figures who have been endowed with the stereotyped features of East and West; and second, through the interaction of the two lovers themselves, both of whom also come to stand for the two parts of the German nation. It is at this second level that the sense of conflict between the two camps is at its keenest.

Several critics have pointed out that the division of Germany is reflected in the Manfred–Rita relationship. Brettschneider, for example:

Die Tragödie eines geteilten Landes in der Tragödie der Trennung zweier Liebender zu konkretisieren, ist ein literarisches Unternehmen, das vielfach versucht wurde.[30]

---

[30] *Zwischen literarischer Autonomie und Staatsdienst*, p. 123. Despite this claim, Brettschneider names no other work. His footnote to H. J. Geisthardt's 'Das Thema der Nation und zwei Literaturen' is of little value, since the latter names only two other works.

Similar broad, but unsubstantiated claims have been made by H. G. Hölsken in *Jüngere Romane aus der DDR* (p. 26) and Arno Hochmuth in *Literatur im Blickpunkt* (p. 193).

The formulation is a nice one, although it misrepresents the issue: the separation of the two is not to be considered in tragic terms, while the 'Trennung zweier Liebender' also requires some commentary. What Rita is faced with does not represent a choice between political conviction and married bliss. Her choice is between life in the GDR and life in the West with someone with whom she was *previously* in love. By the time of Manfred's flight she has outgrown the infatuation and recognised his limitations. It is worth stressing what critics have repeatedly failed to recognise: that Rita's suicide attempt is undertaken not for the love and loss of Manfred, but because love itself has not lived up to her high expectations:

Unbewußt gestattete sie sich einen letzten Fluchtversuch: Nicht mehr aus verzweifelter Liebe, sondern aus Verzweiflung darüber, daß Liebe vergänglich ist wie alles und jedes. (p. 275)

If the novel is in any way tragic, then it is the failure of love as an absolute, and not as an experience, which makes it such.

Neither Manfred nor Rita is fully representative of the state to which each declares allegiance, yet they obviously contain key elements of the personality which East German writers associate with those two states. What is important is that as a personality Rita develops; Manfred, on the other hand, does not. Rita's progress is towards a maturity which is both emotional and political, and it is on both these levels that she is able to reject the claims of Manfred when she visits him in the West.

From the beginning the lovers emerge as starkly contrasting figures, with Rita as the potential socialist, and Manfred as the typical defector. Rita is something of a 'Naturkind': a true product of the 'Dorf'. Naïve, warm-hearted and trusting, she is a sincere and sensitive girl who 'feels' rather than 'analyses'; she also has a deep concern for others. Manfred, more a product of the 'Stadt' (which is frequently contrasted with the 'village', although not, surprisingly, always to the advantage of the latter) appears almost as the polar opposite. Every one of her positive features is negated in his character, with two adjectives being used constantly to describe his actions: 'spöttisch' and 'gleichgültig'. Manfred is a cold, cynical personality; he distrusts all others, is selfish, self-important and ungrateful. Care is taken to explain his emotions in terms of his adolescence, which was endured during the moral turmoil of the later years of the war. Manfred's generation as a whole is seen to have been unable to believe in a new form of society after 1945, while his unfortunate experiences with so-called socialist 'friends', who have behaved in opportunist manner at his expense, have exacerbated his cynicism. It is above all Manfred's parents who have contributed to his attitudes. Their acceptance of National Socialism and then the Socialist Unity Party for personal ends alone has robbed him of any belief in political idealism.

Rita's affair with Manfred begins very much as an infatuation of first love. He is the first to make her think in terms wider than those of the village, and she is prepared to tolerate much for the new freedom of spirit which she has gained. But her political education is more protracted and, in the long run, more satisfying an experience, which eventually helps her to triumph over her emotions both in West Berlin and later in the sanatorium. Moreover, it is a form of maturation which proceeds not from rational insight but from *emotional* appreciation of everyday conflicts which are in essence political. Rita is converted to a new political viewpoint by the example of others and through the desire to emulate them. Once she reaches this new stage she gains a fresh insight into her personal relationships and is thus able to overcome emotional bonds.

It is in her new role as socialist that Rita is able to triumph over the demands and enticements of Manfred and the West. She freely admits that a year ago her reactions would have been totally different (p. 263), but the thought processes in which she indulges during her afternoon in West Berlin reveal a totally different state of mind. Her every reflection and action is that of the socialist, who is saddened by the life encountered in the capitalist part of the world. Another aspect of her transformation is that she is no longer able to speak with Manfred as formerly. Although they have always been basically incompatible in the past, they have nonetheless been able to communicate with each other. On this occasion, however, Christa Wolf makes it clear that their minds are operating on completely different levels, the main difference being that Manfred's private interests are opposed by Rita's new communal concerns. The best illustration of this is Rita's persistent and spontaneous identification with her factory colleagues; such comments only puzzle and irritate the individualist Manfred.

By the time of their final encounter, then, Rita and Manfred meet not primarily as lover and mistress. Although Manfred begins the afternoon by acting in his former role, he quickly realises that Rita is behaving in a different manner. She has already decided before her trip to Berlin on the way in which she must conduct herself. As a consequence these scenes in Berlin – some of the most carefully written of the novel – reveal two different approaches to life rather than just the conclusion to an ill-matched relationship.

Much of the lovers' conversation obviously centres on different aspects of life in East and West. In view of Christa Wolf's bitter attacks on the Federal Republic in such essays as that in 'Notwendiges Streitgespräch' and 'Deutsch sprechen', it is to her credit that she has restrained herself in a work of literature. For although there is criticism of the West in Rita's observations, this is for the most part implicit; and, more important, it is balanced by justified criticism of the East in much of what Manfred says. Some of his remarks are so close to the bone that it is not surprising the novel was considered unfavourably in many quarters. The following outburst, for example, is unprecedented in East German literature:

'Daran will ich gar nicht mehr denken. Diese sinnlosen Schwierigkeiten. Diese übertriebenen Eigenlobtiraden, wenn eine Kleinigkeit glückt. Diese Selbstzerfleischungen. Ich kriege jetzt eine Arbeit, da werden andere extra dafür bezahlt, daß sie mir jede Störung wegorganisieren. So was hab ich mir immer gewünscht. Drüben hab ich das nie – jedenfalls nicht zu meinen Lebzeiten.' (p. 254)

Rita is not the type to criticise openly, and her reaction to the above is consequently not to counterattack but to muse on Meternagel, her main source of inspiration. This thought process suggests to the reader the victory that socialism has won in her mind, and it does so far better than would have any diatribe against the West.

If *Der geteilte Himmel* marks an advance on the presentation of a divided nation, then it is primarily in the movement to a more balanced view of the two German states. Although the image of the West that emerges from the novel conforms in many respects to that already established in propaganda, Christa Wolf makes it clear that a blanket condemnation of the 'other' German state is by no means easy – or justifiable. At one point Rita elaborates on one of the chief difficulties in proving the superiority of the East. She regrets that the distinction between the two is not more clear-cut so that Eastern beliefs could be justified conclusively:

'Alles wäre leicht', sagte Rita zu Schwarzenbach, 'wenn sie dort als "Kannibalen" auf den Straßen herumliefen, oder wenn sie hungerten, oder wenn ihre Frauen rotgeweinte Augen hätten. Aber sie fühlen sich ja wohl. Sie bemitleiden uns ja.' (p. 62)

Another respect in which Christa Wolf has gone beyond the over-simplificatory approach of earlier writers is in her depiction of the defector Manfred. The latter does not leave the Republic solely for the traditional reasons – such as strong capitalist leanings and political immorality – for failings in the GDR itself are the main motivating factor. As Raddatz puts it:

So läßt [Christa Wolf], zum ersten Mal in der DDR-Literatur, auch den 'anderen', den, der geht, Recht haben; Christa Wolfs Manfred ist nicht 'gekauftes Subjekt' und 'Agent des Imperialismus', nicht einmal bloß einer, der 'noch nicht' das Licht des Heils sieht, das zu sehen, den Klügeren, Gläubigeren schon vergönnt ist.[31]

The response of certain East German critics was less enthusiastic. They would obviously have preferred the fault to have lain with Manfred alone, and not with their own society:

Wo ist auch nur an einer Stelle deutlich charakterisiert, daß die Entscheidung Manfreds schließlich ihre Wurzeln in der Existenz des westdeutschen Staates hat? Niemand kann abstreiten, daß Christa Wolf für die falsche Entscheidung zwei Ursachen sieht: die Herkunft und die Erziehung im Herrfurthschen Hause einerseits und widrige Lebensumstände in der DDR andererseits. . .so muß man doch sehen, daß sich in der Vereinfachung, die Christa Wolf bei dem Motiv für das Verlassen der DDR vorgenommen hat, eine falsche Auffassung von der Rolle der DDR verbirgt.[32]

It is ironic that Christa Wolf should be accused of oversimplification, since this is exactly what she has succeeded in avoiding. (A point which is even clearer when the techniques of the novel are set against those of her polemical essays.) When compared with earlier East German novels, *Der geteilte Himmel* marks a considerable advance in the attempt to show the complex nature of any decision for or against one of the German states.

The plot of Hermann Kant's *Die Aula* is strongly autobiographical. As was suggested in Chapter Two, it concerns the life of journalist Robert Iswall, who is invited to deliver one of the speeches to mark the closure of the 'Arbeiter-und-Bauern-

---

[31] *Traditionen und Tendenzen*, p. 380. The same point is made by Durzak (op. cit., p. 275), who quotes a section of Dieter Schlenstedt's 'Motive und Symbole in Christa Wolfs Erzählung "Der geteilte Himmel" ': 'Der Versuch. . .ist poetischer und mehr Durchbruch als andere neuere Bücher, die ähnliche Probleme aufgreifen, sie aber viel didaktischer nehmen. Das Buch Christa Wolfs ist gerade der Versuch, sich der Didaktik zu entledigen.' (Schlenstedt, p. 78; quoted by Durzak, p. 407, fn. 2.)

[32] Martin Reso, '*Der geteilte Himmel' und seine Kritiker*, p. 158; quoted by Hölsken, op. cit., p. 27.

Fakultät'[33] where he studied shortly after the war. The invitation stimulates him into reflections on the early years of the Republic, and his day-to-day activity (which includes a business trip to Hamburg) is constantly interrupted by memories of his former colleagues and their communal adventures. Through constant self-questioning Robert provides a history of his own life, those of his three closest friends, and with this, a history of Germany.

The use of representatives is only one of several ways in which Kant presents divided Germany. It is, in fact, subordinate to his use of the 'traveller' and to his frequent implicit comparisons of East and West. Yet his use of these figures is nonetheless important, not least since it helps us to appreciate why he should have chosen 'Die Aula' as a title.

In *Der geteilte Himmel* divided Germany is partly analysed in terms of the contrast between the 'Bürger' and the 'Sozialisten'. In *Die Aula* this is developed into the conflict between representatives of 'das Alte' and 'das Neue'. What East Germans understand by these concepts has strongly political overtones, as is well illustrated by a quotation from Brecht:

Die Trennung Deutschlands ist eine Trennung zwischen dem Alten und dem Neuen. Die Grenze zwischen DDR und Bundesrepublik scheidet den Teil, in dem das Neue, der Sozialismus, die Macht ausübt, von dem Teil, in dem das Alte, der Kapitalismus regiert. Aber die Macht wird in beiden Teilen bekämpft, und so ist eine Trennung überall in ganz Deutschland zu fühlen, überall kämpft das Neue mit dem Alten, der Sozialismus mit dem Kapitalismus.[34]

Walter Ulbricht has used the terms with specific reference to the writer's task. Speaking at the '11. Plenum der ZK der SED' in 1965, he referred to those 'die es verstehen, Kunstwerke mit nationalem Inhalt zu gestalten, in denen der lebendige Kampf der Menschen zwischen dem Neuen, Fort-

[33] Cf. above, p. 47.
[34] 'Realismus als kämpferische Methode', pp. 552–3. Also quoted by Friedrich Rothe at the beginning of his 'Sozialistischer Realismus in der DDR-Literatur', p. 184.

schrittlichen und dem Alten, Rückständigen. . .interessant gestaltet [wird]'.[35]

The 'old' and the 'new' are standard Communist values which suggest historical and international developments, but in *Die Aula* Kant presents them specifically within the framework of the (1949) Eastern educational system; what the East German reader will detect behind these concepts is therefore not only the conflict of two world ideologies, but also the narrower, national conflict of two educational systems. That of the West is embodied by the old University (to which the 'ABF' is attached) and its reactionary students who 'wollen nichts Neues', while the studying 'Arbeiter und Bauern' ('prächtige *Repräsentanten des Neuen*' – p. 261 [my italics]) represent the 'Arbeiter-und-Bauern Staat'. The symbolic value of 'Altes' und 'Neues' is brought out by their repeated use in the narrative, and not only by the implications of what Kant is presenting.

The major clashes of the old educational order with the new all take place in the 'Hall' of the title. In the first of these, the 'ABF' pioneers are warned of the dangers that await them: 'Hochmut, Vorurteile, Angst um bedrohte Privilegien, Aberglauben und Klassendünkel' (p. 66). These qualities will be recognised as typical of bourgeois society (as prominent in the Federal Republic of 1965 as they were in the Western Zones of Occupation of 1949 and, to a lesser extent, in certain circles of the Soviet Zone, the SBZ), and they are for the most part personified in the Rector of the University, whose boring and totally irrelevant speech is highlighted by his extempore flashback to the difficulties his own worthless faculty encountered, a fine sense of the comic arising from the Rector's seriousness towards his own, rather ridiculous subject and his total obliviousness to the laughter he is arousing. It is not fortuitous that this representative of the reactionary forces is a mineralogist and speaks of an interest in hundreds of thousands of years and in the past, not the present. In this caricature Kant is presenting

[35] 'Zu einigen Fragen der Literatur und Kunst', p. 4.

the traditional image of the university professor and his refusal, if not inability, to accept the new order of society. The Rector sees in the revolutionary government only the hope of a new building for his faculty and he speaks to the 'ABF' in condescending tones. His aloofness and aridity are reflected in the language and contorted structure of his speech, and Kant's summary, also in long, undramatic sentences (and quite untypical of his normal, lively style), perfectly recreates the boring and monotonous tone.[36]

In complete contrast to the Rector stands Völschow, the dynamic Director of the 'ABF' and a representative of the new, progressive society. His speech of welcome is as different from the Rector's in content as it is in style, carrying away the students by its relevance to their particular situation and by its encouragement. Kant reinforces the difference between the

[36] Another representative of the old University order is Professor Noth, the Old Testament Professor whose seminar Robert mistakenly enters. Robert is surprised to find traditional customs still prevailing ('Robert wußte, daß Studenten so grüßten, früher, und er wunderte sich, daß es dies immer noch gab' – p. 24), but at this juncture he is not yet aware of his error. When he does discover he is in the wrong room, he is subjected to the amused contempt of the Professor and his students, who regard him as an oddity. The Professor ridicules his soldier's uniform and the fact he is a worker's son, and Noth's final witticism – the sarcastic remark that Robert's path is not to the 'kleine Propheten', the subject of his seminar, but to the 'große Propheten, die Marx und Engels heißen' (p. 26) – brings the house down.

It cannot be coincidental that the most famous Old Testament scholar of Germany in 1965 (the date of the book's publication) was Professor Martin D. Noth (which Kant has modified to 'D. Noth'), who lectured in Greifswald, Königsberg, and Leipzig until 1945, when he left to go to Bonn. Since the actual date of his departure will probably be blurred in the minds of Kant's readers (or, more probably, they would only know that he lectured in the West), Kant may be attempting to suggest that Noth was still in the Soviet Occupied Zone in 1949 but, appalled by 'das Neue', then left for the more reactionary part of the country, seeing his spiritual home there rather than in the GDR. In view of Noth's treatment of Robert, the implications of this suggestion hardly require commentary.

The Universities as seats of reaction were a common target of early East German literature. The University of Greifswald (which, for autobiographical reasons, is presumed to be the University in question here) has also been exposed in this light by Willi Bredel in *Ein neues Kapitel* (Band 1).

two by making their speeches so stylistically dissimilar: Völschow's is described briefly (in a paragraph, in contrast to the
three sides of the Rector's) and in terse sentences, which suggest
the business-like atmosphere which he always emanates, the
only direct speech of this passage being the forceful quotations
with which he challenges the opposition (p. 66).

The second major clash between old and new occurs when
the 'ABF' attempt to win seats on the Student's Council ('Stu-
dentenrat'). Here the unprogressive nature of the opposition is
displayed by a conservative historian who opposes all but the
most gradual change and boasts that 'wir stehen in einer Tradition, die vorschnelle Neuerungen ausschließt' (p. 201). The
ludicrous nature of this reactionary's arguments is exposed in
his further boast that 'dies ist eine Stadt, in der die erste Dampf-
maschine einundsechzig Jahre nach ihrer Erfindung installiert
wurde' (p. 201). The historian is discredited in the eyes of East
German intellectuals by his implicit rejection of dialectical
materialism and in the eyes of the workers by his views on industrial progress. For the East German, anyone who speaks on
industry in such a myopic manner is to be regarded with disdain, since the importance of industry over all other branches
of activity has been emphasised by the leadership since the
earliest days. Quasi Riek, representing the dynamic 'ABF',
challenges the attitudes of the students, appealing to their moral
sense and their duty towards the new order. Through a rhetorical *tour de force* Quasi wins a seat on the Council, which marks
a clear step forward in the battle against tradition.[37]

[37] Quasi's 'flight' to the West would erode his stature as a representative if it
implied that he had indeed rejected the GDR for the capitalist system, but
there are several suggestions in the text that he was dispatched there under
special instructions from the East German secret service. Numerous critics
have failed to take these suggestions into account, and even the latest publication on the novel, E. W. Herd's otherwise sensitive discussion ('Narrative
Technique in Two Novels by Hermann Kant') refers only to Quasi's secret
meeting with persons unknown shortly before his departure for the West,
and his highly ambiguous comments in the Hamburg pub he now operates.
Other, and equally telling, points include Meibaum's stuttering at the
word 'Riek' (when normally he is never at a loss for an answer – p. 248)

In the first 'Hall' scene, then, representatives of the two attitudes to education are contrasted and the difficulties facing the 'ABF' made clear (a preamble to this scene is that in which Gerd and Robert briefly enter the Hall – but they are so horrified by the archaic majesty of their surroundings that they almost run away). In the second there is a struggle between the two which culminates in a minor triumph for the progressives. In the final, brief scene, total victory for 'das Neue' is presented: all the faculty have passed their 'Abitur' and they are thus able to become full students. The majority do, a good number of them later becoming key figures in GDR society.

The celebration to which Robert's whole life has recently become geared (the 'Abschlußfeier') is also to take place in the Hall, but it is cancelled and a programme is substituted which is more orientated towards 'das Neue und die vor uns liegenden Aufgaben' (p. 427). Robert ironises the changed programme, chiefly because it has been instigated by Meibaum, who is always seen in a comic light, and because the invitation is couched in typical Party jargon; yet from the educational, progressive point of view, lectures on socialism are superior to an evening of anecdotal reminiscences. In 1962 – just as much as in 1949 – the GDR is still looking forwards, albeit on occasions a little too seriously!

If the 'Aula' is to represent anything, then it is the arena of

and his lie that it was customary to remove the files of those who had left the Republic (p. 250); Riebenlamm's evasiveness and sudden departure after being questioned directly on this matter (p. 283); Jakob Filter's uncertainty about Quasi's motivation immediately before he left for the West, together with his rather ambiguous remarks on critical issues; the Party's very lenient attitude towards Jakob, who had acted as pledge ('Bürge') for Quasi's conduct and who was therefore to be held responsible for his 'flight'; Jakob's feeling that the farewell letter Quasi wrote from West Berlin to his girl friend Hella seemed as if it were 'abgeschrieben' (pp. 328–30); and finally, the fact that Quasi has become a barman in the West – as Rose points out in what seems a rather telling line, he hardly ever drank beer while he was in the GDR – in the context of other suggestions, this certainly implies that he was directed by the Party to take up such a job, bars being a traditional rendezvous of spies. As Quasi himself puts it in a metaphorically significant line: 'Ich höre hier so manches; da lernt man' (p. 184).

conflict between the conservative and socialist viewpoints in the educational field.[38] It is into this Hall that decisive moments of 'ABF' history are projected and the progress of the new spirit from trepidation through conflict to domination is charted. As mentioned above, the clash of conservative and socialist principles is symbolic of another problem, namely, that of the conflict of East and West. What for East Germans are the stereotyped features of each country emerge in their respective representatives: the prejudiced arch-conservatives, the Rector and the historian on the one hand, and the dynamic, far-seeing socialists Völschow and Quasi on the other. In terms of character alone Kant thus both presents and evaluates the significance of division as far as the educational sphere is concerned.

By setting his story in a transitional period Kant is able to depict elements of the old society as well as those of the new, but since East Germans are encouraged to regard all reactionary elements as symbolic of the West, this conflict of old and new is, on the symbolic plane, to some considerable extent the conflict of the divided nation. Another example of this is to be found in Robert's reminiscences on the old 'Pommernplatz', now named the 'Platz der Befreiung'. Reflecting on what would need to be changed in order to shoot a film depicting the early days of the Republic, he decides:

Ein paar HO-Schilder müßten verschwinden; da drüben zum Beispiel, wo jetzt 'Obst und Gemüse' steht, müßte wieder 'Kolonialwaren' geschrieben stehen, und vielleicht könnte man den dicken Krämer und Ölschieber mit seiner schmuddeligen Schürze in die Tür stellen; die Neonschrift 'Haus der Thälmann-Pioniere' müßte natürlich auch weg, da gehörte wieder 'Raiffeisen-Bank' dran; das Restaurant hätte wieder 'Nettelbeck-Haus' zu heißen und der Platz der Befreiung wieder Pommernplatz. (p. 259)

Here too we have symbolic presentation of the socialist victory, the progress from capitalism to collectivism. '*Kolonial*waren'

---

[38] For a different view, see Werner Neubert, 'Komisches und Satirisches in Hermann Kants "Aula"', p. 134. Neubert reduces the symbol to nonsense by seeing the Hall in terms of a schoolroom.

is reminiscent of imperialism, 'Raiffeisen-Bank' of capitalism (it is still a prominent West German merchant bank), 'Nettelbeck-Haus' of private enterprise, and 'Pommernplatz' of 'Revanchismus'.[39] The substitutions indicate the move to socialism while reminding the reader – particularly through the reference to the 'Raiffeisen-Bank' – that there has been no similar progress in the West. As commented above, since for the East German reader the concept of 'das Alte' has strong associations with contemporary West German society, on the symbolic plane he will again recognise the gulf between the policies of each part of the divided nation.

Die Aula marks a clear literary advance in the presentation of East and West, not only in the way Kant depicts the conflict between the two in terms of concepts, but also in the style of this novel, which is greatly superior to those previously considered. Few novelists to treat the divided nation have done so in such an ironic and entertaining way as this author, who has successfully integrated a political message into a personal and comic framework. It is undoubtedly for this reason that his novel has enjoyed such publishing success in both parts of the German nation.

Three of the major novels of 1968 were all concerned with the problems of division: Anna Seghers' *Das Vertrauen* (referred to above in connection with the preceding volume of her trilogy, *Die Entscheidung*); Wolfgang Joho's *Das Klassentreffen* (discussed in Chapter 2, pp. 31–3); and Werner Heiduczek's *Abschied von den Engeln*. The first two works could well have been written twenty years previously, so close are they in style to the simple, openly moralistic products of early East German socialist realism. Heiduczek, on the other hand, operates with the less insistently rhetorical methods of the younger generation as a whole. There is no forced optimism

[39] For details of this concept, see Appendix.

in *Abschied von den Engeln*; it reflects the confidence with which East Germans began to regard their part of the nation as the superior one, and which has marked a gradual turning away from all-German issues to those of the GDR alone.

Heiduczek traces the progress of a family which has been separated by the division of Germany. In the West are Max, Professor of Theology, and Anna, owner of an expanding fur business. In the East: Thomas, a newly appointed progressive Headmaster, and Herbert, a high-ranking local government official. The main link between the two sides is provided by the hero, Anna's son Franz, whose disgust at his mother's adultery, combined with an adolescent existential crisis, induces him to escape to his relations in the GDR. His stay there extends longer than he had anticipated. He attends the school where Thomas is Headmaster, falls in love, despairs of life again, but finally comes to recognise that the ideals of Communism can provide the hold on life for which he is searching.

An exchange of letters between Heiduczek and Heinz Plavius, which was reprinted in *Neue Deutsche Literatur*,[40] as well as an article by Harald Korall in the same journal,[41] have elaborated the genesis of *Abschied von den Engeln*: from the simple study of a family into a detailed investigation of life in the two German states. The changing titles reveal the growing prominence of the 'divided nation' theme: from *Die Marulas* (the name of the family) to *Kreuz und Stern*, an attempt to present in symbolic form the different preoccupations of West and East. As Korall puts it:

Der Weg von Franz Goschel, der sein zerrüttetes Elternhaus verläßt wie zuvor schon sein vor Welt und Auseinandersetzung flüchtender Vater... und nacheinander zu den Brüdern seiner Mutter geht, ist ein Weg zu repräsentativen Verhaltensmöglichkeiten in Deutschland. Das Kreuz symbolisiert die Welt des Katholizismus, der die Marulas samt und sonders entstammen und der ihre in der Bundesrepublik lebenden Glieder – Max und Anna – weiter verhaftet sind; der Stern ist Symbol der neuen gesellschaftlichen Ordnung des Sozialismus, in der Herbert

40 'Ein Meinungsaustausch'.
41 'Einmal dies schreiben – Zur Genesis eines Romans'.

und Thomas leben. Hüben und drüben, Ost und West, Kapitalismus und Sozialismus in Deutschland werden nun ganz bewußt einander genenübergestellt. (p. 147)

Korall does not suggest why Heiduczek should have rejected *Kreuz und Stern* as the final title, but the reasons for this decision may be deduced from the new one, which has little significance until well through the novel and even then remains slightly obscure. It seems certain that the author is determined to avoid anything suggestive of the programmatic titles of the 'Aufbauliteratur'.

Heiduczek twice makes the point that the division of Germany is a spiritual one:

Es war kein gerodeter Waldstreifen, der Deutsche von Deutschen trennte. Es war eine Mauer, die in Jahren nach dem Krieg zwischen den Menschen hochgewachsen war mitten durch das Denken und Fühlen eines Volkes, es trennte in Hüben und Drüben und eben einen solchen Satz schreiben ließ, der Tragik und Hoffnung zugleich in sich einschloß. (p. 181)

The above are the reflections of Karl Westphal, a Communist imprisoned in the West for illegal political activity. His daughter Ruth, wife of Herbert, reaches similar conclusions:

Und ihr war durch Franz bewußt geworden, was sich im Grunde genommen in Deutschland vollzog, nicht nur das Offensichtliche, das gegeben war in zwei antagonistischen Gesellschaftsformen, sondern das sich unmerkliche Verändern der Menschen, ihr sich Entfernen voneinander, das sich Herausbilden zweier völlig verschiedener Lebensgefühle. (p. 228)

The above two passages express in direct terms one of the central presuppositions of East German writing on this theme. Further, they encourage the reader to see behind the main figures those qualities which may be considered typical of East and West. Propaganda has, of course, ensured that Heiduczek can rely on his reader's being able to isolate these features, and in this novel it is in fact very much up to the reader to do so. Direct encounters between national representatives – with the opportunity these offer for typical qualities to be drawn out by contrast – are limited to only two occasions.

The most striking structural technique of *Abschied von den Engeln* is montage. The third-person narrative is frequently interrupted by dialogues in the present time, by quotations from those held in the past, and by interior monologue. These insertions all tend to be short and to be set against each other; in particular, phrases of key significance in a character's development are reintroduced at critical moments of his career. The basic advantage of this method is that it lends itself to ironic juxtaposition, and Heiduczek avails himself of this throughout, especially in order to deflate his characters. The representatives of the West, for example, are subjected to more rigorous analysis (in terms of their past being set against their present actions) than those of the East; the failings of Anna in particular are underlined from early in the novel. Her hypocrisy, for example, is exposed by such phrases as 'Was ist mit dir und...' (recalling adultery), 'Gott zum Gruß' (religious bigotry), or 'Pelzsalon "Giselle" ' (advertising gimmickry and profits).

The use of montage can be one of the most forceful means of controlling one's reader's sympathies, but Heiduczek has wisely avoided excessive exploitation of this advantage. His attacks come mainly in the form of plot, and it is therefore up to the reader to isolate the details for himself. Occasionally the implications are made clear in the way suggested above, but most Eastern readers will have little difficulty in recognising that the major representatives of West German society – Anna and her lover Hans – are typically capitalist egoists who embody all the qualities to be expected in such figures: the desire for power and wealth, luxurious living, snobbery, vanity, hypocrisy and immorality. With the sole exception of Max Marula, the enlightened Professor of Theology, the secondary characters of the West display features equally typical of the standard image.

Rather like Meternagel in *Der geteilte Himmel* (who is, of course, implicitly criticised for his unbridled self-sacrifice and dedication to the socialist cause), all the Eastern figures embody a strong sense of moral purpose. Herbert, for example, suffers a minor nervous breakdown through overwork. His wife too devotes herself to the teaching profession far more intensely than is good for her, while Karl Westphal will suffer years of imprisonment and isolation for the sake of his political ideals. Again, it is partly by means of the montage technique that Heiduczek characterises these figures. On the whole the characters of the West are distanced through the montage; we are encouraged to see their present actions or statements through an earlier, usually unfavourable, perspective. The characters of the East, on the other hand, tend to be given greater stature through presentation of earlier periods of their careers: the flashbacks often extend to moments of difficulty or to struggles which have been successfully overcome. The advantages of referring to former personal and political crises are twofold. Not only is deeper motivation provided, but Heiduczek is able to bring out the positive features of his Eastern representatives.

As suggested above, the contrast between the two German states is fully thrown into perspective on only two occasions. The first is the meeting between Max Marula, the Professor of Theology, and Karl Westphal, imprisoned Communist agitator. The second is the family reunion over the grave of Anna, a few pages before the close of the novel.

It is not surprising that Heiduczek has described the meeting of Max and Karl as a 'Gipfeltreffen',[42] for Karl is the most dedicated Communist of the novel, and Max the chief representative of West German Catholicism. Quotations from their discussion are used throughout as part of the montage technique, and the remarks of both figures have an authoritative, aphoristic quality; their function when re-used is obviously quite different from that of the self-deflating remarks of Anna. Moreover, the fact that Max stands in the first instance for a religion, rather than a political ideology, does not reduce his value as a representative of the West. In the standard East

42 'Ein Meinungsaustausch', p. 124.

German view of the Federal Republic, clericalism exerts a significant and pernicious influence on politics.

The conflict between these two characters is not really a dramatic one. The tension that might have accompanied such a key meeting is removed by the resigned attitudes of both speakers, each of whom knows his opponent is unconvinceable. Heiduczek's aim in this scene is to indicate the nature of 'Hoffnung' (a leitmotif of the novel) for the Marxist and the Christian. The development of the discussion is simple, but it is clear from the outset who will 'win'. Further, Karl's arguments, those of the materialist, gain added weight through his present situation (a prison cell) and through the strategic placing of this scene between chapters on Anna's preparation for a mock suicide (amid the decadence of her luxury home) and the actual act of suicide itself, which follows the discussion.

Karl's triumph is made clear not only through the rejection of 'hope' by Anna, the Catholic, but by Max's entry for that day:

Wir haben die Auseinandersetzung mit den Kommunisten bislang günstigenfalls als eine Art geistiger Turnübung betrachtet. Wir waren in unseren Studierstuben immer Sieger geblieben. Wir werden uns daran gewöhnen müssen, in der lebendigen Auseinandersetzung auch besiegt zu werden. (p. 383)

Given the nature of the book and its place of publication, Karl's victory in this matter is clearly inevitable; it is nevertheless well handled. It is all the more surprising, therefore, to note that an *East* German critic should have complained of 'moralism' in such sections. With reference to all characters and scenes set in the West, Klaus Jarmatz has written:

Es lauert die Gefahr, einzelne Figuren nur als wenig fleischgewordenen Abdruck bestimmter Haltungen darzustellen....In den großen weltanschaulichen Auseinandersetzungen zwischen Max und Westphal, die eine gewisse Schlüsselstellung einnehmen, wird zwar die moralische Überlegenheit des Kommunisten Westphal deutlich, unklar bleibt aber die unmittelbar praktische Zielsetzung der weltanschaulichen Haltung. Dadurch tritt gerade in diesen Partien zuweilen ein Moralismus hervor.[43]

[43] 'Variationen über das Glück', p. 889.

In contrast with previous novels, the rhetoric of *Abschied von den Engeln* is remarkably restrained. It is a mark of rising Eastern critical perception that Jarmatz should have chosen to criticise such a feature.

The other instance of direct confrontation between East and West is included in the final pages of the novel. Max and Thomas Marula, meeting over the grave of their sister, exchange views on where Franz should spend the rest of his life:

—Du hast kein Recht darauf, Franz von hier fortgehen zu heißen. Welches Recht hast du auf ihn?
—Ich? Keins. Ich habe es leichtfertig aus der Hand gegeben. Aber du, Max, hast genausowenig eins. Du hättest es sonst vor zehn Monaten schon geltend gemacht. Stellen wir also nicht die Frage nach meinem oder deinem Recht. Stellen wir die Frage nach den besten Möglichkeiten für ihn.
—Den Trick kenne ich: Der Sozialismus hat nicht nur das bessere ökonomische System, er hat auch die besseren Menschen.
—Kein Land, keine Gesellschaft kann sagen, sie habe die besseren Menschen. Besser können immer nur die Möglichkeiten für die Entwicklung ihrer Menschen sein.
—Besser muß durchaus noch nicht gut sein.
—Die Zeit ist zu kostbar für Sophistik, Max.
—Die innere Entscheidung eines Menschen allein hat Bedeutung, nicht die geographische, Hallenbach oder Lohenhagen.
—Mach dir nichts vor, Max, Ihr habt Franz hier nichts mehr zu bieten.
(p. 437)

Max's accusation ('Den Trick kenne ich') gives the impression of Heiduczek's impartiality, yet here, as throughout, the author is carefully controlling his reader's sympathies. It is primarily the content of the speeches which encourages the reader's agreement with the socialist, and not the method of suggestion that Heiduczek uses elsewhere. An example of this is to be found in the concluding lines of this scene:

'Jede Minute stirbt ein Mensch auf der Welt,' sagte Max.
'Und jede Sekunde wird einer geboren,' erwiderte Thomas.

The technique is far less obtrusive than in earlier East German works. Heiduczek 'suggests' (albeit in obviously symbolic terms with the overtones of the theme of 'Hoffnung') rather than 'states' the contrasting backward/forward looking nature of these two attitudes to life. Further, he does this through dialogue, not authorial commentary. The difference is again analogous to that between 'telling' and 'showing'. The conclusions Heiduczek reaches on divided Germany may well be identical with earlier writers, but by suggesting and above all by *demonstrating*, he has produced a partisan image of inter-German relations which is far more convincing than that in the majority of earlier volumes.

4. THE RELATIONSHIP OF DIVIDED GERMANY TO THE THIRD REICH

The third major means by which East German writers have highlighted the differences between the two German states has been to contrast them in terms of their respective relationship with the preceding historical era. This approach is once again closely related to propaganda, for one of the earliest, as well as the most recurrent, accusations levelled against the Federal Republic has been that it closely resembles the Third Reich. While the GDR, it is repeatedly pointed out, bears no comparison with the earlier period, the way of life in West Germany is interpreted as differing only in minor respects from that of the preceding epoch. This dominant image of continuity with only a minimum of change finds its natural conclusion in the description of the West as a 'viertes Reich', a charge which continues to be levelled in every medium and which is also to be found in literature.[1] Surprisingly, there is no consistency in the literary presentation of revived National Socialism. Some see the Federal Republic adopting the policies of the Third Reich without a break, with the Western Occupation Powers assisting the process. Others see a short period of respite after 1945, which is succeeded by evidence of history 'repeating itself', initiated by those Nazis who have escaped punishment. On the whole, however, it is the alleged process of 'restoration' which has most frequently been exposed, and this is a procedure which has been attacked by the majority of writers now living in the GDR.

Possibly the first literary attack on West German restoration was Erich Weinert's 'Genauso hat es damals angefangen', a poem which was published as early as 1946.[2] This work is

[1] E.g. Jurij Brězan, *Eine Liebesgeschichte*, p. 129; Klaus Beuchler, *Aufenthalt vor Bornholm*, p. 153.
[2] The following stanzas are the most significant:
Kaum war das tausendjährige Reich kaputt,
da krochen sie behend, die Hakenrune
rasch aus dem Knopfloch polkend, aus dem Schutt. . .

chronologically exceptional, however, for it was not until the early fifties that presentation of the Federal Republic in terms of its relationship to the Third Reich began to feature as one of the dominant themes in contemporary writing. Since then authors have concentrated on illustrating the most striking factors to unify the two regimes, such as the continued existence of Nazi politicians and industrialists, of identical policies towards Communism, and of the fascist personality, that is, the type under which Nazism (or neo-Nazism) can easily flourish. In most depictions of the Federal Republic there is an insinuation – or even direct observation – that what is being presented finds clear analogies in an earlier period of German history.

It should be emphasised that the East German writer can rely on his reader's aversion to the Third Reich to a much greater degree than can his West German counterpart. Although in the GDR one totalitarian state has to some considerable extent replaced another, there have been extensive attempts to discredit and eradicate all traces of National Socialism in that country – a task which was carried out far more thoroughly than in the

> Schon gehn die meisten wieder durch die Maschen.
> Wie lange noch? Dann steht der Schießverein.
> Denn statt das Land von Nazis reinzuwaschen,
> wäscht man die ganzen Nazis wieder rein.
>
> Das darf sich heut' schon wieder frech vermessen
> und sein Bedauern fassen ins Gebet,
> daß viel zu wenig im KZ gesessen
> und daß es nicht noch mal nach Moskau geht.
>
> . . . . .
>
> Genauso hat es damals angefangen!
> Und wo es aufgehört ist euch bekannt.
> Verschlaft ihr noch einmal, die zu belangen,
> dann reicht bestimmt kein Volk uns mehr die Hand.

Verse attacks on the resurgence of the past have naturally been restricted. Other notable examples include René Schwachhofer's 'Westdeutscher Tatbestand', Jens Gerlach's 'Ich weiß nicht, was soll es bedeuten', and, of course, Brecht's 'Der anachronistische Zug oder Freiheit und Democracy'.

West.[3] By presenting the Federal Republic in terms of the preceding period, the East German writer is therefore availing himself of an established cautionary model, while simultaneously,
and perhaps more importantly, demonstrating that history is
continuing its course or actually repeating itself.

There is a further reason why Hitler's Germany can serve so
useful a function for the writer: East German readers are likely
to detect in even the briefest reference to the Third Reich a
metaphorical allusion to the Federal Republic. Such metaphorical awareness has resulted from the incessant attempts of propaganda to emphasise the connections between the two periods.
As Horst Siebert puts it in his discussion of the East German
school text-book:

Da...suggeriert wird, daß in der BRD die Tradition des Hitler-
faschismus fortgesetzt wird, beinhalten zahlreiche Aussagen über das
dritte Reich, insbesondere über den politischen Einfluß der Unternehmer,
zugleich eine Kritik an den 'westdeutschen Monopolkapitalisten'. Auch
die Darstellung der deutschen Arbeiterbewegung verweist indirekt auf
die gegenwärtige politische und gesellschaftliche Situation in Deutschland...[4]

---

[3] East Germans have made much of this positive aspect of their policy, which
frequently figures in propaganda. See, for example, Alfred Grosser, *L'Allemagne de notre temps*, pp. 495–8. Horst Siebert sums up the schoolbook
presentation of this theme as follows: 'In der DDR hat bereits die neue Zeit
begonnen, hier wurde die deutsche Vergangenheit bewältigt. In der BRD
dagegen herrschen noch die reaktionären Kräfte der Vergangenheit, die
Nazis und die kapitalistischen Ausbeuter'. (*Der andere Teil Deutschlands in
Schulbüchern der BRD und der DDR*, p. 50.)

It should in fairness be added that the East Germans themselves have
been accused of not 'overcoming' the past in one significant respect.
Refugees from the East in particular have frequently stressed that the methods
of the GDR secret police are uncomfortably close to those of Hitler's 'Gestapo'. See, for example, Heinz Brandt, *Ein Traum der nicht entführbar ist*;
Martin Gregor-Dellin, *Der Kandelaber*; Gerhard Zwerenz, *Die Liebe der
toten Männer*. Even Robert Havemann, a writer still living in the East, has
made the same point in his *Fragen Antworten Fragen*.

[4] Siebert, op. cit., p. 22. It should, in fairness, be added that the Federal Republic adopts much the same policy towards the GDR. As Siebert points out,
developments in the 'Zone' are frequently compared with previous ones
in the Third Reich, pp. 98f., 110f.

This is an important point, which has long been overlooked by commentators on East German literature.[5] Further, if certain features of the Third Reich are likely to suggest the contemporary situation in the West, then this factor must greatly enlarge the corpus of fiction to deal with the issues which now divide the German nation. Many war novels, for example, are relevant to this classification, for they deal with a type of 'fascism' which has supposedly been overcome in the GDR but which propaganda maintains is still a salient feature of West German society. The dialectical pattern of thinking which is used so much in the East will also encourage readers to react in this way. The depiction of fascism – either in the past (Third Reich) or in the present (Federal Republic) – is likely to induce awareness of the contrasting antifascism on which the GDR itself is supposedly based. Moreover, the issue of East German 'antifascism' used to be as frequent an element of propaganda as was the neo-Nazism of the West.

The fact that East German writers can rely heavily on the accusations of their country's propaganda is reflected in the composition of many novels. Although some writers depict both Democratic and Federal Republic within a single work, there is really no need for them to do so. The achievements of their own (socialist, antifascist) country can remain implicit, or can at any rate be understated, since the reader is likely to be only too well acquainted with them. As a consequence, writers have been able to choose any one of the following three ways when writing on this theme. The first, and most obvious, has been to depict the situation in both countries within the space of a single work. In

[5] The only other critic to have commented similarly is Werner Brettschneider, who unfortunately restricts his remarks to a footnote:

> Wenn G. Kunert mit *Im Namen der Hüte*, R. Schneider mit *Die Tage in W.* und *Der Tod des Nibelungen* und *Prozeß in Nürnberg* in die deutsche Geschichte vor 1945 zurückgreift so sind dies polemische Darstellungen des 'Faschismus', die nicht der geistigen Überwindung dienen, sondern dem kalten Krieg gegen Westdeutschland, dem das Erbe angelastet wird, von dem man selbst nicht betroffen zu sein vorgibt. (*Zwischen literarischer Autonomie und Staatsdienst*, p. 130.)

view of what is suggested above, it is perhaps not surprising that this is the least commonly employed. A far more popular alternative has been to attack elements of restoration in the West, that is, to prove that the past has not been 'overcome' in that part of the nation, while the GDR, on the other hand, stands – implicitly or explicitly – as a contrasting background. A final method has been to illustrate the manner in which the East has successfully rid itself of the Nazi heritage. In this case it is the West which stands, usually *ex*plicitly,[6] as the background to present events. Again, this method is far less common than the second; for rather than deal with the positive achievements of their own society, writers have preferred to indulge in destructive criticism of their opponents.[7]

[6] There were very few East German novels written between 1945 and 1970 which did not contain at least a single reference to the West or in which the evils of capitalism were not depicted. Even a love story like Herbert Nachbar's *Oben fährt der große Wagen* contains several significant allusions to the other Germany.

[7] This is a common technique of socialist writing in general, and in particular among the older generation. These writers had spent so long attacking capitalism that they found the transition to praising socialism rather daunting. As Wolfgang Joho has admitted:

> Eine der wesentlichsten Ursachen aber dafür, daß mir ein Buch heute nicht mehr so leicht von der Feder geht und ich mich zuweilen frage, ob ich, mit überkommenen und bisher bewährten Methoden arbeitend, nicht den Anschluß verloren habe, betrifft, so glaube ich, die ältere Schriftstellergeneration vor allem und im besonderen.

> Aufgewachsen in einer von antagonistischen Klassengegensätzen beherrschten Gesellschaft und uns orientierend an einer Literatur, die im wesentlichen diesen Antagonismus spiegelte, hatten wir Älteren es bei unserem ersten literarischen Versuch relativ leicht. Thema und Konfliktsituation waren eindeutig gegeben: Kampf gegen die bestehende, als verfault erkannte und für eine künftige sozialistische Ordnung, Feind- und Freundbild waren klar umrissen.

The foundation of the GDR brought with it the demand for a new type of socialist writing, however:

> Nach jahrzehntelangem Kampf und einer jahrelangen Phase des schwierigen Übergangs errang der Sozialismus in der DDR den Sieg. Damit kam zwar nicht das Ende aller zwischenmenschlichen Konflikte, wie manche vorschnell und falsch annahmen, wohl aber näherten wir uns dem Ende der antagonistischen Klassenwidersprüche und der Grundwidersprüche

The main premisses of East German propaganda against the Federal Republic are outlined in the Appendix to this volume. It may now be worth introducing a number of items which have a specific relation to the theme under discussion, material which possesses far more restricted an influence yet which is, nonetheless, likely to offer an important stimulus to writers in particular: the literary critical attacks upon 'restorationist' tendencies in West German writing. These used to be regularly featured in the major literary journals and to form a traditional part of Writers' Conferences.

Whenever the system of the GDR is considered by its leaders, it is almost invariably contrasted with that of the West. Thus Ulbricht in his speech in praise of East German development given on 25 March 1962 ('An die deutsche Nation') did not omit to contrast Eastern success with Western failure. He also castigated the restorationist factions in the Federal Republic:

Westdeutschland befindet sich wieder unter der Herrschaft des Monopolkapitals, der klerikalen Dunkelmänner, der hitlerischen Wehrwirtschaftsführer, der Generale, Richter und Henker des Naziregimes. Unterstützt von den USA, haben sie Deutschland gespalten. Sie haben Westdeutschland der NATO angegliedert und unternehmen andere Schritte, um Westdeutschland völlig aus dem Nationalverband auszugliedern. . . .Bonn rüstet in fieberhaftem Tempo auf und strebt hartnäckig nach der Verfügungsgewalt über Atomwaffen. Die demokratischen Rechte der westdeutschen Bevölkerung werden systematisch abgebaut.[8]

zwischen Individuum und Gesellschaft, von deren Darstellung Generationen von Romanschriftstellern gelebt hatten.

Das bedeutet, daß wir uns mit einer neuen, das heißt bisher unmittelbar am eigenen Leib noch nicht erlebten und darum nicht gestalteten, einer neuen Qualität von Konflikten und zwischenmenschlichen Beziehungen konfrontiert sahen. Sie gilt es, ideologisch und künstlerisch zu bewältigen. ('Der Schriftsteller in der neuen Literaturgesellschaft', p. 21.)

The style of writing here postulated by Joho has remained an unattainable ideal both for him and many of his contemporaries.

[8] 'An die deutsche Nation. Rede vor dem Nationalrat der Nationalen Front des Demokratischen Deutschland auf seiner 11. Tagung am 25. März 1962. Zum Entwurf des "Nationalen Dokuments". Die geschichtliche Aufgabe der DDR und die Zukunft Deutschlands'; quoted from Lingenberg, *Das Fernsehspiel in der DDR*, p. 145.

It is above all the sense of *continuity* between Third Reich and Federal Republic which Eastern politicians are eager to emphasise. The media too, frequently devote much space to important West German public figures whose formative years have been tainted by misdeeds committed during the earlier period, while even in journals such as *Neue Deutsche Literatur* and *Sinn und Form* (after 1962), articles which treat the Federal Republic frequently degenerate into little more than diatribe against the successors of the Third Reich. Kurt Hager, for example, begins an article by referring to 'die Gegner' (a standard term for the West German ruling class), but soon becomes highly emotional when delimiting these 'opponents':

Die Gegner...Die ehemaligen Hitlergenerale und Naziblutrichter, die Bücherverbrenner und Organisatoren von Auschwitz und Maidanek die heute wieder, wie die Verfolgung von Hochhuth zeigt, die geschichtliche Wahrheit und jeden fortschrittlichen Gedanken verfolgen.[9]

For Eastern literary critics the most disconcerting feature of the Federal Republic is naturally the continuity of the National Socialist tradition in literature. In general, these critics have been highly selective in the West German novels which they discuss, choosing either works which themselves attack National Socialist trends in Western society; or which promulgate Nazi ideals and glorify the Nazi tradition. In the first category ('anti-fascist' or 'critical realist') are such works as Paul Schallück's *Engelbert Reinecke*, Christian Geißler's *Anfrage*, and Karllud-wig Opitz's *Im Tornister: Ein Marschallstab!*, while in the second ('neo-fascist') are all works based on war experiences, whether presented as memoirs or as fiction. The most trenchant reviews of such writing used to be those by Günter Cwojdrak in *Neue Deutsche Literatur*, many of which were reprinted in *Die*

[9] 'Freude an jedem gelungenen Werk', p. 63. Hager's choice of concentration camps may appear odd to the Western reader, for whom Belsen, Dachau, and Buchenwald are all more infamous than the little-known Maidanek. This selection is more meaningful to the East German, however: the emphasis is on camps not only liberated by the Russians, but also situated in East Prussia, which immediately raises the issue of West German 'Ostpolitik', linking it with former fascist atrocities.

literarische Aufrüstung and *Eine Prise Polemik*. Klaus Ziermann too has devoted himself to criticism of this sort, and his
Romane vom Fließband is a lengthy and detailed study of the
most striking Nazi elements still obtaining in many Western
novels and popular weeklies. The very titles of these critical
studies usually reveal their purpose and reinforce the reader's
image of the West through their sensational quality, whether or
not the review is actually read. Taking an example from each
of the two major journals, we find Werner Liersch entitling his
review of Ina Seidel's *Michaela* 'Roman der Restauration' (in
Neue Deutsche Literatur); while Ziermann's survey of West
German paperbacks features as 'Einbruch der Barbaren. Anmerkungen zur Taschenbuchproduktion in Westdeutschland'
(in *Sinn und Form*). Even the quality of school textbooks is not
overlooked, as in the appropriately dramatic title of Günther
Deicke's review 'Hitler war Bundespräsident. Untertanentreue
und Unwissenheit im westdeutschen Schulbuch'. Other significant titles include 'Die zweite Literatur',[10] 'Braune Presse',[11]
and 'Braune Zensur',[12] while the East German view of Western
'progress' is well summarised by Klaus Hermsdorf in the
following line, with which he begins a typical attack: 'Die
gesellschaftliche Entwicklung in der BRD als restaurative,
geschichtlich regressive Bewegung. . .'.[13]

So convinced are East German writers of the fascistic nature
of the Federal Republic that they have appealed to their Western counterparts in the following terms:

Den Künstlern und Schriftstellern Westdeutschlands sagen wir: Sie
stehen heute vor der Entscheidung, entweder der Restauration einer
unmenschlichen Vergangenheit zu dienen und jenen Kräften den Weg
zu bahnen, die den Untergang des deutschen Volkes besiegeln. . .[14]

[10] Günter Cwojdrak in *NDL*.
[11] Stephan Hermlin in *Sinn und Form*.
[12] Richard Christ in *NDL*.
[13] 'Aufforderung zur Tat', p. 143.
[14] 'Erklärung der Deutschen Akademie der Künste, auf der außerordentlichen
Plenartagung am 30. Mai 1962, vorgetragen von Stephan Hermlin.'

The process of restoration is here seen as avoidable, but on other occasions it is seen as complete. The editors of *Neue Deutsche Literatur*, for example, have spoken of:

die nationale Entscheidung gegen die faschistische und imperialistische Vergangenheit (*die in Westdeutschland noch Gegenwart ist*)...[15]

Such propaganda has left a distinctive mark on contemporary East German literature. Analysing the relationship between past and present in the Federal Republic has been a common theme since the early fifties and constitutes an important aspect of 'Vergangenheitsbewältigung', that is, 'coming to terms with the past'.[16] This high-sounding, commonly used, but rather nebulous term is decidedly misleading, however, since the prime concern of most East Germans is to demonstrate the opposite, that there has been no attempt in the West to learn anything at all from the lessons of history. It is only when dealing with their own society that these writers suggest any progress has been made; further, they suggest that there is a clear relationship between successful 'Vergangenheitsbewältigung' and the establishment of a socialist state.

In this chapter I should like to discuss a number of works which contrast Federal and Democratic Republic in terms of their respective relationship to the Third Reich, concentrating on Franz Fühmann's *Böhmen am Meer*, Herbert Nachbar's *Haus unterm Regen*, and Günter de Bruyn's 'Renata'. In each of these the author aims to examine some particular aspect of

---

[15] 'Der Jahreskonferenz entgegen. Der Stand der Literatur und die Aufgaben der Schriftsteller in der DDR', p. 190. [My italics.]

[16] The concept has been used freely and often rather loosely by West German critics. The East Germans, on the other hand, have provided an official definition:

> Es ist die Pflicht der ganzen Nation, die Vergangenheit sorgfältig zu prüfen, schonungslos nationale Selbstkritik zu üben, aus ihrer Geschichte die richtigen Folgerungen für die Zukunft abzuleiten. Das allein heißt Vergangenheit bewältigen. Es ist die ernste Pflicht jedes Künstlers und Schriftstellers, als Sprecher und Lehrer der Nation aus Lauf und Beispiel der Geschichte Gegenwart und Zukunft zu erläutern und zu gestalten. ('Erklärung der Deutschen Akademie der Künste', p. 325.)

the different way in which East and West reacted to the situation after 1945, the conclusion being that the West did not respond to the moral demands of Hitler's heritage, whereas the East clearly did. The following analyses are intended to illustrate the potential strengths and limitations of the three possible approaches mentioned above (pp. 117–18). Discussion moves from (1) those works set in both East and West; to (2) those set principally in the East; and finally to (3) those set principally in the West.

Franz Fühmann's *Böhmen am Meer* is an exceptional work in that its theme concerns 'Vergangenheitsbewältigung' (or its failure) in *both* German states: the author is as intent on attacking restorative movements in the West as he is in praising the socialist success in ridding itself of all elements of fascism. The story amplifies Fühmann's earlier and shorter studies in this field and marks his most decisive step into political literature. Prior to this *Erzählung* most of his fiction had been concerned with the war and the fascist mentality, but never directly with the political situation in the Federal Republic.[17]

17 Since East German writers are strongly encouraged to study criticism of their work and to follow the suggestions of the Party, *Böhmen am Meer* may be seen as a response to criticism of Fühmann's earlier collection of short stories, *Stürzende Schatten.* These are politically 'relevant' in that they deal with the horrors of fascism, but, as Rosemarie Heise pointed out in her review, although Fühmann treats the war from a contemporary, humanist point of view, he nevertheless ignores the concrete manner in which fascism has been overcome by the new socialist German Democratic Republic. Only by demonstrating this can any sense of 'Bewältigung' be proved:

Es fehlt den Erzählungen Fühmanns etwas für den Leser der Gegenwart schlechthin Unentbehrliches: Die Orientierung im Jetzt und Hier, die Anleitung zum Handeln, durch das allein die faschistische Vergangenheit wirklich überwunden werden könnte. Dazu aber bedürfte es eben mehr als nur der bloßen Entlarvung: Nur durch die Gestaltung ihrer tätigen Überwindung in unserer sozialistischen Gegenwart wird die faschistische Vergangenheit für den Leser als überwindbar erkannt, aber auch – *angesichts der Situation in Westdeutschland* – als noch zu überwinden bewußt. ('Die Bürde der Vergangenheit', p. 133) [My italics.]
(Contd overleaf)

The plot of *Böhmen am Meer* is relatively simple. An East German writer, in search of a rest from the demanding nature of his vocation, travels to the remote resort 'Z.' (presumably Ziesendorf) on the Baltic coast. To his regret, he finds that his duties as a socialist prevent him from enjoying the long-awaited holiday. The discovery that his landlady, Frau Traugott, is frequently petrified by an uncontrollable fear of the sea – and yet paradoxically refuses to move away from it – forces him to probe the origins of her strange affliction. His investigations in the village itself prove fruitless, however; the only clue of possible value is that Frau Traugott once worked for 'Baron von L.',[18] a rich Sudeten landowner whom the narrator himself remembers from childhood. By coincidence, the Baron is shortly to speak at a 'Sudetendeutsches Heimattreffen' (a meeting of Sudeten refugees who are now petitioning the West German government to undertake action for the return of their lands),[19] and so the narrator, hoping an encounter might stimulate his memory, travels to West Berlin for the occasion. The ceremony proves a horrifying spectacle but nevertheless enables him to recall a critical moment of the past and thus to resolve the mystery which surrounds his heroine: her fear of the sea arises from the unsuccessful suicide attempt after dismissal from the Baron's service in 1939. There still remains the problem of why Frau Traugott will not leave the coast, however, which is only resolved in the final page. Returning to Z. for the heroine's for-

The reviewer may have been flattered to find that in his next two works on the past – *Böhmen am Meer* and *Das Judenauto* – Fühmann followed her recommendation almost to the letter.

[18] In view of the strongly autobiographical nature of the story, the reference is in all probability to Lodgman von Auen, leader of the 'Sudetendeutsche Landsmannschaft' between 1951 and 1959. The impression given in Fühmann's interview with Sauter (cf. below, p. 135) is that the real Baron was as evil a figure as is represented by the story, but personal communications on this topic have suggested a different view. Fühmann, it seems, has exaggerated the aggressive and revanchist features depicted for both literary and ideological effect.

[19] For brief details of the 'Heimatvertriebenen' see footnote to 'Landsmannschaften' above, p. 14.

tieth birthday, the narrator suddenly realises that it is the generosity of the villagers which has induced her to stay among them. Accustomed only to the brutality of pre-war, feudalistic society, she suffers under the delusion that kindness of the sort she has experienced in this village is not to be found anywhere else in the Republic.

The repeated use of the word 'Vergangenheit' at climactic points of the narrative stresses the dominant theme of *Böhmen am Meer*: 'coming to terms with the past' in both Democratic and Federal Republic. The criterion by which the two states are measured is their success or failure in assimilating their heritage, and Fühmann dramatically illustrates that whereas the East has successfully faced the historical situation, the West has failed to do so.[20] Whilst this failure is forcefully demonstrated in a single scene, most of the story is devoted to illustrating the contrasting humanitarian spirit which prevails in the East. Fühmann achieves this mainly by establishing his narrator (a former Sudeten German who is now a citizen of the GDR) as a representative figure of his generation and the new society, and thus allows his observations on past and present to suggest the antifascist attitude which characterises the Democratic Republic.

The most decisive scene of the story takes place in West Berlin, to which the narrator has travelled in order to hear the Baron von L. The Baron is now leader of a group of 'revanchists'[21] who are violently campaigning for a return to their former possessions in the Sudetenland, and the narrator describes in detail the nature of the refugees by which he is surrounded. Although the choice of the Sudetenland is coincidental – since the story is based on fact[22] – this territory serves Fühmann's theme particularly well. The Sudetenland provided one

20 Werner Baum also makes this point in his perceptive study of the story: 'Es wird zugleich der große nationale Konflikt sichtbar, der darin begründet ist, daß in Westdeutschland die Lehren aus der Vergangenheit *nicht* gezogen wurden.' (*Bedeutung und Gestalt*, p. 85)

21 Details of the East German view of 'Revanchismus' are included in the Appendix.

22 Cf. below, pp. 134-5.

of the most important preludes to the Second World War, and Hitler's claims on it are probably better known than those he made on any other part of Europe. This factor should enable even the poorly-informed reader immediately to recognise the parallels which begin to emerge between the revanchists' actions and those of Hitler, for the manner in which the nationalistic ceremony is conducted bears a strong resemblance to comparable demonstrations during the thirties. The narrator's journey consequently begins to appear very much like one into the Third Reich.[23]

Fühmann takes special care in emphasising the degree to which the Third Reich has been revived in contemporary Western society. His aim is not merely to demonstrate that isolated elements of the former epoch are present, but that the periods are in practically all respects identical. Accusations are made on several levels. First, on the emotional plane, as in the horrified reactions to the incredible situation: 'und die Vergangenheit war aufgestanden' (p. 396); 'es war, als wäre die Zeit stehengeblieben' (p. 398); 'es war das Jahr 1938 und war es doch nicht...' (p. 398). Other details reveal a more specific link between the two periods, such as the sartorial symbolism of the following: a youth in the 1955 ceremony is described as 'ein fünfzehnjähriger *in schwarzer Hose und weißem Hemd* mit Binde und Rune trat nach vorn...' (p. 396). Only three lines later the narrator describes in a flashback how: 'ein junger Mann.. .*in schwarzen Stiefelhosen und weißem Hemd*, führt lachend einen alten Rabbiner am Bart durch die Straßen' (p. 397). [My italics in both quotations.] This flashback gives a context to the present moment, as do a number of others. The narrator, stimulated by the similarity of present events with

---

[23] This metaphor is a common one. Other striking examples include Brigitte Reimann's *Die Geschwister*, in which the heroine warns her brother on the implications of flight to the West: 'Du hast nicht einmal begriffen, daß dein Schritt über die Grenze ein Schritt zurück in die Vergangenheit ist', p. 232. Herbert Nachbar sees defection in exactly the same terms in *Haus unterm Regen*: 'Ist jemals der Gedanke an Flucht aufgetaucht? Wohin denn Flucht? In die Vergangenheit, in das Wolfsgesetz?', p. 188.

those of 1938, relives the past with critical awareness, a point which has been made by both Werner Baum[24] and Hans-Joachim Bernhard. Bernhard, for example, comments as follows:

Ein großer Vorzug der Erzählung beruht darauf, wie der Dichter... Gegenwärtiges mit Vergangenem verklammert. Die durch den Gang der Erzählung provozierten Erinnerungen werden immer wieder aus der Sicht der inzwischen gesammelten Erfahrungen des Dichters korrigiert.[25]

The skilful use of flashback is clearly no literary innovation, but Bernhard overlooks one aspect that may well be new to East German fiction. The temporal shifts are most effective in those passages where the reader cannot tell whether past or present is uppermost in the narrator's mind, for Fühmann alternates between the two without indicating which is being experienced. This ambiguity obviously points to the very fact he is aiming to stress: the disturbing similarity of the two epochs. By the sustained use of seascape imagery Fühmann gives these sections a strong sense of unity, so that the two periods are bound to one another and the consequences of the past seen as potential consequences of the present. An element of prophecy thus enters the *Erzählung*, similar to that in Heinrich Böll's *Billard um halb zehn* or Günter Grass's *Hundejahre*. As Guy Stern has pointed out, such an element is common to a number of works that concern 'Vergangenheitsbewältigung':

Diese Werke sind oft aus der didaktischen Absicht, der Gleichsetzung von Damals und Heute, so angelegt, daß durch geschickte Rückblenden...die Vergangenheit, ja manchmal sogar eine prophetisch erschaute Zukunft der Gegenwart gegenübergestellt wird.[26]

The strength of Fühmann's best flashbacks lies in this ability to put into perspective through historical analogy. By demonstrating that the Third Reich has a modern parallel he suggests the continuity of the National Socialist tradition in the West.

The National Socialist tradition is, of course, promulgated

---

[24] *Bedeutung und Gestalt*, p. 93.
[25] 'Nationale Thematik in der Erzählung', p. 154.
[26] 'Prolegomena zu einer Studie der deutschen Nachkriegsliteratur', p. 246.

by former Nazis, in particular the Baron von L. He too has changed only in minor details. On the first occasion (in a flashback to 1938) he is seen as 'einen schlanken, gepflegten Herrn mit kurzem blondem Haar und kurzgestutztem Backenbart; er hatte eine randlose große Brille mit goldenem Bügel auf der Nase, und er rauchte eine Zigarre' (p. 376). On the second occasion (1955) these characteristics are repeated: 'Er hatte sich wenig verändert, nur Haar und Backenbart waren grau geworden; er trug eine schmale randlose Brille mit goldenem Bügel und rauchte eine Zigarre...' (p. 398). Here Fühmann passes over the physical attributes and concentrates on the affluent features ('goldene Brille'; 'Zigarre'). Apart from the spectacles changing from 'groß' to 'schmal' (which offers a neat aperçu on the author's maturation), the Baron has remained the same feudal lord that he was in 1938.

One of the most recurrent themes of Fühmann's work is, as J.-H. Sauter has put it, 'das Motiv der intellektuellen Manipulation [seiner] Generation durch den Faschismus'.[27] In practically every work which concerns the fascist period, Fühmann exposes the devious attempts by which the minds of the young have been perverted. What he now attempts in *Böhmen am Meer* is to demonstrate that comparable forms of indoctrination are still in use in the Federal Republic and that the experience of National Socialism is an indispensable foundation for the policies of the present Western regime. The climax of the *Erzählung* actually demonstrates that the organisers of the 'Sudetendeutsches Heimattreffen' can wholly rely on the Nazi heritage in order to stimulate the mass into an emotional fervour.

When the narrator arrives in West Berlin he is surprised to find that the refugees' conversation covers every topic but their homeland. In one sense this demonstrates that Western capitalists are not even committed to their cause, but the striking change which is effected through the playing of the 'Egerländer

[27] 'Interview mit Franz Fühmann', p. 48.

Marsch' (which has strong National Socialist connotations) demonstrates that they can be instantaneously aroused by memories of the past: 'und jählings verzerrten sich die Mienen...' (p. 395). In a moment they revert from harmless gossips to savage neo-Nazis, a point which is reinforced by the imagery. Previously described in terms of a quiet stream, they are now seen as a blind, hurtling current. The immediate transformation betrays that their conditioning under the Third Reich has by no means been eradicated. This march, it has been pointed out earlier in the story, was the major means used by the Nazis to enflame the Sudeten Germans in 1938. Its present effect proves that the mass has not yet been able – or willing – to free itself from the conditioning to which it was subjected during the Third Reich, and that the necessary stimulus will produce exactly the same reflex that the Nazis were able to obtain. This point is further reinforced by the crowd's violent reaction to the speech of the Baron, who mesmerises his audience with his rhetoric. As I have argued elsewhere, the Baron's emotional clichés as well as his theme are closely modelled on those of Hitler.[28] His demagogic control of the crowd allows him to rouse it into a nationalistic outburst, through which the demonstration attains its supreme parallel with the Third Reich.

One of the most repulsive aspects of this ceremony is the exploitation of the young for nationalist ends: the sight of innocent children being forced to parade in the 'Volkstracht' of a country they have never known fills the narrator with anger. Contrasting the scene before him with his experience of how refugees are treated in the East, he is able to generalise on the different approach of the two German states to a problem which both of them had to face shortly after the war:

in dem einen Deutschland gab man den Umsiedlern ein Stück Land und eine Wohnung und eine ehrliche Arbeit, und in dem anderen Deutschland steckte man ihre Kinder in tote Trachten und speiste sie ab mit einer Hoffnung, die mörderisch war. (p. 397)

[28] 'Franz Fühmann's "Böhmen am Meer": A Socialist Version of "The Winter's Tale"', p. 587.

The logic here is patently false, for apart from the sweeping generalisation, East and West are not compared on the same plane. The conclusion may deceive, however, since each aspect of the comparison has been anticipated: in the section preceding this sentence Fühmann's skilful use of flashback has enabled him to demonstrate both the exploitation of children and the humanitarianism which exists in the GDR. The above sentence represents a natural conclusion to this section in that it restates these two facts in crystallised form; yet while both of them may be true, they are not opposites, and should not be juxtaposed as such.

But the most striking feature of this sentence is the emotional overtones. The connotations of simplicity conveyed by 'Land', 'Wohnung', and 'ehrliche Arbeit' contrast sharply with those of the metaphorical 'steckte man ihre Kinder in *tote* Trachten' and '*speiste sie ab* mit einer *Hoffnung*, die *mörderisch* war' [my italics]. The actual choice of metaphor is clearly rhetorical: 'Steckte man ihre Kinder' and 'speiste sie ab' suggests manipulation of the crowd by its leaders. The opinion that the Western exiles are in fact conditioned has already been suggested verbally, but just as the parents are seen to be puppets in the hands of the demagogues, so too are the children seen – in turn – to be victims of their parents. Through the repetition of a key clause Fühmann is able to discredit the latter's conduct:

Dies sei die Tracht ihrer Heimat, *hatte man ihnen*, den jungen Westfalen und Bayern und Hessen und Friesen und Württembergern und Berlinern, *gesagt*; es sei die Tracht ihrer Heimat, und sie müßten sie mit Stolz tragen, *hatte man ihnen gesagt*. . .(p. 396 [my italics])

The repetition both attracts the attention of the reader and also suggests that the author is distancing himself from the action. The use of the indefinite pronoun is equally subtle; rather than kind and gentle parents, an anonymous persuasive force is seen to be operating.

The view that the West is conditioned against Communism is

common enough in East German propaganda,[29] but Fühmann gives it a further dimension in *Böhmen am Meer* which will be particularly clear to those who are acquainted with his other works, both early (notably *Kameraden* [1955]) and late (*Der Jongleur im Kino* [1970]). Present Western methods are seen to be not only immoral but atavistic, relying as they do on one of the most repulsive – yet effective – facets of Nazi techniques.[30]

Although Fühmann's attack on the West comes principally

---

[29] For further details, see my ' "Conditioned against us..." The East German View of the Federal Republic'.

It is ironical that the same point should be made by a West German, Wolf Wondratschek: 'Die Angst vor Kommunisten gehört immer noch zu unserer Erziehung', *Früher begann der Tag mit einer Schußwunde*, p. 9.

[30] It might well be questioned whether Fühmann, in drawing attention to such pressures in the Third Reich, is not also drawing attention to the same – or more intense – pressures in his own society. Marcel Reich-Ranicki has in fact suggested that this is the reason why some of Fühmann's work has found little favour with the authorities: his preoccupation with totalitarian aspects of the Third Reich might easily remind readers of similar methods being employed in the GDR today (*Literatur der kleinen Schritte*, pp. 261–263). This problem may have worried censors in the early days of the Republic, but it has long been overcome terminologically, in a manner which is reminiscent of George Orwell's *Nineteen Eighty-Four*. Just as the leadership distinguishes between Western armament ('for war') and Eastern armament ('to maintain the peace'), so too is conditioning in both Germanies seen in different ways. That of the East is 'Bewußtseinsbildung', the education of citizens into humanist ideals, while that of the West is 'antikommunistische Hetze', 'Meinungsmanipulation', or 'kapitalistische Massenführung', control of the masses for capitalist ends. The fact that the method is in both cases the same is quietly overlooked. What *is* emphasised is that West German techniques are directly related to those of the Third Reich!

Jürgen Rühle has made a similar point to Ranicki's, but with reference to different writers:

Wer beispielsweise heute in der sowjetisch besetzten Zone Falladas *Jeder stirbt für sich allein* oder Zweigs *Beil von Wandsbek* liest, wird natürlich empört sein über die Verbrechen des Nationalsozialismus, noch mehr aber wird ihn die teuflische Parallelität erregen zwischen der vergangenen und der gegenwärtigen Dikatur. Das war der Grund warum die Funktionäre diesen Büchern mißtrauten, warum sie den Film, der nach dem Zweig-Roman gedreht wurde, verboten. ('Schwierigkeiten der Verständigung', p. 71.)

in the guise of an indictment of revanchist activity, this does not mean that his critique excludes Western society as a whole. Able to rely on a reader who is wholly prepared to believe that the Federal Republic condones the revanchists' methods, Fühmann can understate his broader attack. Two brief examples will suffice; both of them relate events in the exiles' ceremony to national attitudes.

In a reference to the children dressed in 'Volkstracht', the narrator comments: 'die Kinder...vom Strudel der Kameras und Mikrophone, von Scheinwerfern geblendet' (p. 396). While Fühmann could clearly have stressed the fervour of the press (on behalf of their readers) much more, he can rely on the background knowledge – and resultant prejudgment – of his Communist reader, who will form from the few details a picture of whatever magnitude he wishes.

Another subordinate clause which contains a far broader attack is the narrator's rhetorically perfect outburst as he leaves the ceremony:

ich lief die Straße hinunter und eilte der S-Bahn zu, um in das Berlin zurückzufahren, *in dem die Mörder ohne Freiheit sind*...(p. 400 [my italics])

The attack here is more direct than in the first example, and Fühmann also supplies a point of contrast (i.e. East Berlin) in order to set the present actions in their social and political framework. In the rest of the story, however, he generally relies upon the moral awareness of his reader to supply the criterion against which the revanchists' activities must be judged.

In suggesting that the above was 'rhetorically perfect', I was, of course, using the concept of 'rhetoric' in its original sense. As F. J. Stopp has reminded us, its object is 'not to demonstrate truth but to produce the conviction that the truth has in fact been demonstrated',[31] a formulation which sums up Fühmann's technique rather well. For although true murderers are obviously not 'free' in the Federal Republic, the author has

---

[31] *The Art of Exposition in Lessing's Prose Works*, p. 38.

been able to suggest – with apparent logic – that they actually are. By considering the sequence of the stages through which this claim is advanced, it is possible to distinguish the central rhetorical pivot of the whole *Erzählung*.

In the above quotation Fühmann is generalising from a specific example, but he is also using a terminology which is both broad and emotive. The impact made by this passage is similar to that discussed above (pp. 129–30): the elements of the contrast (murderers of the West: justice of the East) are not compatible, but they have been introduced in the preceding section, in which the rather tenuous view that the Baron is a murderer is skilfully presented. So too is the moment at which the narrator remembers the succession of circumstances that led to Frau Traugott's attempted suicide. The turning point is the Baron's demand for the return of the Sudetenland:

Der Redner erhob seine Stimme; er hatte bisher in klagendem Ton das deutsche Schicksal bejammert, und nun hob er die Stimme, um zu drohen. 'Unsere Forderung ist nur recht und billig!' schrie er. (p. 198)

It is the word 'billig' which stimulates the narrator into recalling how the Baron, on learning that his unmarried maid (i.e. Frau Traugott) was pregnant, had suggested his wife engage a Czech maid instead, since these were 'billiger'. The connection between the two different uses of the word is slight, but Fühmann attempts to forestall objections through his preceding deliberations on the peculiar human ability to recall certain events through a single word or gesture. Even more questionable are the grounds on which he accuses the Baron of 'murdering' Hermine: harsh dismissal from service is hardly a legal definition of the term, whether or not this leads to attempted suicide! Ironically, this potentially serious weakness of the plot may pass unnoticed, for it is a discrepancy only evident on close examination. Since the narrator is appealing principally to our emotions at this point, the reader is unlikely to be distracted by nice questions of guilt. As soon as the narrator hears the word 'billig' he violently denounces the Baron as a murderer (using the emotive 'Mörder' four times within as many lines) and only then does he proceed to describe the vital succession of events in which the Baron was implicated. A passage of self-accusation follows, in which he raises the persistent motif of personal guilt (here his passive observation of the events) and then he once more condemns the Baron ('Mörder' again being used on four occasions). Through the constant use of the 'murderer' concept Fühmann persuades his reader that the Baron's crime is far greater than is actually the case. Although the former has only metaphorically 'destroyed' Hermine, the frequent repetition of a word normally used literally conduces the impression that his act must be considered in the traditional sense. In both the passages in which these accusations are made, the villain is seen on the platform in his capacity as leader of the revanchists and is therefore prejudged as a murderer – like Hitler. He is, at any rate, firmly associated in our minds with Nazi actions, and the dismissal of a maid appears as only one more facet of the criminal fascist mentality.

The issue could, of course, have been made far more clearcut. It would have been simple to depict the Baron maltreating Hermine or forcing her into suicide in a more sensational manner and therefore fully meriting his description as a murderer. That Fühmann avoids what many other East Germans would have eagerly exploited may arise from either of two factors. First, that he wished to follow the plot of his model, Shakespeare's *The Winter's Tale*, as clearly as possible;[32] or that this is an authentic detail in a writer renowned for his strong autobiographical penchant and his sincerity.

The extent to which this story does in fact rely on Fühmann's personal experience was made clear in a recent discussion between him and J.-H. Sauter. The central features are all derived from a chance encounter:

Das Thema in konkreter Form lief mir eigentlich über den Weg. Die Heldin dieser Geschichte, Frau Traugott, existiert, es gibt sie wirklich.

[32] For details of the parallels between the two works, see my 'Franz Fühmann's "Böhmen am Meer": A Socialist Version of "The Winter's Tale" '.

Ich könnte Ihnen Namen, Ort und Hausnummer sagen. Ich traf dieser Frau genauso, wie ich sie geschildert habe, verstört und an ihrer Umgebung, ich meine der Landschaft, in der sie nun lebte, leidend. Ich habe mich mit ihr unterhalten, auch mit ihrem Sohn, der übrigens wirklich auf die Kapitänschule ging. Das andere ist dann frei erfunden.[33]

Earlier in the same interview Fühmann comments at length on the motivation for the story, as well as his intentions in writing it. The passage is worth quoting in its entirety, since it explains his recurrent interest in the past as well as some of the points he was trying to make.

Sauter raises a question concerning 'Die Fahrt nach Stalingrad':

SAUTER:

In Ihrem Einzelschicksal erfaßten Sie das Schicksal eines großen Teils Ihrer Generation und umrissen zugleich die Forderungen des Tages. Zielen Sie nicht bei dieser Dichtung zugleich auf zusätzliche Dimensionen ab, wenn man bedenkt, daß zur Zeit ihrer Entstehung im westdeutschen Staat sich das erneut zu etablieren beginnt, was Sie als tödlich erfahren hatten?

FÜHMANN:

Gewiß, das gibt einen mächtigen Anstoß. Ich möchte es Ihnen an einem andern Beispiel zeigen. Als ich meine Erzählung *Böhmen am Meer* schrieb, da hatte ich die Hoffnung oder auch den festen Vorsatz, daß sie die letzte Arbeit zum Thema Krieg, Vergangenheit undsoweiter sei, und dann mußte ich um dieser Erzählung willen zu einem dieser 'Heimattreffen' gehen, um einfach einmal zu sehen, wie so etwas ausschaut. Ich war da, und es war für mich ein so bestürzendes Erlebnis, daß ich wirklich faßungslos – oft gebraucht dieses Wort, aber ich war wirklich fassungslos – dastand und dachte, die Zeit wäre stehengeblieben, und ich sei irgendwo im Sudetengau im Jahre 1938 – es waren also dieselben Losungen, und es waren dieselben Märsche, es waren dieselben Uniformen, und es waren dieselben Reden, und es waren dieselben Fahnen und Trommeln und Wimpel und Runen und weißen Strümpfe, und es waren dieselben Lieder, und es waren zum Teil sogar dieselben Personen, die da standen und, als sei nichts gewesen, als sei jetzt das Jahr 1938, wieder diesen ganzen fürchterlichen Mechanismus aufzogen. Da kam mich sehr und zwingend das Gefühl an, daß es nicht von meinem subjektiven Wollen und Entscheiden abhängt, ob die Auseinandersetzung mit der Vergangenheit erledigt ist. Aus dieser Erkenntnis

[33] 'Interview mit Franz Fühmann', pp. 50–1.

kam dann der Gedanke, das zu schreiben, was dann später das *Judenauto* geworden ist. Die Vergangenheit ist leider nicht tot, und ich werde mich daher wohl noch lange mit diesem Thema beschäftigen. (loc. cit., pp. 40–1)

This reply contains a number of phrases which actually occur in the story, some of which are quoted above (p. 126).

Although much of *Böhmen am Meer* concerns the private life of its narrator, the increasing concentration first on another person (Frau Traugott) and then on the political situation, is suggestive of a growing awareness of duty. The socialist writer's concern is not with the personal pleasures related in the first pages, but with larger and more important political and moral questions. So although the narrative begins with an account of private bliss, its climax appropriately falls in a scene in which the two German states are contrasted. Yet the sense of contrast lies not only in the narrator's open juxtapositioning of East and West (as quoted above, p. 129), nor in his incontrovertible demonstration of those factors which unify Nazi past and Western present. It depends equally, if not more, upon the ability of the (East German) reader to supply a moral standpoint from which the whole revanchist campaign can be exposed. Given such a reader, a considerable proportion of the story will be experienced as a conflict of fascism and humanitarianism, of West and East.

Although Fühmann's conclusions are identical with those of propaganda, the author is able to transcend any stock quality they would consequently have possessed by grounding his plot in such a convincing, private world. The issue is never presented in explicitly political terms or in the assertive extremism of propaganda, but within the framework of a sensitive individual's holiday experience. Those juxtapositions in which a blunt contrast is effected are skilfully anticipated, seeming to spring naturally from the plot, while even when commenting directly on West Germany Fühmann is careful to avoid the excesses to which many of his fellow writers have succumbed.

The 'revanchist' movement – as exemplified in the ceremonies of those who call themselves the 'Heimatvertriebenen' – has also been exposed by Manfred Bieler. In *Bonifaz oder Der Matrose in der Flasche*, a novel published in 1963 (before his move to the West), Bieler satirises a wide range of West German phenomena; significantly, his climax is an attack on the revanchist and militarist schooling against the GDR which is supposedly encouraged in the Federal Republic.

Bonifaz, a picaresque hero, is involved in a number of escapades in the West, all of which confirm its image (in the East) as morally corrupt and restorationist. In his final experience before returning to the Soviet Zone he becomes involved in a gathering of the newly formed 'Neue Nase Partei', which is organised by ex-Nazis and masks its aggressive intentions behind a euphemistic title. It is referred to at one point as 'die Neue Alldeutsche Trutz-Organisation [cf. NATO], die hier eine Ausstellung für die Selbstverteidigung gemacht hat', when the exhibition in question is in fact a 'Bombenausstellung' with plans for attacking the East openly on view.

Bieler's principal means of discrediting the West German organisers of this demonstration is similar to Fühmann's: he reveals affinities between present actions and similar ones in the Third Reich. Not only are the leaders the same, but the methods are basically unchanged, stirring music, marching, flags, banners and demagogy being the most prominent. The aim of the ceremony is to arouse support for the policy of annexing the East by force, in particular the town of 'Roßbach',[34] which lies only a few miles across the border. The banners all proclaim

---

[34] 'Roßbach' is seen as an imaginary town near the border, but the name is clearly symbolic. Roßbach is a village near Leipzig, the site of Frederick the Great's worst defeat (1757) in the Seven Years War. In Arnim's 'Der tolle Invalide auf dem Fort Ratonneau', for example, 'Roßbach' is seen as a blemish on Prussian history: 'Wenn doch so ein Teufel in alle unsre kommandierende Generale führe, so hätten wir kein zweites Roßbach zu fürchten. . .' (*Sämtliche Romane und Erzählungen* Vol. 2, p. 737). In the present case Roßbach would suggest the wounded pride of the Federal Republic.

The later references to 'Roßbach' could conceivably refer to Gerhart

this in a variety of ways, but the most striking, as well as the most common slogan, is that which offers a verbal parallel to the pre-war German situation: ROSSBACH – HEIM INS REICH. As Fühmann has reminded us in *Das Judenauto*, the determination to bring territories 'heim ins Reich' was common in the years before 1939.[35] It has since been given a fresh existence by East German propaganda to characterise the aims of the revanchist movement in the Federal Republic, and by using it Bieler is adhering to the stereotyped image of these chauvinists as neo- or ex-Nazis. Bieler's attack on the ceremony can, however, be criticised for its rather clumsy use of a Nazi framework: the satiric effect could have been obtained without such exaggerated use of National Socialist elements. *Böhmen am Meer* is far superior in this respect. The parallels which Fühmann draws with the Third Reich are far more judiciously integrated into the plot than Bieler's comparatively crude jibes and his open mockery.

Robert Andrews has found both *Bonifaz* and Bieler's 'Das verschluckte Herzogtum' examples of comedy, pure and simple,[36] but there seems to me a bitter, serious note in much of the humour in both works. This is, I feel, particularly true of the bomb show, just as it is true of an earlier suggestion that Nazis are only biding their time until it is again propitious for them to emerge from concealment. Bieler describes the glass prison in which some of them are confined as 'eine Herberge für vorläufig Überflüssige'. 'Überflüssige' is euphemistic and may raise a certain amusement, but the unexpected 'vorläufig' possesses a warning overtone. Andrews overlooks the concern with which Nazism is considered in the East; citizens of the GDR are encouraged to consider the ethical and political aspects

Roßbach, the famous SA leader, whose biography was written by Arnolt Bronnen in 1930.

[35] See in particular the Chapter 'Die Berge herunter', pp. 41–53.

[36] 'A Comic Novel from East Germany: Manfred Bieler, "Bonifaz oder Der Matrose in der Flasche" '.

of a work as much as its formal qualities, and they will therefore be unlikely to consider these episodes on a purely literary plane.

It should not, however, be forgotten that Bieler's novel does represent the sole 'humorous' attempt to depict the Federal Republic in terms of the Third Reich. The satire of all the works discussed in this chapter is of a far more serious intent than that to be detected in the novels introduced in other chapters. The 'traveller' and, to a lesser extent, the 'representative', have offered far greater opportunities for levity than has the backcloth of Hitlerism.

The works discussed thus far in this chapter are set in both East and West Germany. Herbert Nachbar's *Haus unterm Regen* is more typical of contemporary fiction, for it is set in the East alone, with the West featuring only in occasional references. Despite the geographical limitation, however, the work quite clearly seeks to investigate the attitude of both parts of the German nation to their common heritage.

Nachbar's novel is built around a problem faced by two lovers. Christoph, a pilot in the East German Air Force, is forbidden to marry Henriette since her father, a war criminal, now lives in the Federal Republic. As Christoph reluctantly explains: 'Nach einer Bestimmung können Flugzeugführer eine Frau nur dann heiraten, wenn die Frau keine Verwandten ersten Grades in Westdeutschland oder im kapitalistischen Ausland hat' (p. 35). Christoph wishes to marry Henriette and is prepared to sacrifice his career to do so, in spite of contrary advice. Henriette, on the other hand, realises the vital part that flying plays in his life and is not prepared to marry him if, in order to do so, he must renounce that career. An insoluble situation thus arises and remains unresolved at the end of the novel, although a hope is raised that the Air Force may decide to relax its regulations in this particular instance. The potential danger of the circumstances slowly emerges: although there is no *present* possibility that Henriette would utilise her privileged position (as the wife of a pilot) to obtain secret information, there is nevertheless the chance that her relationship with her father might in future lead her into criminal activities.

Haus unterm Regen falls into the second category of works mentioned above, that is, those in which the past is seen to be overcome by the new socialist society. Against this is the explicit West German background, in which the past is still very much alive. The main stumbling block to the happiness of Christoph and Henriette is, of course, that the latter's father was not only a Nazi, but a war criminal. It is implied that he would have been punished for his misdeeds if he had lived in the GDR, but he has escaped from justice and lives unmolested in the West. The book accordingly embodies the Eastern accusation that acknowledged war criminals openly live without fear in the Federal Republic. As Henriette's grandfather, Otto, muses to himself: 'Nach einem schlimmen Krieg entstehen zwei deutsche Staaten. In einem wird aufgeräumt mit den Verbrechen und mit den Verbrechern der Vergangenheit. Im anderen nicht' (p. 216). The same issue is raised by Christoph in an imaginary conversation with his Group Captain. Among the reasons he advances to prove that Henriette would never leave for the West is the fact that 'Sie vermißt in Westdeutschland die ehrliche Abrechnung mit der Vergangenheit' (p. 53). It is noteworthy that the actual words 'Abrechnung mit der Vergangenheit' are introduced, not only at this point but also later by Otto, who realises his guilt in not informing Henriette of her father's true character. In a passage of self-accusation he reflects on the way in which he has brought up his granddaughter:

Ich habe ihr gegenüber nicht gespart mit Antworten auf Fragen, die *sie* stellte. Auch die Abrechnung mit der Vergangenheit Deutschlands, aus der mir Schande für die Familie gekommen war, habe ich ihr erleichtert – aber den entscheidenden Schritt, die Abrechnung mit dem Beweis in der eigenen Familie, diesen Schritt habe ich versäumt. Warum wundere ich mich eigentlich, wenn die Vergangenheit mir nachläuft wie ein räudiger Köter? Was tat ich denn, um das Tier zu verscheuchen? (p. 77)

Because the GDR has purportedly solved the problem at a national level, Otto has shelved the familial aspect; forced to confront the results of his actions, he finally realises the necessity of resolving the question at a personal level and so breaks the silence he has maintained over his son. Otto must bear a certain guilt through his silence, but he does at least inwardly recognise this. Contrasted with the actions of his age-group in the West, his conduct is far less reprehensible. The attitude of his contemporaries in the other state is brought up by Christoph:

Und drüben marschieren sie schon wieder, es sind nicht mehr nur Alte, es sind auch welche nachgewachsen. Hab ich mir eigentlich noch nie klargemacht, aber es stimmt. Da marschieren die Alten und hinter ihnen ein Gefolge von Jungen, die so erzogen wurden, wie es die Alten wollten. Tatsächlich, man denkt gar nicht dran, daß im alten Geist junge Menschen denken. Bei uns? Keine Frage. Wir haben die Zeit genutzt. (p. 144)

In these final comments, as in all Nachbar's other pronouncements on the two states, the contrast is boldly and confidently asserted. The other significant features raised in this passage are the idea of 'intellektuelle Manipulation', which was emphasised so strongly by Fühmann; and the movement from 'ich' to 'wir' as Christoph develops his social/political deliberations.

Like so many East German novels, *Haus unterm Regen* has as one of its themes the conflict between individual and community: the social desires of the individual versus the moral and political claims of the state. The clash of the two – which is not really a clash, given that all appreciate the problems involved and are eager to seek compromise – is precipitated by the fact that there are two Germanies which have followed different aims, the significance of which mounts as political aspects increasingly impinge on the action. Otto's son also begins to stand for a larger entity than Nazism alone. By constantly identifying him with the West as a whole, Nachbar makes the Berlin wall (the erection of which is featured in the novel) seem all the more desirable.

Yet the open existence of Otto's son in the Federal Republic acquires full significance through extra-literary means: the information supplied by mass media. Whilst the West may never be featured directly in the novel and the Nazi presented only through the eyes of others, the East German reader will nevertheless expand the basic outline of the fascist mentality which emerges through his acquaintance with many factual cases. It is a one-sided picture of fascism – and by extension, of West German attitudes – which is presented, since it rests on only one character. But since no other offers a counter-balance, the West in seen exclusively in terms of his most striking qualities. Through a rhetorical trick Nachbar suggests the similarity of many others in the West to this criminal. Christoph, musing on him, resolves that: 'ich werde auf ihn schießen, falls er *und seinesgleichen* unser Land überfallen' (p. 231 [my italics]). Fühmann employs the same method as he generalises on the repulsive figure of the Baron in *Böhmen am Meer*: 'er war ein Mörder, wie seinesgleichen Mörder sind. . .' (p. 399).

The issue of 'coming to terms with the past' is raised almost programmatically in *Haus unterm Regen,* and by using such phrases as 'Abrechnung mit der Vergangenheit' Nachbar relates the familial problem around which the plot is centred to much larger national issues. Although the case is an individual one, its general relevance is suggested by the fact that it is habitually referred to in such nationally significant terms. Throughout the story the East as a whole is seen to have successfully triumphed over its heritage. Failings in that part of the nation are only material ones, and it is interesting to note that the author does not desist from suggesting some of these (p. 164). As in several previous examples, frankness in the sphere of self-criticism gives the impression of a sincere approach to all aspects that are considered.

Haus unterm Regen employs an exceptionally large number of references to the Federal Republic and the Third Reich. Most novels contain only occasional allusions (albeit at critical points of the narrative) to remind readers of the contrasting situation in the other part of the nation.[37] In Fries's *Der Weg nach Oobliadooh*, for example, such allusions are far less common. The first occurs as the anti-heroes Arlecq and Paasch muse on a schoolteacher they both knew:

Ebenden mein ich, sagt Paasch. Soll nachm Westen sein. Begreif ich nicht, sagt Arlecq und schließt die Augen. Einen besseren Sommer haben sie drüben auch nicht. Der Zigarettenrauch steilt sich an den Sonnenstrahlen hoch. Aber bessere Pensionen für Nazis, sagt Paasch. (p. 107)

Fries handles this reference to Federal Republic and Third Reich particularly well. The issue is not treated with either the gravity or the terminology which might be expected, the unconcerned tone of the speakers contrasting sharply with the content of their remarks. The concept of the 'mental set' (as mentioned in Chapter One) is again relevant, however, for the writer can clearly rely on his reader's recognising the implications of such statements and can thus understate the issue. Paasch introduces the example of 'Republikflucht' remarkably casually ('soll nachm Westen sein') and Arlecq continues the levity by his whimsical reduction of the difference (or the lack of one) between the two states to a question of weather. The following description of the peaceful scene might seem irrelevant, but it serves a function similar to that of the 'pregnant' pause before the shattering climax. The (East German) reader's emotions will have been aroused by Arlecq's feigned ignorance, and they will now be heightened by the contrasting tempo and obvious diversion into insignificant description. Harmony is restored by the climactic succinctness of Paasch's reply, with the host of suggestions which it embodies.

Another example is to be found in Arlecq's account of what life in the West was really like. After a brief visit to West Berlin he and Paasch have returned to the East, and Arlecq is now supplying his girlfriend Anne with an explanation for

---

[37] E.g. Karl-Heinz Jakobs, *Beschreibung eines Sommers*; Herbert Nachbar, *Oben fährt der große Wagen*; Herbert Otto, *Zum Beispiel Josef*.

their change of heart. The first part of his answer is clearly given tongue-in-cheek, but that does not apply to the second:

Die Unterschiede waren zu groß, sagte er zu Anne. Wenn du das verstehst: dreizehn Jahre andere Gewohnheiten. Und die Polizei im Lager sah aus wie aus einem Hitler-Film. (p. 269)

Once again, a single, simple allusion suffices to make a broad allegation. Authors of the sixties can rely so fully on their reader's 'mental set' that many conceal their critique within a subordinate clause. De Bruyn, for example, in *Buridans Esel*:

Gegen diesen schlechten Ruf...hat man sich zu wehren...da achtet man ein bißchen aufeinander, damit nicht wieder Zustände einreißen wie vor fünfundvierzig oder wie jenseits der Mauer, das ist man der neuen Zeit und den Heranwachsenden doch schuldig. p. 39)

This example, like Fries's, illustrates the way in which writers can now confidently understate the issue of West German restoration. It also reveals the progress which has been made since the fifties, when such accusations were usually made directly and repeatedly within many novels.

The works referred to above are set in the Democratic Republic and use the Nazism of the West as their main point of contrast. The corollary to this, a Federal Republic setting with the East as a contrast, is also to be found in a number of novels. But for that matter, any work by an East German writer which is set in the West is by implication concerned with division, for the Eastern reader is bound to supply a criterion by which Western actions can be measured. The mental process involved will be similar to that detectable in the observer of satire, which, as J. P. Stern has reminded us, relies for its effect 'on a reader who will supply the moral or aesthetic norm against which the experience that is being presented...will be measured'.[38] East German writers do not, however, rely on

[38] Introduction to Arthur Schnitzler's *Liebelei, Leutnant Gustl, Die letzten Masken*, p. 38.

their reader's instinctively providing this contrastive element. There are very few books set in the West in which there is not at least a minor reference to the Democratic Republic.

I should like to consider two works which fall into this category, both of which first appeared in *NDL*: Eberhard Panitz's 'Das Gesicht einer Mutter' (1960), and Hans-Dieter Linstedt's 'Rheinische Geschichte' (1966). Although neither of these is particularly well written, their very mediocrity is typical of this approach to the issue of division, and it is worth remarking in this respect that no author of note seems to have used this means of contrasting the two Germanies. The reason for the choice of other approaches may lie partly in the fact that accomplished writers rarely set their works in a milieu with which they are unacquainted: and since few (if any) East Germans have an intimate knowledge of West German society, most are doubtless reluctant to portray it in any depth. Those who have nevertheless done so have tended, I feel, to base their work on the image of propaganda: there is, at any rate, the strong impression of caricature in these presentations of the West, and the sense of authenticity which characterises many novels which employ the 'traveller' motif is lacking from works in this category. For this reason I shall consider these two examples only briefly. Both betray the overt techniques usually associated with propagandist writing.

'Das Gesicht einer Mutter' concerns the history of a mother in post-First World War and National Socialist Germany, the terrors of the Second World War, and finally, the survival of a Nazi mentality in the Federal Republic. This is evident not only in the support which is given to acknowledged ex-Nazis (a point Panitz tends to overstate in the story), but also in the view that history is about to repeat itself. One of the most disturbing images of the story is that of Nazi manoeuvres on the banks of the Elbe shortly before the invasion of Poland. The final section contains an almost identical image, but on this occasion of 'Bundeswehr' manoeuvres, which are taking place in exactly the same spot. The similarity of situation (and of the vocabulary used to describe it) firmly links the two scenes in the reader's mind:

Es ist ein heller Morgen, und rechts und links vom Weg wirbelt es den Sand der Heide hoch, denn die Panzer sind wieder da, die marschierenden Soldaten und die Kanonenrohre am Horizont. So als hätte nie der Krieg an diesem Fluß ein schauerliches Ende gefunden, rasselt und donnert es ringsum, schrillen Kommandostimmen und hämmern Maschinengewehre den Takt. (p. 37)

The horror of the situation – a gruesome history repeating itself – is partly relieved by the following sentence. The bank of the Elbe is, of course, the border between Federal and Democratic Republic, and it offers a note of hope – if not for the unfortunate mother, then at least for her son: 'Nur das Ufer der Elbe ist verwaist, eine Grenze, und das andere Ufer ist für Jörg Dobbertin bisher ein unbekanntes Land'. This suggestion of hope for Jörg (who is, like his mother, a victim of the capitalist system) is consolidated in the final line, where his chances of progress are adumbrated. He has been seen 'mehrmals in Gesellschaft eines Mannes...der weithin als "Roter" gilt'. This conclusion is on the note of 'Ausweg DDR', as Jörg Lingenberg puts it with reference to the 'Fernsehspiel'.[39] The GDR is seen as the only viable alternative to the evil, neo-Nazi situation in the West.

Many works set in the West hardly rise above the level of propaganda, a failing due to their frequent and crassly presented analogies between Federal Republic and Third Reich. It is to a certain extent surprising that writers have tended to overemphasise such analogies. In consideration of the frequency with which propaganda has established a sense of continuity between the two periods in question, the reader might well expect authors to operate with a subtle series of allusions to the epoch with which contemporary Germany is to be compared. To adopt the terminology of Herman Meyer, 'conspicuous'

[39] *Das Fernsehspiel in der DDR*, pp. 236–9.

references could easily be replaced by more 'cryptic' ones.[40] This is, however, by no means the case. The parallels are often presented directly, and in a manner which may strike the West European as decidedly over-explicit. An example of this overtly tendentious approach is to be found in Hans-Dieter Linstedt's 'Rheinische Geschichte', the story of an East German school-teacher, Hans Eckweiler, who returns to his native Rheinland village during a visit to a pedagogic conference in Mainz. The resemblances between past and present are to him the most remarkable feature of the Federal Republic, and they give rise to a number of comments, of which the following are the most striking:

Hans ist zumute, als habe man hier die Zeit einfach 25 Jahre zurück-gedreht. (p. 61)

Aber sein Gegenüber ist geblieben, was er vor Jahrzehnten schon war. Die Zeit ist stehengeblieben, in ihm und um ihn. (p. 63)

[Hans is reminded of a poem:] 'Deutschland, du liebe Mördergrube', heißt es darin. Du liebe Mördergrube! 'Wo es rückwarts aufwärts geht...'
Rückwärts aufwärts! Und wo das Abwärtsgehen den Abwärtsgehenden wie ein anderes Aufwärts vorkommt. (p. 68)

[Hans:] 'Ehrlich gesagt, mir war unerträglich, in einem Städtchen atmen zu müssen, in dem das Alte wieder Auferstehung feiert...' (p. 73) etc.

Throughout there are frequent explicit references to the GDR, while the final paragraph, consisting of a single sentence, reinforces the theme: 'Wie schön ist es, denkt Hans Eckweiler, heimzukehren, endlich heimzukehren' (p. 95), meaning, of course, to his new spiritual home. The idea is once again 'Ausweg DDR', but in far more overt a manner than that employed by Panitz. Time and again the narrator's comments are rendered superfluous by the clear direction of the plot.

I should like to conclude this chapter by considering a work

[40] *The Poetics of Quotation in the European Novel*, p. 7.

which falls into none of the above three categories, but which nevertheless depicts the West exclusively in terms of its relationship to the Third Reich. Günter de Bruyn's 'Renata' marks a break from the traditional approach to Western restoration by considering contemporary attitudes from the Polish point of view. The story illustrates in particular the manner in which the Poles distinguish between two types of German, between 'die Faschisten' and 'die Deutschen'. Although not stated, there are implications that this distinction is essentially one between Federal and Democratic Republic.

'Renata' is in the first instance a love story. Michael Schwartz, a West Berlin schoolteacher on a visit to Poland, meets Renata, a nurse, in a railway carriage. For both the experience proves 'love at first sight', but Renata is considerably distressed to learn of Michael's nationality. The Polish reaction to the concept of 'Germany' is compared with an unconditioned reflex:

[Renata] ich dachte: er ist ein Deutscher, und erschrak dabei, weil ich an Papa dachte und an die Zeit der Okkupation. Das ist nun einmal so: die Gedankenverbindung zwischen Deutschland und Wehrmacht ist so eng wie zwischen Krieg und Tod. Wie die Augen auf grelles Licht durch Zusammenziehen der Pupille, reagieren unsere Gedanken auf das Wort 'deutsch' durch Einengung auf grau Uniformierte. Und wie das Auge erst nach einer gewissen Zeit wieder sehfähig wird, können wir dann weiterdenken und Unterschiede sehen. (p. 80)

Overcoming her initial fear, Renata agrees to meet Michael later in the day, when they dine and visit a 'Tanzbar' together. After a period of elation Renata breaks down and relates an obsessive childhood experience in which she was abused and assaulted by a German. That figure, as both she and her lover realise, was none other than Michael himself. It is for this reason that she decides there is no future for the two of them; she will never be able to forget his background and what she and her family suffered during the war. She also fears that their idyllic dreams will prove hollow when they have to face reality. Michael leaves with regret, but is changed by the confrontation. It has brought home to him a number of features concerning his own past and that of the Federal Republic. He is now resolved to change himself and the present political system, which, he has been brought to realise, does not differ too markedly from that of the Third Reich.

The reader's attention is held by two factors: the development of the relationship between Michael and Renata, and the conversion of Michael to a committed point of view. From the first pages a hint is given of the importance that politics are to play. Michael feels self-conscious in Poland and for that reason speaks little: 'Ich hatte viel geschwiegen in den Tagen meiner polnischen Reise, weil es mir unangenehm war, als Deutscher erkannt zu werden. Niemand hatte mir Veranlassung dazu gegeben, alle waren mir freundlich, ja herzlich begegnet, aber trotzdem war mir zumute wie einem Menschen mit schlechtem Gewissen' (p. 74). The suspicion that the Poles are presenting a façade and that all Germans are hated in that country is corrected in the next sentence: 'Mein Bruder, dessen Hochzeit Anlaß meiner Reise gewesen war, hatte mir gesagt, daß man hier zwischen Deutschen und Faschisten unterscheiden könne und ihm heute niemand mehr seine Herkunft vorwerfe'. An important distinction is raised here, and it is one that is repeated at several other points in the story. The use of the ambiguous term 'fascist' serves a particularly useful function, for it has two points of reference in contemporary East German society. First, to former supporters of the Third Reich; and second, to their successors in the Federal Republic. Since the Republic as a whole is commonly referred to as 'fascist' or 'neo-fascist', while the GDR is constantly presented as a country of anti-fascism, the distinction between 'Deutschen' and 'Faschisten' may consequently appear to the reader as that between the two Germanies.

The concept of fascism is reintroduced only two pages later in Michael's reflections on his visit to Auschwitz. As his group passes a pile of prisoners' hair which was to be used for commercial purposes, Michael is impressed by the Poles' terminology:

'Die Faschisten haben verstanden, aus allem Kapital zu schlagen!' sagte der polnische Freund meines Bruders dazu. Die Faschisten? Sehr großzügig ist diese Trennung von Faschisten und Deutschen. Macht sie es für uns überflüssig, ein schlechtes Gewissen zu haben, wenn wir an dem Haarberg vorübergehen? (p. 76)

'Faschisten' carries a heavy ironic weight within the above passage, while the choice of the slightly unusual 'Kapital' (with its obvious connotations of 'Kapitalisten') offers the attentive reader a set of wider implications to what is basically a historical issue. The visit to Auschwitz itself raises the question of national guilt, which will be heightened for the East German reader by the knowledge that former concentration camp personnel live an open existence in the West.[41] The fact that the Federal Republic allows such figures large pensions – and must therefore acquiesce in their former atrocities – is a common feature of propaganda. There are many articles on this subject, and the title of one of them is particularly relevant to this chapter: F. Faber's 'Unbewältigte Vergangenheit'.[42]

But the most remarkable aspect of the above quotation, as of this section as a whole, is that Michael feels no guilt for the

---

[41] There are numerous literary illustrations of this theme. One work, which offers an exposé of National Socialist criminals in general, is Rolf Schneider's 'Die Unbewältigten', a radio play based on the 1963 Herterich affair in the Federal Republic. The play concerns the continued existence of several notable National Socialist figures in positions of supreme power in the West, against whom opposition is a long and perilous process. For Schneider, the most alarming feature of the affair is that a large number of Western citizens violently oppose any attack on these former criminals. The fact that such citizens vilify the hero with terms like 'Kommunistenschwein' (p. 145) reinforces the view that the conflict in the play is again basically that of humanism and fascism, East and West.

Another illustration is to be found in Stephan Hermlin's 'Die Kommandeuse', a short story on the uprising of 17 June 1953. Here a daughter learns from her father that the West actually prefers former Nazis above others: ['Sie hatte danach von ihrem Vater aus Hannover einen Brief bekommen –] dort kümmere sich kein Mensch um einen, im Gegenteil, seine frühere Tätigkeit im Reichssicherheitshauptamt sei für die Justiz eigentlich eine Empfehlung gewesen', p. 226.

[42] Faber's article denounces the policy whereby Nazi criminals are given preferential treatment in the law courts as well as premature release.

events of Auschwitz.[43] His obsession with the past is illustrated by his frequent musings on aspects of the Third Reich – and even allowing for the free-ranging diary form, there is often only the barest link between these and what has preceded – yet for all this, little if any sense of shame emerges. Although the idea of a 'guilty conscience' is mentioned on the second page, it becomes clear that Michael feels no responsibility for previous occurrences. While this in itself might be understandable, the fact that he is not prepared to prevent their recurrence illustrates the culpable nature of his attitude. By acting in this way he is, of course, revealing another important aspect of the typically Western citizen as he is seen by the GDR.

By the end of the opening section of the story, Michael has already been characterised as a typical West German. But the process is continued over much more of the development: there is almost an element of caricature, in fact, as he repeatedly lives up to the image he has presented in the first pages.

In his early discussion with Renata, for example, two important facets of the West German mentality (as seen by the East) are raised. One is political disinterest, introduced when Michael rejects the view that West German girls are interested only in 'Mode und Kochrezepte': 'Nein, aber sie nehmen die Politik nicht so ernst. Und ich glaube, seien Sie nicht böse deshalb, daß sie sorgloser leben so!' (p. 87). The other aspect is revanchism. Renata asks him his attitude – as a teacher – towards territories East of the Oder–Neiße line. She receives an immediate retort:

---

[43] Karl-Heinz Jakobs has also used the image of the concentration camp to bring out West Germans' total lack of concern for the events of the past. In 'Weimarnovelle' two lovers pay a harrowing visit to Buchenwald and then return to Weimar where they encounter a group of visitors from the West. As these figures get progressively intoxicated, they lose their inhibitions and begin acting as they did during the war, singing Nazi songs and expressing Nazi sentiments. The immorality of their nostalgia for the past (and the suggestion that they are behaving as they would in the Federal Republic) is set into relief by (a) the reactions of East German public and police; and (b) the backcloth of Buchenwald, symbol of the evil potential these visitors embody.

[Renata:] 'Und – die polnischen Westgebiete?'
[Michael:] 'Die deutschen Ostgebiete?' (p. 82)

The decisiveness of this reply makes it clear that any political interest is dominated by a strong sense of nationalism.

Apathy in the face of true political issues is reinforced shortly afterwards during Michael's conversation with a taxi driver:

'Wissen Sie, daß Frank, der sogennante Reichsminister von dort aus sein blutiges Terrorregime führte?' fragte der Chauffeur... 'So etwas vergißt man nicht!' sagte er. 'Vielleicht wird in Deutschland zu viel vergessen!' Ich hatte ihm gesagt, daß ich aus Westberlin kam, und hatte gewußt, daß so etwas wieder kommen würde. 'Bei uns kümmert man sich nicht so viel um Politik, wenn es einem gut geht.' Ich merkte, daß ich rot wurde, weil ich wußte, wie dumm dieses Argument war...(p. 84)

A growing sense of responsibility is evident here, but Michael is still inwardly hostile to political pressure of this nature. His failing is the traditional 'Bildung'-oriented German's inability to take sufficient interest in politics, and the implicit historical framework within which this apathy should be seen is given a sudden emphasis in the driver's blunt response to the above:

'Da wird es ein neuer Hitler leicht haben!' sagte er ruhig, ohne sich nach mir umzudrehen. (p. 84)

As was suggested earlier in this chapter, the bogey of National Socialism is far more ominous a threat to the East German than to the West. For the former the driver's harsh analogy will consequently have the quality of a trump card. There is, of course, little doubt that concern for political awareness is taken far more seriously in the GDR than in the West and that many East Germans show a genuine concern over Western political disinterest. Horror is often expressed that the majority of Western citizens should be in the control of scheming right-wing factions and fascists who manipulate them for their own ends.[44] As a report in *Die Zeit* indicated, East German youth is far better politically informed than their Western counterparts,[45] while defectors to the Federal Republic have often been

[44] See, for example, Ernst Richert, *Das zweite Deutschland*, p. 120.
[45] R. Eser, 'Jugend in der DDR'.

disgruntled by the political ignorance and complacency of their new aquaintances.[46] The traditional West German reply is that socialists subordinate everything to politics, as in the following remark in Werner Heiduczek's *Abschied von den Engeln*. But both the initial comment and its counterstatement are to be seen in the context of past – and present – German history:

—Ihr in der DDR habt die sonderbare Art, alles der Politik unter-zuordnen, selbst ein Gespräch beim Abendbrot.
—Der unpolitische Mensch ist der am meisten manipulierte Mensch, der willfährigste, der bis zum Jüngsten Tag betrogene. (p. 76)

Exploitation of the individual for political purposes, already noted in *Böhmen am Meer* and *Bonifaz*, is again suggested in 'Renata'. The taxi driver, continuing his series of direct warnings, enquires into the 'Heimatvertriebenen' and warns of their danger. Referring to Michael's mother, who belongs to the 'schlesische Landsmannschaft', he comments:

'In politischer Hinsicht seid ihr aus den kapitalistischen Ländern manchmal wie Kinder. Angst kann einem werden dabei. Ihre Mutter hängt an der alten Heimat, gut, ich achte ihren Schmerz, aber merkt sie denn nicht, wie sie mißbraucht wird?'

The taxi driver is using 'kapitalistisch' advisedly here. His accusation is not levelled against West Germany, but against the West in general. His criterion, of course, is the standards of the Communist bloc.

In contrast to Renata, who is presented as an intelligent and well-informed personality, Michael appears rather naive, unprofound and complacent, a point which de Bruyn can reinforce stylistically owing to his use of the (alternating) first person form. Michael's deliberations on the question of German, and especially personal, guilt, show an escapist attitude, and although he believes that former Nazi criminals are again in positions of power in the West, he does not see why he should oppose them, since to do so would probably involve sacrificing all he

---

[46] See *Ich bin Bürger der DDR und lebe in der BRD*, edited by Barbara Grunert-Bronnen.

has thus far achieved. This is very much a question of 'qui s'excuse, s'accuse', and offends the moral norm not only of the East German reader. Through the sole directly moralising comment of the story ('da wird es ein neuer Hitler leicht haben'), de Bruyn has supplied an international norm against which both regressive tendencies as well as complacency towards them can be measured.

The evening Michael spends with Renata breaks away from such politically significant elements into a rather idyllic atmosphere, but this is soon broken by Renata's breakdown and the relation of her horrific childhood experience. It is this which finally effects the decisive change in Michael, bringing him to the realisation of latent destructive urges and forcing him into a decision. From this point all the typically complacent features previously enumerated are rejected. His cynical, materialist attitude to his profession is replaced by a moral one, and he is also prepared to sacrifice his career, which his new course will probably make inevitable. Ute, his girl friend, confronts him with arguments similar to those he used earlier in the story and thus symbolises his former self, but Michael remains intransigent, determined to resist all those whose attitude is reminiscent of an earlier epoch. In a comment applicable to both then and now, he delivers a moral critique: 'Jeder ist verantwortlich für das, was er nicht zu verhindern sucht' (p. 99).

What de Bruyn is attacking in 'Renata' is not West German ignorance on matters of restoration, but deliberate suppression of unwelcome facts in the interests of a secure living. The immorality of such a *Weltanschauung* as 'leben und leben lassen' was castigated in *Das Klassentreffen*, while here, as in *Böhmen am Meer*, it is given a historical antecedent. The immorality of most Germans' behaviour under the Third Reich is taken as self-evident.

The main success of 'Renata' lies in the manner in which de Bruyn has balanced the love story with the theme of political conversion, making the exploration of personal guilt as important as the critique of West German attitudes. Michael's *volte face*, convincing motivation of which could have been potentially difficult, is especially well handled. Here the author uses the structure for a clearly rhetorical purpose rather than the aesthetic function it serves in the rest of the story. The action is related by Michael and Renata in turn, almost in diary form, each being allotted five separate sections. Up to the end of section eight (Renata's story from the Third Reich) both have followed a strictly chronological sequence in the presentation of their experiences, but this is now suddenly broken. By the time Renata has finished her story, we have guessed that the culprit is Michael; this is confirmed by the beginning of section nine, in which we are plunged directly into an argument between him and his West Berlin girl friend Ute, who is attempting to dissuade him from a new attitude towards West German policy. It is only after this argument that Michael returns to the chronology expected and describes his immediate reactions to Renata's story. By juxtaposing Michael's guilty conduct with his attempts to redeem himself, de Bruyn gives credibility to this action. He depicts Michael as determined to fight against not only what he used to represent in the Third Reich (i.e. the despicable 'Mitläufer', the half-hearted but nevertheless participating Nazi), but also what he used to represent before his encounter with Renata – the descendant of the former, a complacent 'Bundesbürger' who inwardly opposes the restorationist aspects of contemporary society yet does nothing to change them.

The conflict between Ute and Michael has an important thematic significance, for in their disagreement over the attitude to be adopted in modern society, two diametrically opposed viewpoints emerge: that of the cynical 'Bundesbürger', and that of the Communist. Whereas previously the presentation of a divided German nation was dependent on the East German reader supplying a normative background (of his own state's achievements and outlook) to the neo-Nazism of the West, the difference between the two states is now more openly presented through the conflict of two representative points of view (as in the works examined in Chapter 3). That Michael's new attitude is in fact Communist is stressed by Ute ('Du bist in einem Tage Kommunist geworden!') and he is further identified with the GDR through his desire to come into contact with illegal Eastern agents and to teach the true facts concerning the Oder–Neiße border.

A final point should be made about Michael's decision, which is linked with the concept of 'Vergangenheitsbewältigung', the theme which links all the works discussed in this chapter. Whereas a failure to draw any lessons from the events of the past is evident in all those West Germans considered in *Böhmen am Meer, Bonifaz,* 'Das Gesicht einer Mutter', etc., 'Renata' depicts a successful attempt to confront and overcome one's heritage. But de Bruyn stresses that this attempt can only be successful on a private level: it is made abundantly clear that Michael's actions will lead to his forfeiting his position and all else he has attained in a society which, as a whole, still refuses to acknowledge the moral liabilities which were imposed by acceptance of the ideology of the Third Reich.

5. CONCLUSION

The conclusions of the preceding chapters are contained within those chapters themselves, and there is therefore little point in repeating them all here. There are, however, a number of more general remarks which can be made about the development of the theme 'divided Germany', as also the actual image of the two German states which has been presented in literature. Finally, the distinctive nature of East German writers' treatment of this theme can be set into perspective by a short survey of the West German works on this topic.

The two Germanies have repeatedly been contrasted by the propagandists of both countries, and Günther Wallraff has neatly summed up the attitudes which they sought to arouse. As he puts it in the first two stanzas of his satirical 'Hier und Dort':

Hier	und	Dort
I Hier freiheit dort knechtschaft		II hier gleichheit dort ausbeutung
hier wohlstand dort armut		hier aufbau dort zerfall
hier friedfertigkeit dort kriegslüsternheit		hier friedensheer dort kriegstreiber
hier liebe dort hass		hier leben dort tod
dort satan hier gott		dort böse hier gut

The image of divided Germany which appeared in GDR fiction of the fifties unfortunately often corresponded to this simplistic view, while practically every one of the wide range of crimes and failings of which the Federal Republic stands accused has been featured in literature.[1] These failings have been balanced, of course, by all the contrasting positive achievements of the socialist regime in the Democratic Republic. Nevertheless, although this view of East and West has remained basically unchanged in propaganda over the last twenty-five years, Eastern literature has revealed a movement away from such oversimplification of the national image, together with considerable development in the general manner of its presentation. In addition, certain writers have drawn attention to features which have *not* been included in propaganda.

The first striking advance has been in the movement to a more balanced appraisal of the two states. In early novels the West is presented as totally evil, and there is an eagerness to make the agents of the Federal Republic responsible for every failure that occurs in the GDR. The 'sabotage' motif recurs in a great number of the 'Aufbau' novels set on the land or in industry, and the West is continually depicted as attempting to undermine all progress in the East. In works such as Hans Lorbeer's *Die Sieben ist eine gute Zahl*, Rudolf Fischer's *Martin Hoop IV*, Werner Reinowski's *Der kleine Kopf* and Hans Marchwitza's *Roheisen*, Western agents, bribed or blackmailed, are repeatedly shown attempting to disrupt the Eastern economy. The Federal Republic itself figures only occasionally, the reader being encouraged to consider it mainly in terms of the saboteurs it sends to the East.

1961 marks a watershed: from this point one finds many more novels set in both East and West, while the actual presentation of each country becomes more convincing. Since an open border is necessary for many plots, a number of works written after erection of the Berlin Wall are nevertheless concerned with the same period as those written earlier; their treatment of this period is, however, quite different. This is a significant feature, for the circumstances of those years obviously cannot have altered – what has changed is the writers' attitude towards them.

[1] For details of the accusations of propaganda, see Appendix.

Other features of writing after 1961 are that not all failings are attributed exclusively to Western infiltrators, there is less idealisation of Eastern Party members and of 'positive heroes' acting as counterbalances to Western representative figures, and the West itself is not so frequently depicted as completely hostile. In this respect the literary image of the West deviates considerably from that of propaganda. A further deviation from the official standpoint is that refugees are no longer considered as purely contemptible figures, and the failings of GDR society – not just blackmail or the attractions of the West – are shown to be responsible for the defection of many intellectuals. It is this self-criticism which is so welcome in the literature of the sixties, particularly in works which are also sharply critical of the Federal Republic: *Der geteilte Himmel*, *Eine Tüte Erdnüsse*, and *Zeugnis zu dritt*, for example. And in novels where criticism of the East is subdued (e.g. *Die Aula* and *Abschied von den Engeln*), the attempts to disparage the West are also kept in moderation.

Exceptions to this pattern are generally provided in novels by the older generation (such as Anna Seghers and Wolfgang Joho), a point which suggests it would be false to assume that the appearance of a less exaggerated image of East and West marked a true development in individual writers. It is different authors – those who first began to write in the sixties – rather than a change of attitude, which have mainly determined this situation. The older generation were in general far more committed writers than the younger ones: members of the Communist Party when to be so was illegal, they obeyed the call for partisan literature far more readily than a generation which had not experienced repression during the Third Reich and which was less willing to blind itself to the initial failings of the Democratic Republic. Important contributory factors were that the Cold War was at its most intense during the fifties and that literature reflected the fervour with which politicians attacked the West. Also, once the frontier with the West was closed there was no necessity for such overtly didactic methods – writers no longer needed to persuade their fellows not to defect to the West by suggesting life there was as evil as had previously been claimed.

Younger writers have not only presented a more balanced image of East and West, but they have also drawn attention to two other features which are not included in the crass accusations of propaganda. First, they have shown concern for the way division has affected human relations between East and West, often centring on the problem of 'communication'. An example of this is to be found in Kurt Steiniger's *Der Schöpfungstage sind nicht sechs*, in which Martin Dill, a citizen of the GDR, is invited by his brother to take up a position in the (Federal Republic) 'Bundespost'. The invitation forces Martin into speculation:

Ein seltsamer Abend. Wie war es gekommen? Brüder gehörten nicht zur selben Familie. Mutter und Sohn waren getrennt, nicht nur durch die Grenze, sondern noch mehr durch Ideen und Verhältnisse, durch Gedanken und Worte. Verschieden alles. Zeitungen, Briefe, Bücher – in einer Sprache geschrieben, sind kaum lesbar hier oder dort. Anders die Tage und die Abende. Was sollte man tun? Es war da. So entstanden nach dem Krieg. Sollte dies Land ewig getrennt bleiben? Nein. Aber wo gab es den Ausweg? Konnte man keine Brücke entdecken? Ach, Autos und Ideen lassen sich nicht vereinigen. Ebensowenig Korpsbrüder und Arbeiter, Playboys und Bauern, gesundes Brot und hochkarätiger Glanz. Vieles liegt zwischen Deutschland und Deutschland, zwischen dem Beamten und dem Funktionär, zwischen Söhnen und Söhnen. (p. 510)

Martin's feelings of uncertainty and regret are typical. In many other novels there is a sense of unease in the presence of citizens from the other state, and both Christa Wolf (in *Der geteilte Himmel*) and Brigitte Reimann (in *Die Geschwister*) have commented on this fact in remarkably similar terms. Reimann's heroine, on a visit to West Berlin, is surprised that the strange people around her speak the same language ('Sie sprachen Deutsch, und ich hörte die deutschen Vokabeln und kam mir dennoch vor wie eine unerkannte Reisende in einem fremden

Land' – p. 60), while Wolf's heroine also experiences distinct unease in West Berlin ('Man ist schlimmer als im Ausland, weil man die eigene Sprache hört. Man ist auf schreckliche Weise in der Fremde' – p. 252). The sensation of feeling oneself in another country figures again in Jurij Brězan's *Eine Liebesgeschichte* (p. 91), Fritz Rudolf Fries's *Der Weg nach Oobliadooh* (p. 268), Uwe Johnson's *Das dritte Buch über Achim* (p. 316), Hermann Kant's *Die Aula* (p. 108), Wolfgang Joho's *Das Klassentreffen* (pp. 29, 54), Horst Mönnich's *Einreisegenehmigung* (p. 148), Hans von Oettingen's *Das Skalpell* (p. 142), and Herbert Plate's *Das soll der Mensch nicht scheiden* (p. 251).

The feeling of disorientation is sometimes exacerbated by linguistic difficulties. This too is hinted at in the quotation from Steiniger, and it has been brought out repeatedly by Uwe Johnson. In *Mutmaßungen über Jakob*, for example, the East German Jakob is unable to establish a point of contact with the members of a West German 'Männergesangverein' ('aber es war kein Reden mit ihnen, sie verstanden ihn nicht' – p. 282), while in *Das dritte Buch über Achim* the West German Karsch has initial difficulties with the language of the East ('er fand sich nicht in die Sprache des Landes' – p. 20). In *Zwei Ansichten* the issue is raised in passing on several occasions, but it is only in the more pointed 'Eine Reise wegwohin, 1960', that the problems are explained more fully. Karsch is here seen to be highly conscious of his linguistic deficiencies:

Er lernte den veränderten Sinn der Fremdworte, die in seinem Land nicht mehr benutzt wurden oder gar nicht, die zweiten Fälle von Struktur und Perspektive schrieb er auf mit anwachsendem Mitwissen, er lernte diese Sprache nie so gut, daß er sie zur Verständigung hätte benutzen können. Selbst im umgänglichen Reden der gewöhnlichen Leute fand er sich kaum unauffällig zurecht, da ihm zehn Jahre dieser Geschichte fehlten; sie erkannten ihn ohne Mühe. (pp. 39–40)

A more total breakdown of communication has been suggested by several of the Eastern poets. Günter Kunert, for example, in 'Wo Deutschland lag...', suggests a metaphorical plane beyond the literal one:

> Wo Deutschland lag, liegen zwei Länder,
> Zwei Länder liegen dort
> Und es trennt sie
> mehr als eine Grenze.
> Die gleiche Sprache sprechen sie,
> Die gleiche,
> Aber können sich nicht verstehen, weil
> Sie eine andere Sprache sprechen,
> Eine andere,
> Denn sie sind zwei Länder, zwei Länder
> Sind sie, und liegen, wo Deutschland lag.

The final manner in which certain writers have deviated from propaganda lies in their suggestion that division is regrettable, a point which is featured both in Kunert's poem as well as in the above quotation from Steiniger. This is not a theme of the politicians, who are far more intent on making accusations as to who is responsible for the present situation, but it is to be found in many works by the younger writers. And although they too may lay blame for present circumstances, they also recognise the tragedy that division has meant for the German nation as a whole. And this, ironically, is one of the main themes of what was probably the very first fictional presentation of divided Germany, Eduard Claudius's short sketch 'Mensch auf der Grenze' (1948).

Besides these developments in the image of the two German states, there has been a significant change in the actual manner of its presentation. This lies mainly in the movement from 'telling' to 'showing' which was elaborated in Chapter 3. There has been a marked difference between the literature of the fifties and the sixties in this respect: not only in less direct presentation of information and judgments, but particularly in the move away from 'telling' in its derogatory sense of 'moralising'.

The reasons advanced for the movement to a more realistic national image again hold good for this change in technique, while a further explanation may lie in the changing conception of the purpose of literature between the fifties and the sixties. The writer's audience in the early years of the Republic consisted mainly of the politically non-committed. Distrustful of politics after the collapse of National Socialism, the majority of Germans remained sceptical of the new socialist state and its ideals; the aim of writers in this period was therefore principally to *convert* these waverers to the socialist cause, and they attempted to do so with the methods which they thought appropriate. The audience of the sixties, and particularly the late sixties, was largely different. As was suggested above, writers no longer needed to urge their fellows not to escape to the West, for escape had been made impossible; nor did they need to argue quite so lengthily that socialism would eventually triumph, for modest economic success had already been achieved. This changed relationship between writer and reader allowed the younger generation of writers in general to respond with works which no longer attempted in the first instance to persuade; instead, they could rely on the moral support of a reader who shared their attitudes.[2] Works of the former category continued to be written, of course, by the older generation and also by younger writers of more limited talent such as Christa Borchert, Gertrud Bradatsch, and Hans von Oettingen. In these, however, there is little sense of community between writer and reader.

The difference between these two categories is, I think, well summed up by the concepts of 'art' and 'propaganda' as they have been elaborated by Ronald Peacock. In *Criticism and Personal Taste* he distinguishes between the two at some length and concludes with the following remarks:

[2] The best information on the changing attitude of East Germans towards their state is provided by Hans Apel in *Die DDR 1962–64–66*. His main conclusions here are summarised in 'Bericht über das "Staatsgefühl" der DDR-Bevölkerung'.

A point I want to clarify, however, is a difference between art and propaganda that is crucial and makes it impossible to confuse the two. It is essential to distinguish between poetic works based on given beliefs (like the work of the metaphysical religious poets), susceptible in consequence of fulfilling a natural function for readers who share those beliefs; and works which aim to convert unbelievers to views not previously held. The function involved in the former case is organic, legitimate, genetically and causally natural, and necessary. In the latter case there is an imposed didactic purpose. (p. 44)

This seems a distinction which can usefully be applied to the works discussed in earlier chapters. All these were concerned with propagating a particular point of view, and they did so with not only differing methods, but also with differing degrees of success. In Chapter 2, for example, a distinction was drawn between works such as Wolfgang Joho's *Das Klassentreffen*, in which the artistic purpose was subordinate to the writer's propagandist aim, and works like Hermann Kant's *Die Aula*, in which the moral was contained within the artistic framework. A similar pattern was evident in Chapters 3 and 4. The use of representative figures, as well as the method of contrasting Federal and Democratic Republic in terms of their relationship to the Third Reich, were exploited with the same degree of artistic success or failure. The overt, indeed, occasionally crass, methods of Anna Seghers and Hans-Dieter Linstedt, for example, contrasted with the far more concealed rhetoric of Werner Heiduczek and Günter de Bruyn.

The failure of the less successful works lies, I feel, in their *unnecessary* reliance on a conspicuous moral. As Peacock suggests, 'propaganda' aims to convert unbelievers to views not previously held, and its expected audience should therefore be a non-socialist one. Such an audience certainly existed in the GDR of the 'Aufbau' years, but as already suggested, it did not do so after the mid- or even early-sixties. A number of books written after that date do take into account the changed nature of this audience, but many do not, and it is these works, in which the overtly didactic method is superfluous, that fully merit the designation of 'propaganda'.

Peacock's distinction is relevant to all East German works, of course, and not only those concerning the division of Germany. The 'imposed didactic purpose' of many novels stands in clear contrast to the innate rhetoric of those in which the writer is relying on a belief he shares with his reader.

In the preceding chapters of this volume there have been only occasional references to West German works concerned with the divided nation. I should now like to consider briefly the approach of Western writers to the division of Germany, and to draw some comparisons and contrasts between works written in West and East. This should bring out the differing perspective which East German writers have tended to adopt.

There are, I would submit, three important reasons why fiction of the Federal Republic treating this subject should differ from that written in the GDR. First, writers have not been regularly encouraged by politicians to write on the problems of division, and, furthermore, to present them in a particular way. (Although there have, of course, been numerous appeals by literary critics that writers devote their energies to this subject.[3]) Second, authors writing in the West have no cause to fear overt censorship, particularly as far as their presentation of the East is concerned – which is not the case with their GDR counterparts. And third, one can assume a different ideological outlook from writers living in the Federal Republic, a country in which the Communist Party was illegal for most of the fifties and sixties. Socialist writers such as Wolf Biermann and Peter Hacks, whose politics conflicted with those of the Western regime, tended to leave the Federal Republic for the GDR.

Works on the divided Germany which have been published in the Federal Republic are as diverse in content as they are in

---

[3] See, for example, the works by West German critics quoted at the beginning of Chapter One, as well as Hans Werner Richter's collection of open letters and appeals by both writers and critics, *Die Mauer oder der 13. August.*

style. They range from Peter Handke's 'Horrorgeschichte', in which two students from West Berlin cross into the Eastern half of the city ('Das Umfallen der Kegel von einer bäuerlichen Kegelbahn'), to the crass anti-Communist propaganda of the anonymous *Dreimal durch den Zaun*.[4] In certain novels the depiction of division is almost coincidental – in Ursula Trauberg's *Vorleben*, for example, which is concerned with the emotional development of a murderess. Those sections which take place in the East are mainly non-political, and the author seems to have no interest in inter-German problems, even though both parts of the nation are depicted within her work. (For this reason such volumes have been excluded from the following list.) Other novels, on the other hand, reveal their author's passionate concern with the political aspects of division – Dieter Meichsner's *Die Studenten von Berlin*, for example – while yet others deal with the political situation in the GDR alone, using the Federal Republic as an implicit or explicit positive contrast: Zwerenz's *Die Liebe der toten Männer* and *Aufs Rad geflochten*, as well as works by Wolfgang Leonhard and Fritz Schenk.

These works can be divided into two categories. First, those by writers who have lived in the West since shortly after the war, which include :

Stefan Andres, *Die Dumme*; Joachim Burkhardt, *Zum Beispiel im Juni*; Daniel Christoff, *Schaukelstühle*; Gerd Gaiser, *Am Paß Nascondo*; Peter Handke, 'Das Umfallen der Kegel von einer bäuerlichen Kegelbahn'; Horst Mönnich, *Einreisegenehmigung*; Margarete Norweg, 'Zonengrenze'; Wolfgang Paul, *Einladung ins andere Deutschland*; Herbert Plate, *Das soll der Mensch nicht scheiden*; Theodor Plievier, *Berlin*; Helmut Putz, *Die Abenteuer des braven Kommunisten Schwejk*; Arno Schmidt, *Das steinerne Herz*; Wolfdietrich Schnurre, 'Der Zwiespalt', I & II, *Das Los unserer Stadt*; Johannes Mario Simmel, *Lieb Vaterland magst ruhig sein*.

And second, those by refugees from the East. These are

---

[4] The facile nature of this story, which was published by the 'Bundesministerium für gesamtdeutsche Fragen', has been ridiculed by Peter Milger in 'Wildwest an der Zonengrenze'.

usually based on personal experiences and use a first-person or diary form:

Jürgen Beckelmann, *Lachender Abschied*; Heinz Brandt, *Ein Traum, der nicht entführbar ist. Mein Weg zwischen Ost und West*; Ute Erb, *Die Kette an deinem Hals*; Martin Gregor-Dellin, *Der Kandelaber*; Uwe Johnson, *Mutmaßungen über Jakob, Das dritte Buch über Achim, Karsch, und andere Prosa, Zwei Ansichten*, 'Eine Kneipe geht verloren'; Walter Kempowski, *Uns geht's ja noch gold*; Hans-Christian Kirsch, *Die zweite Flucht, Deutschlandlied*; Eckart Kroneberg, *Der Grenzgänger*; Wolfgang Leonhard, *Die Revolution entläßt ihre Kinder*; Dieter Meichsner, *Die Studenten von Berlin*; Eva Müthel, *Für dich blüht kein Baum*; Fritz Schenk, *Im Vorzimmer der Diktatur*; Ursula Sigismund, *Grenzgänger*; Catrin Sonntag, *Mein letztes Jahr*; Gerhard Zwerenz, *Die Liebe der toten Männer, Aufs Rad geflochten, Ärgernisse. Von der Maas bis an die Memel*.

Generalisation on these works is difficult, since there are fewer clear patterns than in East German writing. Four main points are that (1) refugees from the East are more likely to treat this subject than are West Germans proper (2) the theme is more commonly a peripheral than a central one (3) the hero is often an intellectual (a choice which facilitates criticism of Party machinery from the inside) (4) except in the fiction of Uwe Johnson, the perspective of works published in the Federal Republic tends to be hostile to the GDR. Surprisingly, however, many refugees are also hostile to the Federal Republic. As Gerhard Zwerenz has put it: 'Wir Ost-West-Flüchtlinge sind gewohnt und angehalten, beide Welten zu kritisieren'.[5] This is clearly the case among intellectuals, for whom the capitalism and materialism of the West often represents a disappointment. In contrast to those who have left the East because of hatred of Communism, these writers are idealists who have left because they feel the ideals of Communism have been abused there; but they discover that sentiments of this sort are regarded askance in the Federal Republic. And it is perhaps significant that those few writers who know both East and West equally well should find serious faults with both parts of the German nation.

[5] *Ärgernisse*, p. 25.

There is only one major respect in which works published in the East resemble those of the West, and that is in their presentation of the other country in terms of the Third Reich. For the East, the Federal Republic is continuing the imperialist policies of Hitler's Germany and using ex-Nazis to do it; for the West, on the other hand, the Democratic Republic is continuing the terrorist repressive activities normally associated with the police state of the preceding epoch.

Considering the large number of books published in the Federal Republic (particularly in comparison with the Democratic Republic), it is surprising that relatively so few should deal with the problems of the divided nation. For although many authors have made occasional allusions to the East in their work,[6] it is (to my knowledge) only in those works listed above that division occupies a position of any prominence.

Since 1970 there has been a marked fall in the number of East German works to treat divided Germany. I have, in fact, been able to trace only two novels in which it is a central issue: Renate Feyl's *Das dritte Auge war aus Glas*, and Hans von Oettingen's *Das Skalpell*. Nevertheless, it has shown far less of a decline as a peripheral motif, and Hermann Kant's shift of emphasis between *Die Aula* (1965) and *Das Impressum* (1972)

[6] Taking random examples from the four major novelists now writing in German, one finds Böll's Hans Schnier (*Ansichten eines Clowns*) recalling an unsuccessful visit to Erfurt, and a humorous attack on the Federal Republic's non-recognition of the East in *Ende einer Dienstfahrt*. Frisch alludes equally scantily. *Mein Name sei Gantenbein* contains two references to the issue of 'reunification', and when in *Homo Faber* the character of the Communist Piper is introduced, it is almost coincidental that he now lives in East Germany. Despite his play on 17 June 1953 (*Die Plebejer proben den Aufstand*), Grass's interest in the two Germanies is very restricted in his novels. There are several allusions to the East in *Hundejahre* (especially in the 101st of the 'Materniaden'), but there is only one in *Die Blechtrommel*. *örtlich betäubt* may be set in West Berlin, but it is concerned with a non-German issue: the war in Vietnam. Finally, in Walser's *Halbzeit* one of the hero's friends lives in East Germany, but the issue of the two states is never developed; nor is it in *Das Einhorn*, where again there are only occasional, unsystematic references to the fact that Germany is divided.

is symptomatic of a general trend. In the earlier work the issue of division is a key one, but in the more recent one it has been relegated to a subsidiary role.

The chief and obvious reason for this movement is most probably that other issues have gained in importance – the emergence of a new society in the GDR, for example, with the wide range of themes that this has brought with it. By 1970 the question of division was by no means as urgent as it had once been, and the existence of two separate sovereign German states is presented without question in most Eastern novels written after this date. In these the West is often a sinister background, but it is rarely featured in any depth. By this stage of the GDR's development a wide-ranging presentation of the West is hardly necessary, however. Thanks to the work of both politicians and authors, the occasional allusion will suffice to suggest a comprehensive 'mental set' which has been steadily consolidated in the reader's mind since even before the foundation of the two German Republics.

APPENDIX

Since East German literature cannot be fully appreciated without some acquaintance with the major forces which affect both writers and readers in the GDR, the following outline attempts to trace those social and ideological factors which have influenced the fictional presentation, as well as the reception, of the theme 'divided Germany'. It is important that the approach of the foreign reader be informed by the conditions under which this literature has been produced, for these differ so radically from those in the non-socialist countries that even a high degree of empathy cannot compensate for their ignorance. As David Daiches has pointed out, one of the main values of sociologically informed criticism is that it can

help us to avoid making mistakes about the nature of the work of literature which we have before us, by throwing light on its function or on the conventions with reference to which certain aspects of it are to be understood.[1]

Without some awareness of the 'conventions' upon which East German fiction is based, as well as its 'function' in a socialist state, the foreign reader's understanding of this literature will be at best imperfect.[2]

[1] *Critical Approaches to Literature*, p. 364.

[2] The following concentrates upon influences which are likely to play a significant role in determining the attitudes of both writers and readers. For the general structure of East German society, and for details of other forms of pressure, see in particular: David Childs, *East Germany*; Ernst Richert, *Das zweite Deutschland*; Hermann Rudolph, *Die Gesellschaft der DDR – eine deutsche Möglichkeit?*; Jean Edward Smith, *Germany beyond the Wall. People, Politics and Prosperity*; Kurt Sontheimer and Wilhelm Bleek, *Die DDR. Politik, Gesellschaft, Wirtschaft*; Rüdiger Thomas, *Modell DDR. Die kalkulierte Emanzipation*.

In all advanced societies the system of mass media can have a significant effect on both the cultural demands of the populace as well as on the attitude of writers towards social and political problems. This is particularly true of Communist societies, in which mass media are part of a larger propaganda system, are centrally controlled, and have the specific aim of influencing judgment.

The purpose of mass media in the GDR may be interpreted as the following:
(1) to spread the ideals of Marxism-Leninism
(2) to assist the development of the individual to full socialist maturity
(3) to support the leadership of the GDR
(4) to combat all fascist, capitalist and bourgeois tendencies.[3]

Clearly, a political criterion is applied to all means of communication, and the controllers of this system are consequently subject to a number of restrictions in their presentation of material. Reproach for failure to conform, as well as acts of censorship, are usually unnecessary, however, and this for two reasons. First, all those concerned with the media receive basic training in political commentary at various institutes;[4] and second, perhaps more important, candidates for such influential positions are usually selected only if they have shown themselves to be politically reliable. Mass media consequently display a policy of full support for the Party's decisions, and in the case of material on the divided nation, they inevitably reflect the opinions which have been determined by the former.

[3] Abstracted from Hermann Meyn, *Massenmedien in der Bundesrepublik Deutschland*, p. 101. Much of the section devoted to the GDR is drawn from E. M. Herrmann, *Zur Theorie und Praxis der Presse in der Sowjetischen Besatzungszone Deutschlands*. The other works on the press, *Die Presse in der Sowjetzone* ('Bonner Fachbericht') and Hans Schimanski's *Leitgedanken und Methoden der kommunistischen Indoktrination*, are also highly derivative.

[4] Journalists and radio and TV editors receive their training at the 'Fakultät für Journalistik der Karl-Marx-Universität, Leipzig' (Miss Herrmann devotes a considerable section of her book to the work of this large faculty). Writers are given assistance in the 'Arbeitsgemeinschaften junger Autoren' (organ-

The press, for example, is a particularly carefully controlled source of support for the Party. Supervised by the 'Abteilung für Agitation und Propaganda beim ZK der SED' and the 'Presseamt beim Vorsitzenden des Ministerrats', journalists are obliged to plan their editions well in advance. In contrast to Western newspapers, comparatively little space is devoted to recent 'news'; much consists of themes which have been prepared some time previously, and many of these used to be directed against some aspect of the West. Speaking of the monthly module on which journalists used to operate, Meyn quoted the following as typical examples of anti-Western topics:

Themen für einen Monatsplan sind zum Beispiel 'Flüchtlingsstrom aus der BRD in die DDR', das Passierscheinabkommen oder auch ein Bundeswehrgeneral. Wenn beispielsweise der General 'Thema des Monats' ist, dann darf kein Tag vergehen, an dem nicht irgendein Bericht über eine Episode aus dem Leben des 'Nazi-Generals' erscheint. (p. 104)

To assist journalists in their arguments, handouts are circularised on Party policy and its justification ('Argumentationsanweisungen')[5]. Even the actual 'news' is regulated – apart from their reporting local events, newspapers are obliged to rely on the central agency ('Allgemeiner Deutscher Nachrichtendienst') for their information. This too is under the supervision of the 'Vorsitzender des Ministerrats' and is organised by fully reliable Party supporters. The need for actual censorship is therefore rare. As early as 1963 Miss Herrmann could disparagingly state that 'Die Presse der SBZ unterliegt heute der perfektionierten Lenkung und Kontrolle durch die SED'.[6]

One explanation of the fact that the Republic has not been obliged to exercise its repressive powers to any great degree is most probably that censorship nowadays is more a subconscious, personal factor rather than institutionalised repres-

ised by the 'Deutscher Schriftstellerverband') and full professional training at the 'J. R. Becher Institut' in Leipzig.

[5] Herrmann, op. cit., p. 62.
[6] Ibid., p. 65.

sion of unwelcome ideas. Journalists, not wishing to have their work openly rejected and their careers threatened, presumably tend to avoid contentious statements.

TV and radio are also responsible to the SED. Like journalists, producers and editors are encouraged to follow an orthodox policy. They are advised in their selection by the 'Staatlicher Rundfunkkomitee' and their aim is to present as much material as possible that is propagandist.[7] The term 'Propaganda' does not incidentally, have the negative connotations of its English (or, for that matter, the West German) equivalent. 'Propaganda' is basically the spreading of the ideology of Marxism-Leninism, and it has consequently a highly positive function.[8] There exists a widespread West European conviction that the citizens of the Communist bloc are unaware of the aims and methods of such propaganda, but this is far from the truth. Mass media are openly acknowledged to have an essentially educative function, and their efficacy is widely discussed in such national journals as *Einheit, Funk und Fernsehen der DDR*, and *Neue Deutsche Presse*. Their success is even mentioned in the bestselling non-fictional work of the Republic, the *Geschichte der deutschen Arbeiterbewegung*:

In der kurzen Zeit seines Bestehens wuchs der deutsche Fernsehfunk zu einem Intrument der ideologisch-kulturellen Erziehung mit einem großen Wirkungsbereich und bedeutendem Einfluß auf die Bewußtseins-bildung der Massen heran. (Vol. 3, p. 235)

Mass media have been an extremely successful means of propagating socialist ideals (a point on which both East *and* West agree!),[9] but they are not the only method adopted by the SED. The most traditional means of communication, that of personal contact, is still regarded as an indispensable aid to

---

[7] For further details, see the first chapter of Jörg Lingenberg's *Das Fernsehspiel in der DDR*.

[8] This frequently overlooked fact is stressed by Fritz Raddatz in 'DDR-Literatur und marxistische Ästhetik', p. 41.

[9] Though for different reasons – the West to prove the danger of mass media propaganda, the East to prove its humanist function. For a West German view of Eastern success, see Richert, *Das zweite Deutschland*, Chapter 8.

constructing the goal of the complete socialist society. Thus Marxism-Leninism is taught as a basic subject in all schools, and courses and discussion of socialist development in the GDR are also compulsory for all students in higher education, irrespective of the Faculty to which they belong. School textbooks are written from an overtly Communist point of view,[10] and teaching is always geared to ideological requirements, journals for teachers offering examples of how material can be best presented from the Communist standpoint. In the case of literature, for example, *Deutschunterricht*[11] offers interpretations and suggested classroom presentations of both modern and classical works, demonstrating in each case how they can contribute to the development of the socialist personality. A typical example is that by Heinz Sallmon, Liesel Rumland, and Wilfried Bütow, 'Grundpositionen des Literaturunterrichts bei der Verwirklichung der Forderungen des neuen Lehrplans und der Aufgabenstellung für die staatsbürgerliche Erziehung', which demonstrates the manner in which a teacher can most profitably utilise fiction and drama in order to inspire his pupils to strive for socialist ideals. The authors' opening premiss is the following:

Wenn die ideologische Bildung und Erziehung als zentrale Aufgabe bei der Herausbildung sozialistischer Persönlichkeiten Ergebnis der Gesamtheit des Unterrichts ist, so ergibt sich daraus die Forderung, sowohl Ziele und Inhalt als auch Methoden, Mittel und Organisationsformen des Literaturunterrichts unter dem Aspekt der ideologischen Bildung und Erziehung zu planen und zu realisieren.

Even literature which is written specifically for children includes a clear political bias. As has been illustrated by Lothar

---

[10] Cf. P. R. Lücke, *Das Schulbuch in der Sowjetzone. Lehrbücher im Dienst totalitärer Propaganda*. As the title suggests, this book is based on anti-communist premisses; Lücke's examples are nonetheless instructive. The most informative and reliable study of East German education is that by Arthur Hearnden, *Bildungspolitik in der BRD und der DDR*; a slightly modified and abridged version has appeared in English translation, *Education in the Two Germanies*.

[11] Published bi-monthly in Frankfurt an der Oder. Not to be confused with the West German *Der Deutschunterricht*, published in Stuttgart.

von Balluseck in 'Die guten und die bösen Deutschen', stories for children and adolescents (as well as 'Unterhaltungs- und Trivialliteratur') are often aimed at producing a hatred of capitalism and imperialism, while at the same time consolidating the Eastern reader's love of his own country. The major enemy is invariably the Federal Republic.

Literature has long been recognised by Communists as a key ideological weapon, as dangerous as it can be useful. In Soviet Russia, for example, dissentient writers have been persecuted and even killed, precisely because Communists believe literature is a vital force in the class struggle. To our knowledge, East German writers have never been killed for their beliefs, but several have certainly been persecuted for them: among others, Wolf Biermann, Peter Huchel, Erich Loest, and Gerhard Zwerenz. In addition, a good number have had difficulties of one sort or another in finding a publisher in their own country.[12] Manfred Bieler, who was also put under pressure at several stages of his career in the GDR, has suggested it is not only writers who run risks, but also the cultural politicians who allow their works to reach the general public. Referring to the peculiarly high position accorded to the writer in a socialist society, he commented:

Er wird auf einer Sänfte vor dieser Gesellschaft hergetragen. Seiner Eitelkeit, seinem Selbstbewußtsein wird an einer höchst empfindlichen

---

[12] For some general remarks on the questions of censorship and publishing problems in the GDR, see H. P. Anderle, 'DDR. Der Zensurapparat im Kopf'. Although there has been a process of liberalisation in the East (particularly since the election of Erich Honecker as successor to Walter Ulbricht in 1971), nonconformist writers still face certain difficulties. Authors whose works deviate radically from the Party line are now not rejected outright, but they are rather encouraged to change those works in accordance with the suggestions of the official censors. If a writer refuses to make such alterations, then it is likely his work will either be rejected by the publishers to whom he submits, or that it will be published in a limited edition only. There remains, of course, the possibility of publication in the Federal Republic, but authors publish there only with considerable reluctance. This procedure has, however, proved the only feasible method for Wolf Biermann and also for certain works by Stefan Heym.

Stelle geschmeichelt, denn er hat eine ungleich größere Wirkung als im Westen. So ist über den Film, der nach meinem Roman 'Das Kaninchen bin ich' 1965 in der DDR gedreht wurde, ein Minister gestürzt.[13]

But literature is not only regarded as an adverse force. When directed properly it can be of great value in the class struggle, and its important role in helping to strengthen the GDR has been emphasised not only by literary critics, but also by the political leadership. Many of the foremost politicians (i.e. those of the 'Politbüro') have expressed a high estimation of the Arts in the new society.

Pieck stressed the importance of art as early as 1946, Ulbricht in 1948,[14] and in 1951 Grotewohl paraphrased Lenin in a frequently quoted speech of 31 August: '*Literatur und bildende Künste sind der Politik untergeordnet*, aber es ist klar, daß sie einen starken Einfluß auf die Politik ausüben'.[15] Kurt Hager, the leading cultural theorist, suggests much the same some fourteen years later, illustrating the consistency of East German thought on the function of literature:

Aber es ist klar, daß diese große Aufgabe einer modernen wissenschaftlich-technischen Gestaltung der Industrie und Landwirtschaft umfassend gebildete Menschen voraussetzt und daß bei der Bildung dieser Menschen Literatur und Kunst eine bedeutende Rolle zu spielen haben. Deshalb ist im Programm der SED der umfassende Aufbau des Sozialismus nicht nur als ein ökonomischer und wissenschaftlich-technischer Prozeß, sondern zugleich auch als ein tiefgreifender ideologisch-kultureller Prozeß dargestellt. Es handelt sich tatsächlich um zwei Seiten einer einheitlichen großen gesellschaftlichen Entwicklung.[16]

It is therefore not surprising to find that the views of the

---

13 *Die Welt der Literatur*, 16 January 1969, p. 10; quoted by Raddatz, *Traditionen und Tendenzen*, p. 395.

14 Speeches by both Pieck and Ulbricht are quoted by H. J. Geerdts in 'Gedanken zur Diskussion über die sozialistische Nationalkultur nach 1945'. Ulbricht's reveal marked evidence of Zhdanov's Moscow speeches of the preceding year.

15 First printed in *Neues Deutschland*, 2 September 1951; reprinted in Schubbe, *Dokumente zur Kunst-, Literatur- und Kulturpolitik der SED*, p. 209. [Italics in original.]

16 'Freude an jedem gelungenen Werk', p. 65.

writers themselves on the nature of their art are geared to the process of social change. The first paragraph of the manifesto ('Erklärung') of GDR writers at their first Writers' Conference ran as follows:

Die Literatur gehört unablöslich zum Wesen unserer sozialistischen Gesellschaft. Sie ist Teil des Entwicklungsprozesses, in dem sich das Volk auf die Höhe des historischen Bewußtseins erhebt. Aus dem Leben entspringend, wirkt die Literatur auf das Leben zurück, auf das Denken, Fühlen und Handeln der Menschen; sie verändert und befähigt zum Verändern. Von diesen Gedanken überzeugt, stärken wir Schriftsteller mit unserer literarischen Arbeit die Deutsche Demokratische Republik.[17]

Individual comments on the nature and function of art do not differ substantially from this basic premiss. Authors regularly express similar views on literature and its aims in the official organ of the Writers' Union, *Neue Deutsche Literatur*.

The fact that it was Ulbricht himself – and not the Minister for Culture – who launched the 'Bitterfelder Bewegung',[18] arguably the most important event in East German literary history, is a further indication of how highly literature is valued in the GDR. Moreover, culture is intended not only for an intellectual élite, as is, so it is often claimed, that of the Federal Republic, but is a major factor in the education of the nation as a whole. The Minister for Culture has far more power and responsibility than any comparable West European Minister, and the GDR is one of the few states to include a cultural policy in its constitution.[19]

Since such a leading role is allotted to artists in Communist ideology, it is appropriate that they should be encouraged to fully utilise their creative ability for ideological ends. This encouragement mainly takes the form of conferences and the pronouncements in the official organ *NDL*, where aims and

---

[17] *Neues Deutschland*, 5 November 1966; quoted from *SBZ-Archiv* 17 (1966), p. 352.

[18] For general details of Ulbricht's speeches and of the 'Bitterfelder Weg' in general, see the appropriate entries in Konrad Franke's *Die Literatur der Deutschen Demokratischen Republik*.

[19] Artikel 18.

methods are fully discussed from a socialist point of view. *NDL* is also a major outlet for literary criticism, which is another planned stimulus for writers. Reviewers, like writers themselves, are left in no doubt about their duty to the Party, and it is their function to criticise writing which deviates too widely from the Party line. For the Communist, value can only be accredited to those works which express positively the ideals of Communism or which assist the development to the Communist utopia; partisanship ('Parteilichkeit') is in fact raised to an aesthetic category to which stylistic criteria are seen to be of secondary importance. Thus, for example, we find Kurt Hager expressing a basic tenet of Marxist literary aesthetics as (in a paraphrase of Lenin) he emphasises the paramountcy of content over form:

Wir stehen auf dem Standpunkt, und ich glaube, der Standpunkt ist richtig, gerade auch für das literarische Schaffen, daß man ohne ideologische Klarheit, ohne konsequente sozialistische Parteilichkeit, keine Position beziehen und kein wirkliches Kunstwerk schaffen kann.[20]

Even literary criticism fulfills a political function in a Communist state. To quote a typical statement:

Die Literaturkritik ist Bestandteil des gesamtgesellschaftlichen Prozesses zur Entwicklung des vollendeten sozialistischen Gesellschaftsystems... Die Aufgabe der Literaturkritik besteht im Sozialismus vor allem darin...daß sie teilnimmt an der Entwicklung sozialistischer Persönlichkeiten.[21]

Like literature, criticism is essentially a tool, 'ein Werkzeug zur Veränderung der Welt'.[22] It has as its purpose the perfection of the socialist state, and it achieves this in two principal ways. First, in its constructive criticism to the writer and in suggestion of the subjects worthy of contemporary treatment (including, as indicated in Chapter 1, divided Germany); and

[20] 'Freude an jedem gelungenen Werk', p. 67.
[21] *Neue Deutsche Presse* 1969, no. 4; quoted in *Blick nach drüben*, 6 May 1969, p. 19.
[22] H. G. Thalheim and D. Schiller, 'Diskussion zu aktuellen Aufgaben der Literaturwissenschaft', p. 9.

second, in assisting the reader to choose works of art which have the highest aesthetic value. As was suggested above, ideological conformity is one of the most important Marxist aesthetic criteria; readers will therefore only be recommended those works which faithfully reflect the Party line.

Ideological and social forces upon writers and readers in the GDR have resulted in the presentation of a single, uniform image of the German nation as a whole, and particularly of the Federal Republic. This image of the West which is presented in Eastern non-literary media is worthy of elaboration in some depth, since it is basic to an understanding of the suggestive elements of East German prose. Much of the work analysed in the central chapters of this book rests upon suggestion for its effect, and since the success of this literary device relies almost entirely upon the reader's acquaintance with the weaknesses under attack (an acquaintance the East German writer can presuppose in his – East German – reader), it is important to ensure that foreign readers are also aware of these writers' presuppositions.

There are relatively few studies of anti-Western propaganda in the GDR. One of the most helpful is that by Horst Siebert, who centres his attention on the image of the West presented in the East German schoolbook. But owing to the fact that all parts of the GDR propaganda system substantiate one another, Siebert's findings are relevant to the image presented by mass media as a whole.

In his conclusion, Siebert summarises the criticism of the 'other' German state which is to be found in the schoolbooks of both East and West. This provides a broad, but not exhaustive, survey:

1. Das andere System ist asozial und inhuman, die Bevölkerung wird vom Staat ausgebeutet. . .
2. Die jeweils andere Regierung hat die deutsche Teilung verschuldet, das Potsdamer Abkommen gebrochen und verhindert die Wiedervereinigung. Die Konsolidierung des eigenen Separatstaates (Gründung,

Aufrüstung, Bündnispolitik) wird als Reaktion auf Maßnahmen der anderen Seite interpretiert. Die andere Regierung wird beschuldigt, die eigenen Wiedervereinigungsvorschläge nicht zur Kenntnis zu nehmen und ein Gesamtdeutschland nur durch gewaltsame Unterjochung des anderen Teils anzustreben.

3. Der andere Staat ist lediglich Ausführungsorgan einer der beiden Großmächte. Die Regierung erfüllt Handlangerdienste der USA bzw. UdSSR und dient als militärischer Stützpunkt und Prellbock.

4. Das andere System ist zum Scheitern verurteilt, die Mängel sind systembedingt und keine Übergangserscheinungen. Die Frage, ob es 'drüben besser' werden wird, wird verneint. Die eigene Ordnung gilt als prinzipiell überlegen.

5. Im jeweils anderen Teil besteht eine unüberbrückbare Kluft zwischen Bevölkerung und Regierung. Dem Volk werden Mitgefühl und Solidarität entgegengebracht, der Staat wird im Interesse der unterdrückten Bevölkerung bekämpft und abgelehnt. Demgegenüber wird eine weitgehende Interessenidentität zwischen dem eigenen Staat und der Gesellschaft vorausgesetzt.

6. Der andere Teil Deutschlands wird nach seiner Verfassungswirklichkeit, der eigene nach der idealen Norm beurteilt. Trotz gelegentlicher Einschränkungen (in den westdeutschen Schulbüchern) wird für das eigene Land eine grundsätzliche Kongruenz von Verfassungsrecht und -wirklichkeit suggeriert.

7. Jedes Schulbuch nimmt für seinen Teilstaat die Sympathie und Unterstützung des Auslands, vor allem der blockfreien Staaten in Anspruch, der andere Teil wird als außenpolitisch isoliert betrachtet. Als Beweis wird von beiden Seiten die Hallstein-Doktrin angeführt.

8. Die Möglichkeiten einer Wiedervereinigung werden allein von der Bereitschaft der anderen politischen Führung abhängig gemacht. Die eigenen Machthaber haben alles Erdenkliche zur Annäherung der beiden Teilstaaten getan. In der DDR wird dabei nachdrücklicher festgestellt, daß ein Gesamtdeutschland nur unter sozialistischen Vorzeichen möglich ist.

9. Stärkste Beachtung finden die Wirtschaftsverhältnisse des anderen Teils, während die Kultur und das Bildungswesen (von relativ seltenen Hinweisen auf den westdeutschen Bildungsnotstand abgesehen) kaum behandelt werden.

10. Jeder Teilstaat nimmt für sich allein die Verwirklichung von Freiheit, Demokratie und sozialer Gerechtigkeit in Anspruch.

The image of the West presented in schoolbooks is less forceful than that of other media, in which a number of other features are evident. First, the consistent *association of the Federal Republic with the Third Reich*. West German policy is seen to be a continuation of Hitler's, and the men in charge of government and the civil service are seen as ex-Nazis. Further, the 'fascist' mentality appears to be promulgated in as many ways as possible.

Neo-Nazi policies are supported by the leaders of a *monopoly capitalism*, and just as former Nazis are seen to be in control in the political arena, so too are former industrialists in control of industry. As is repeatedly pointed out, many of these were responsible for the production of inhuman weapons of war (produced, moreover, under conditions of forced labour), and they should therefore be treated as war criminals. On the contrary, they are congratulated and assisted by politicians in their exploitation of the working class and in their amassing huge personal fortunes. They long for war in order to be able to expand even further, and they exercise considerable control over major governmental policy decisions, particularly those concerning the East. Indeed, Uwe Johnson has neatly summed up the Eastern view of these ogres by referring to them as 'kriegslüsterne Barone der Ruhrindustrie',[23] and the opening pages of Anna Seghers' *Die Entscheidung* provide an illustration of practically every one of the above points. The speaker is the propagandist Richard Hagen, and the firm contrast he makes at the end is typical of propaganda as a whole – the East always provides a positive alternative to the West:

'Der alte Besitzer dieser Fabrik sitzt jetzt im Westen in sicherer Obhut. Er hat Millionen am Krieg verdient, der unser eigenes Land und halb Europa verwüstet hat und Millionen Menschen ermordet. Man kann sagen, er hat Millionen an jeder Million Toter verdient. Jetzt ist er auf neue Kriege aus, auf neue Bombengeschäfte. Dafür läuft im Westen wieder seine Fabrik. Dafür arbeiten sie dort. – Wofür läuft hier unsere Fabrik? Wofür arbeiten wir hier?' (p. 12)

An important section of monopoly capitalism is the *monopoly press*. Apart from a few independent papers, which are fighting

[23] 'Eine Reise wegwohin, 1960', p. 50.

a losing battle, the West German press is controlled by the exploiting class. It wholeheartedly supports governmental policy and seeks to discredit the GDR at every available opportunity.

The *militarism* of the Federal Republic is also frequently criticised, for as a member of NATO West Germany is assumed to be the most likely aggressor in the event of attack. The wall erected in Berlin is interpreted as a protective measure against this force and the persistent infiltration which it organises through West Berlin. The 'antifaschistischer Schutzwall' (to give the official term) is therefore principally designed to keep people out rather than to keep them in!

West German soldiers are seen to be thoroughly indoctrinated against the East, and the massive armament policy (described by Hermann Kant as 'sinn- und augenfälligster Bestandteil der westdeutschen Entwicklung'[24]), which has as its goal the acquisition of nuclear weapons, is undertaken not only so that West Germany can dominate Europe, but also in order to win back land that is no longer 'German'.

This policy of *Revanchism* used to be another frequently criticised feature of West German politics. 'Revanchismus' is the East German term for the (now defunct) policy of the Federal Republic towards formerly German territory which currently lies to the East of the Oder–Neiße boundary with Poland. The GDR used to emphasise that the West was determined to regain this land at all costs, even to the extent of using military force. Those who were expelled from these territories in 1945 were, it was claimed, openly encouraged to believe that they would soon be able to return to their homeland: East Germany and East Prussia would be annexed once again. The ceremonies held by these expellees have been repeatedly attacked in the mass media (as well as in Eastern literature) and are referred to as 'Revanchistentreffen'. (The West, of course, refers to them as 'Heimattreffen', and to the expellees themselves as 'Heimatvertriebene'.)

[24] 'Macht und Ohnmacht einer Literatur', p. 69.

Justice is seen to be arbitrary, judges being mainly former Nazis who are interested in protecting the *status quo* and who are supported by a brutal police and counter-espionage service. Opposition to the state is dealt with harshly, but relatives of those in high positions or with contacts in government or industry have little to fear if they are caught indulging in criminal acts which are non-political.

The West German *way of life* is dominated by the most repulsive aspects of the USA. These are referred to as both the 'amerikanische Lebensweise' and the 'american way of life' [sic], and they include such decadent symptoms as 'Ansteigen der Kriminalität, des Rowdytums, der sexuellen Entartung'; 'Überhandnehmen der Gangsterliteratur, der Horrorfilme'; 'Mißachtung der Menschenwürde und die Bereitschaft zu Mord und Brutalität'.[25] A further symptom is the striving for material wealth and power, especially among the upper classes. (Predictably, such activity never leads to true happiness.)

Other elements of the image of the West include: the pernicious influence of the Church in political and social matters; gambling; drunkenness; political disinterest; hatred and fear of Communism; the rigid class structure.

The East German image of the West is to be found at all levels of broadcasting and publishing, ranging from the official organ of the SED, *Neues Deutschland*, to the satirical magazine *Eulenspiegel*, which frequently pokes fun at its own government's policy. It has shown little development between the early years of the Republic and 1970 (changes have normally consisted in additions rather than modifications), and it has encouraged writers to adopt a fixed attitude towards the West. Many of these have, in turn, incorporated this image in their work, thus compounding the view of the other Germany as an aggressive, immoral, fascist and capitalist state, which stands in total contrast to the aims and achievements of its Eastern neighbours.

[25] Taken from the entry 'Amerikanische Lebensweise' in *Meyers Neues Lexikon*; quoted by Lingenberg, *Das Fernsehspiel in der DDR*, p. 167.

BIBLIOGRAPHY

The following bibliography is divided into two main parts, of which only Section I(a) is intended to be exhaustive. This lists all East German fiction that I have been able to trace in which the theme of 'divided Germany' is a central one; it also includes works in which the subject plays a minor role and which are mentioned in the course of this volume. Section I(b) contains a selection of novels on this theme by writers now living in the Federal Republic.

The list of secondary literature is not intended to be comprehensive. Section II(a) includes only those volumes and articles which are mentioned in the course of my argument together with a selection of other material which was of particular value in studying broader developments in East German literature or the work of individual writers. For bibliographical details of works on GDR literature in general, the reader is advised to consult the bibliographies of John Flores, Bernhard Greiner, and Hans Jürgen Geerdts. Section II(b) contains publication details of other works which have been mentioned, but which are not of direct relevance to the treatment of 'divided Germany'.

Wherever possible, quotations given above have always been from the first edition of the work in question. Owing to manifold difficulties in obtaining such editions of East German novels, it has unfortunately on occasion been necessary to quote from editions other than the first. Indication is given of where this has proved necessary.

Unless otherwise stated, all references to Berlin are to the East German section of that city.

The division is as follows:

PRIMARY LITERATURE

I(a) *East German fiction*

Beuchler, Klaus, *Aufenthalt vor Bornholm*, Rostock, 1969
Bieler, Manfred, *Bonifaz oder Der Matrose in der Flasche*, Berlin und Weimar, 1963
Borchert, Christa, 'Bedrohung der Stadt Bor', *Bedrohung der Stadt Bor*, Berlin, 1967, pp. 135–210.
Bradatsch, Gertrud, 'Die Schwestern', *Begegnung. Anthologie neuer Frzähler*, edited by Joachim Schmidt, Rostock, 1969, pp. 255–86

Brězan, Jurij, *Eine Liebesgeschichte*, Berlin, 1963. Quotation from the edition by Verlag der Nation, Berlin, 1969.

Bruyn, Günter de, 'Renata', *NDL*, 8, No. 7 (July 1960), 73–102

Der Hohlweg, Halle, 1963

Buridans Esel, Halle, 1968. Quotation from the West German edition, München, 1971

Claudius, Eduard, 'Mensch auf der Grenze', *Literarische Revue*, 3 (1948), 484–6

Menschen auf unserer Seite, Berlin, 1951

Von der Liebe soll man nicht nur sprechen, Berlin, 1957

Feyl, Renate, *Das dritte Auge war aus Glas. Eine Studentengeschichte*. Rudolstadt, 1971

Fischer, Rudolf, *Martin Hoop IV*, Berlin, 1955

Fries, Fritz Rudolf, *Der Weg nach Oobliadooh*, Frankfurt am Main, 1966

'Der Fernsehkrieg', *Der Fernsehkrieg*, Halle, 1969, pp. 143–58

Fühmann, Franz, *Böhmen am Meer*, Rostock, 1962. Quotation from the collection *König Ödipus. Gesammelte Erzählungen*, Berlin und Weimar, 1966, pp. 356–403

'Zum ersten Mal: Deutschland', *Das Judenauto. Vierzehn Tage aus zwei Jahrzehnten*, Berlin und Weimar, 1962, pp. 174–85

Geerdts, Hans Jürgen, 'Feststellung zur Person', *NDL*, 8, No. 10 (October 1960), 53–4

Gloger, Gotthold, *Philomela Kleespieß trug die Fahne*, Berlin, 1953

Gotsche, Otto, *Tiefe Furchen. Roman des deutschen Dorfes*, Halle, 1949

Greulich, E. R., 'Die Gangster und der Grindige', *Manuela. Erzählungen*, Berlin, 1970, pp. 213–91

Hauptmann, Helmut, *Ivi*, Halle, 1969

Havemann, Robert, *Fragen Antworten Fragen. Aus der Biographie eines deutschen Marxisten*, München, 1970

Heiduczek, Werner, *Abschied von den Engeln*, Berlin, 1968

Held, Wolfgang, *Die Nachtschicht*, Weimar, 1959

Heym, Stefan, *Schatten und Licht. Geschichten aus einem geteilten Lande*, Leipzig, 1960 (includes 'Der Bazillus', 'Mein verrückter Bruder', 'Im Netz', 'Der Präsentkorb')

5 Tage im Juni, München, Gütersloh, Wien, 1974

Huhn, Kurt, 'Und als ich über die Grenze kam', *NDL*, 15, No. 5 (May 1967), 68–102

Hurny, Albert, 'Begegnung 1960', *NDL*, 11, No. 4 (April 1963), 117–41

Jakobs, Karl-Heinz, 'Weimarnovelle', *NDL*, 8, No. 2 (February 1960), 68–81

Beschreibung eines Sommers, Berlin, 1961

Jendryschik, Manfred, 'Tramp', *NDL*, 19, No. 7 (July 1971), 43–6

Joho, Wolfgang, *Es gibt kein Erbarmen*, Berlin und Weimar, 1961

Das Klassentreffen. Geschichte einer Reise, Berlin und Weimar, 1968

Kammer, Katharina, 'Weg ohne Wahl'. *Der Unterschied. Erzählungen*, Halle, 1959, pp. 35–48

Kant, Hermann, *Die Aula*, Berlin, 1965

Das Impressum, Berlin, 1972

BIBLIOGRAPHY

Kraft, Ruth, *Menschen im Gegenwind*, Berlin, 1965
Kraze, Hanne-Heide, *Üb immer Treu und Redlichkeit...*, Berlin, 1965
Kupsch, Joachim, *Gefährlicher Sommer*, Halle, 1955
Laudon, Hasso, *Semesterferien in Berlin*, Halle, 1959
Linstedt, Hans-Dieter, 'Rheinische Geschichte', *NDL*, 14, No. 1 (January 1966), 129–64. Also in '*Wie sie uns sehen.*' *Schriftsteller der DDR über die Bundesrepublik*, edited by K. H. Brokerhoff, pp. 38–95; quotations from this edition
Loest, Erich, *Die Westmark fällt weiter*, Halle, 1952
Lorbeer, Hans, *Die Sieben ist eine gute Zahl*, Halle, 1953
Marchwitza, Hans, *Roheisen*, Berlin, 1955
Meng, Manfred, *Eine Tüte Erdnüsse*, Berlin, 1969
Meyer, Helmut, *Lena in Berlin*, Berlin, 1962
Morgner, Irmtraut, *Ein Haus am Rand der Stadt*, Berlin, 1962
Nachbar, Herbert, *Haus unterm Regen*, Berlin und Weimar, 1965
Neutsch, Erik, *Spur der Steine*, Halle, 1964
Noll, Dieter, *Die Abenteuer des Werner Holt. Roman einer Heimkehr*, Berlin und Weimar, 1964
Oettingen, Hans von, *Rostiger Ruhm*, Berlin, 1967
  Das Skalpell, Berlin, 1971
Panitz, Eberhard, *Flucht*, Berlin, 1956
  In drei Teufels Namen, Berlin, 1958
  'Die Verhaftung', *NDL*, 8, No. 8 (August 1960), 45–88
  'Das Gesicht einer Mutter', *NDL*, 8, No. 12 (December 1960), 3–37
Petersen, Jan, *Der Fall Dr. Wagner*, Berlin, 1954
Pollátschek, Walter, *Herren des Landes*, Berlin, 1951
Reimann, Brigitte, *Die Geschwister*, Berlin, 1963. Quotation from the edition by Verlag Neues Leben, Berlin, 1964
Reinowski, Werner, *Der kleine Kopf*, Halle, 1952
  Vom Weizen fällt die Spreu, Halle, 1952
Richter, Egon, *Zeugnis zu dritt*, Rostock, 1967
Schmoll, Werner, *Mit siebzehn ist man noch kein Held*, Halle, 1963
Schubert, Dieter, *Acht Unzen Träume*, Berlin, 1967
Schuhmacher, Ernst, 'Bundeswehrleutnant 1962', *NDL*, 11, No. 3 (March 1963), 39–59
Schwarz, J. C., *Das gespaltene Herz*, Berlin, 1962
Seghers, Anna, *Die Entscheidung*, Berlin und Weimar, 1959
  Das Vertrauen, Berlin und Weimar, 1968
  'Eine Begegnung', '*Manuskripte.*' *Almanach neuer Prosa und Lyrik*, edited by J. Ret, A. Roscher, H. Sachs, Halle, 1969, pp. 309–11
Steinhaußen, Klaus, 'Kähling kehrt zurück', *NDL*, 8, No. 2 (February 1960), 3–37. (A shortened version of *Der Rückkehrer*, Halle, 1960)
Steiniger, Kurt, *Der Schöpfungstage sind nicht sechs*, Halle, 1965
Steinmann, Hans-Jürgen, *Die größere Liebe*, Berlin, 1960
Strittmatter, Erwin, *Ole Bienkopp*, Berlin und Weimar, 1963
Thürk, Harry, *Der Narr und das schwarzhaarige Mädchen*, Weimar, 1958
Wangenheim, Inge von, *Einer Mutter Sohn*, Berlin, 1958

'Reise ins Gestern', *NDL*, 15, No. 1 (January 1967), 84–141. (A shortened version of *Reise ins Gestern*. *Blick auf eine Stadt*, Halle, 1967)

Waterstradt, Berta, 'Der Familienmensch', *NDL*, 18, No. 1 (January 1970), 108–16

Werner, Ruth, *Über hundert Berge*, Berlin, 1965

Wohlgemuth, Joachim, *Verlobung in Hullerbusch*, Berlin, 1969

Wolf, Christa, *Der geteilte Himmel*, Halle, 1963. Quotation from the 14th edition, Halle, 1968

I(b) *West German fiction*

Andres, Stefan, *Die Dumme*, München, 1969

Anon., *Dreimal durch den Zaun*, Bonn, 1963 [published by the 'Bundesministerium für gesamtdeutsche Fragen']

Beckelmann, Jürgen, *Lachender Abschied*, Wuppertal-Barmen, 1969

Brandt, Heinz, *Ein Traum, der nicht entführbar ist. Mein Weg zwischen Ost und West*, München, 1967

Burkhardt, Joachim, *Zum Beispiel im Juni*, Zürich, Stuttgart, 1965

Christoff, Daniel, *Schaukelstühle*, Hamburg, 1964

Erb, Ute, *Die Kette an deinem Hals. Aufzeichnungen eines zornigen jungen Mädchens aus Mitteldeutschland*, Frankfurt am Main, 1960

Gaiser, Gerd, *Am Paß Nascondo*, München, 1960

Gregor-Dellin, Martin, *Der Kandelaber*, Olten und Freiburg im Br., 1962

Handke, Peter, 'Das Umfallen der Kegel von einer bäuerlichen Kegelbahn', *Der gewöhnliche Schrecken. Horrorgeschichten*, edited by Peter Handke, Salzburg, 1969, pp. 112–21

John, Otto, *Zweimal kam ich heim. Vom Verschwörer zum Schützer der Verfassung*, Düsseldorf, Wien, 1969

Johnson, Uwe, *Mutmaßungen über Jakob*, Frankfurt am Main, 1959

Das dritte Buch über Achim, Frankfurt am Main, 1961

Karsch, und andere Prosa, Frankfurt am Main, 1964

'Eine Kneipe geht verloren', *Kursbuch* 1 (1965), 47–72

Zwei Ansichten, Frankfurt am Main, 1965

Kempowski, Walter, *Uns geht's ja noch gold. Roman einer Familie*, München, 1972

Kirsch, Hans Christian, *Die zweite Flucht*, München, 1963

Deutschlandlied, Wiesbaden, 1969

Kroneberg, Eckart, *Der Grenzgänger*, Olten und Freiburg im Br., 1960

Leonhard, Wolfgang, *Die Revolution entläßt ihre Kinder*, Köln, [West] Berlin, 1955

Meichsner, Dieter, *Die Studenten von Berlin*, Hamburg, 1954

Mönnich, Horst, *Einreisegenehmigung. Ein Deutscher fährt nach Deutschland*, Hamburg, 1967

Müthel, Eva, *Für dich blüht kein Baum*, Frankfurt am Main, 1957

Norweg, Margarethe, 'Zonengrenze', *Liebe in unserer Zeit*, edited by Rolf Hochhuth, Hamburg, 1961, pp. 336–56

Olivier, Stefan, *Jedem das Seine*, Hamburg, 1961

BIBLIOGRAPHY

Paul, Wolfgang, *Einladung ins andere Deutschland*, Frankfurt am Main, 1967
Plate, Herbert, *Das soll der Mensch nicht scheiden*, Hamburg, 1960
Plievier, Theodor, *Berlin*, München, Wien, Basel, 1954
Putz, Helmut, *Die Abenteuer des braven Kommunisten Schwejk*, München
    und Esslingen, 1965
Schenk, Fritz, *Im Vorzimmer der Diktatur*, Köln, [West] Berlin, 1962
Schmidt, Arno, *Das steinerne Herz. Historischer Roman aus dem Jahre 1954*,
    Karlsruhe, 1956
Schnurre, Wolfdietrich, *Das Los unserer Stadt*, Olten und Freiburg im Br.,
    1959
'Der Zwiespalt', I & II, *Die Erzählungen*, Olten und Freiburg im Br., 1966,
    pp. 308–27
Sigismund, Ursula, *Grenzgänger*, Freiburg im Br., 1970
Simmel, Johannes Mario, *Lieb Vaterland magst ruhig sein*, München, 1965
Sonntag, Catrin, *Mein letztes Jahr. Mitteldeutsches Tagebuch*, München, 1966
Zwerenz, Gerhard, *Die Liebe der toten Männer*, Köln, [West] Berlin, 1959
Aufs Rad geflochten, Köln, [West] Berlin, 1959
Ärgernisse. Von der Maas bis an die Memel, Köln, [West] Berlin, 1961

SECONDARY LITERATURE

II(a) *Works of direct relevance to the theme 'divided Germany'*

Ahl, Herbert, 'Dichter des gespaltenen Deutschland. *Uwe Johnson*', *Literar-
    ische Portraits*, München und Wien, 1962, pp. 7–14
Anderle, Hans Peter, *Mitteldeutsche Erzähler. Eine Studie mit Proben und
    Porträts*, Köln, 1965
'DDR. Der Zensurapparat im Kopf', *Die Grenzen literarischer Freiheit.
    22 Beiträge über Zensur im In- und Ausland*, edited by Dieter Zimmer,
    Hamburg, 1966, pp. 150–8
Andrews, Robert C., '*Anna Seghers' Die Entscheidung*', *German Life &
    Letters*, 15 (1961–2), 259–63
'A Comic Novel from East Germany: Manfred Bieler, "Bonifaz oder Der
    Matrose in der Flasche" ', *German Life & Letters*, 20 (1966–7), 101–6
Apel, Hans, *Die DDR 1962–64–66*, [West] Berlin, 1967
'Bericht über das "Staatsgefühl" der DDR-Bevölkerung', *Frankfurter Hefte*,
    22 (1967), 169–78
Auer, Annemarie, '*Standorte-Erkundungen*.' *Acht kritische Versuche*, Halle,
    1967
Balluseck, Lothar von, *Dichter im Dienst. Der sozialistische Realismus in der
    deutschen Literatur*, 2nd, revised edition, Wiesbaden, 1963
'Die guten und die bösen Deutschen. Das Freund-Feind-Bild im Schrift-
    tum der DDR', *Aus Politik und Zeitgeschichte. Beilage zur Wochen-
    zeitung 'Das Parlament'*, B47/71, 20 November 1971
Baring, Arnulf, *Uprising in East Germany June 17, 1953* (translated from the
    German *Der 17. Juni 1953* by Gerald Onn), Ithaca, N.J., and London,
    1972

Baum, Werner, *Bedeutung und Gestalt. Über die sozialistische Novelle*, Halle, 1968

Bernhard, Hans-Joachim, 'Nationale Thematik in der Erzählung', *NDL*, 11, No. 5 (May 1963), 152–5

Bienek, Horst, *Werkstattgespräche mit Schriftstellern*, München, 1962

Bilke, Jörg B., 'Auf den Spuren der Wirklichkeit. DDR-Literatur: Traditionen, Tendenzen, Möglichkeiten', *Der Deutschunterricht*, 21, No. 5 (September 1969), 24–60
'Planziel Literaturgesellschaft oder Gibt es zwei deutsche Literaturen?', *Aus Politik und Zeitgeschichte. Beilage zur Wochenzeitung 'Das Parlament'*, B51/71, 18 December 1971

Blöcker, Günther, 'Roman der beiden Deutschland', *Kritisches Lesebuch*, [West] Berlin, 1962, pp. 191–5

Bock, Sigrid, 'Die schlafende bessere Zukunft ins Heute bringen. Zum Menschenbild in der Erzählung "Böhmen am Meer" von Franz Fühmann', *Konturen und Perspektiven. Zum Menschenbild in der Gegenwartsliteratur der Sowjetunion und der Deutschen Demokratischen Republik*, edited by the 'Arbeitsgruppe Sowjetische Gegenwartsliteratur am Institut für Slawistik der Deutschen Akademie der Wissenschaften in Berlin' [Leitung: A. Hiersche], Berlin, 1969, pp. 141–66

Boeschenstein, Hermann, 'Zur Erzähl-Thematik in der Literatur der DDR', *Trivium*, Special Publications 1, '*Erfahrung und Überlieferung*', *Festschrift for C. P. Magill*, Cardiff, 1974, pp. 166–84

Bornscheuer, Lothar, 'Wahlverwandtes? Zu Kants *Aula* und Heißenbüttels *D'Alemberts Ende*', *Basis. Jahrbuch für deutsche Gegenwartsliteratur*, 4 (1973), 201–34

Brandt, Sabine, 'Die Entscheidung der Anna Seghers. Ein Roman als Purgatorium', *Der Monat*, 12, No. 139 (April 1960), 77–81

Brandt, Willy, 'Bericht zur Lage der Nation', 14 January 1970; 'Bericht zur Lage der Nation', 28 January 1971. These speeches are contained in the *Verhandlungen des Deutschen Bundestages. 6. Wahlperiode. Stenographische Berichte*, Vol. 71, pp. 839–47, and Vol. 74, pp. 5043–51 respectively

Brecht, Bertolt, 'Realismus als kämpferische Methode', *Gesammelte Werke* Vol. 8, Frankfurt am Main, 1967, pp. 552–5

Brettschneider, Werner, *Zwischen literarischer Autonomie und Staatsdienst. Die Literatur in der DDR*, [West] Berlin, 1972

Brewer, Jim, et al., 'A Working Bibliography for the Study of the GDR', *New German Critique*, 1, No. 2 (Spring, 1974), 124–51

Brokerhoff, Karl Heinz, '*Wie sie uns sehen.' Schriftsteller der DDR über die Bundesrepublik*, Bonn-Bad Godesberg, 1970
'*Mit Liedern und Granaten.' DDR-Schulbücher über Soldaten in Ost und West*, Bonn-Bad Godesberg, 1972

Bundesministerium für gesamtdeutsche Fragen, *Die Presse in der Sowjetzone* [Bonner Fachbericht], Bonn, n.d.

Childs, David, *East Germany*, London, 1969

Christ, Richard, 'Braune Zensur', *NDL*, 14, No. 8 (August 1966), 176–7

Claudius, Eduard, *Paradies ohne Seligkeit*, Berlin, 1955

Cock, Mary, *The Presentation of Personality in the Novels of Max Frisch and Uwe Johnson*, unpublished D.Phil. dissertation, Oxford, 1969

'Uwe Johnson: An Interpretation of Two Novels', *Modern Language Review*, 69 (1974), 348–58

Crips, Liliane, 'La politique culturelle [de la RDA] de 1959 à 1971', *Allemagne d'Aujourdhui*, Nouvelle Série Nos. 37–38 (March–June 1973), 126–42

Cunliffe, W. Gordon, 'Uwe Johnson's Anti-Liberalism', *Mosaic*, 5, No. 3 (Spring 1972), 19–25

Cwojdrak, Günter, *Die literarische Aufrüstung*, Berlin, 1957

'Die zweite Literatur', *NDL*, 9, No. 5 (May 1961), 77–92

Eine Prise Polemik, Halle, 1965

Deicke, Günther, 'Hitler war Bundespräsident. Untertanentreue und Unwissenheit im westdeutschen Schulbuch', *NDL*, 8, No. 10 (October 1960) 141–3

Demetz, Peter, 'Literature in Ulbricht's Germany', *Problems in Communism*, 11 (1962), 15–21

Marx, Engels, and the Poets. Origins of Marxist Literary Criticism, revised, enlarged, and translated from the German *Marx, Engels und die Dichter* by Jeffrey L. Sammons, Chicago and London, 1967

Dening, Richard G., 'East German Literature and Technological Change', *Technology and Society*, 4, No. 1 (November 1967), 30–1

Deuerlein, Ernst, *Deutschland 1963–1970*, Hannover, 1972

Deutsche Akademie der Künste, 'Erklärung der Deutschen Akademie der Künste. Auf der außerordentlichen Plenartagung am 30. Mai 1962 vorgetragen von Stephan Hermlin', *Sinn und Form*, 14 (1962), 325–6

Dönhoff, Marion Gräfin, Rudolf Walter Leonhardt, and Theo Sommer, *Reise in ein fernes Land. Bericht über Kultur, Wirtschaft und Politik in der DDR*, Hamburg, 1964

Dunnett, Alan D., *Die Schilderung des Lebens in den zwei deutschen Staaten im frühen Werk Uwe Johnsons*, unpublished M. ès L. dissertation, Caen, 1975

Durzak, Manfred, *Der deutsche Roman der Gegenwart*, 2nd, revised edition, Stuttgart, 1973

Edwards, Gwyneth E., *The Theory of Socialist Realism and its Practical Application in East German Prose Fiction 1945–1966*, unpublished M.A. dissertation, University College of Wales, Aberystwyth, 1972

Ehlers, H., ' "Böhmen am Meer" – Erzähler und Erlebnis', *Sinn und Form*, 16 (1964), 475–8

Enzensberger, Hans Magnus, 'Die große Ausnahme. Über Uwe Johnson', *Einzelheiten*, Frankfurt am Main, 1962, pp. 234–9

Eser, Ruprecht, 'Jugend in der DDR', *Die Zeit*, 11 April 1969, p. 7

Faber, Franz, 'Unbewältigte Vergangenheit', *NDL*, 11, No. 1 (January 1963), 213–15

Feitknecht, Thomas, *Die sozialistische Heimat. Zum Selbstverständnis neuerer DDR-Romane*, Berlin und Frankfurt am Main, 1971

Flores, John, *Poetry in East Germany. Adjustments, Visions, and Provocations, 1945–1970,* New Haven, Conn., and London, 1971

Franke, Karl, 'Berichte über die DDR – Nachgelesen. Beiträge zum Deutschland-Bild', *Frankfurter Hefte,* 21 (1966), 383–9

Franke, Konrad, *Die Literatur der Deutschen Demokratischen Republik,* 2nd, revised edition, München und Zürich, 1974

Geerdts, Hans Jürgen, 'Gedanken zur Diskussion über die sozialistische Nationalkultur', *Weimarer Beiträge,* 9 (1963), 100–149

Geerdts (ed.), *Literatur der DDR in Einzeldarstellungen,* Stuttgart, 1972

Geisthardt, Hans Joachim, 'Das Thema der Nation und zwei Literaturen', *NDL,* 14, No. 6 (June 1966), 48–69

Good, Colin H., *The German Language and the Communist Ideology. Studies in Usage and Meaning in the special Language of East German Communism,* unpublished Ph.D. dissertation, Bristol, 1971. Some of this material is incorporated into *Die deutsche Sprache und die kommunistische Ideologie,* Bern, Frankfurt am Main, 1975

'Uwe Johnson's Treatment of the Narrative in "Mutmaßungen über Jakob" ', *German Life & Letters,* 24 (1970–71), 358–70

Greiner, Bernhard, *Von der Allegorie zur Idylle: Die Literatur der Arbeitswelt in der DDR,* Heidelberg, 1974

Grosser, Alfred, *L'Allemagne de notre temps 1945–1970,* Paris, 1970. A German translation appeared simultaneously with the publication of the French original: *Deutschlandbilanz,* München, 1970, while an English translation appeared in the following year: *Germany in Our Time. A Political History of the Postwar Years,* London, 1971

Grunert-Bronnen, Barbara (ed.), *Ich bin Bürger der DDR und lebe in der Bundesrepublik. 12 Interviews,* München, 1970

Haase, Horst, et al., *Geschichte der deutschen Literatur von den Anfängen bis zur Gegenwart. Elfter Band: Literatur der Deutschen Demokratischen Republik,* Berlin, 1976

Hager, Kurt, 'Freude an jedem gelungenen Werk', *NDL,* 11, No. 8 (August 1963), 61–72

Hearnden, Arthur, *Bildungspolitik in der BRD und der DDR,* Düsseldorf, 1973; English translation *Education in the Two Germanies,* Oxford, 1974

Heiduczek, Werner, and Heinz Plavius, 'Ein Meinungsaustausch', *NDL,* 16, No. 8 (August 1968), 117–25

Heise, Rosemarie, 'Die Bürde der Vergangenheit', *NDL,* 7, No. 8 (August 1959), 132–4

'Das große Thema', *NDL,* 11, No. 6 (June 1963), 148–53

Herd, E. W., 'Narrative Technique in Two Novels by Herman Kant', *Trivium,* Special Publications 1, *'Erfahrung und Überlieferung',* Festschrift for C. P. Magill, Cardiff, 1974, pp. 185–96

Hermlin, Stephan, 'Braune Presse', *Sinn und Form,* 20 (1968), 1015–18

Hermsdorf, Klaus, 'Aufforderung zur Tat', *NDL,* 8, No. 11 (November 1960), 143–7

'Die nationale Bedeutung der sozialistischen Nationalliteratur', *Weimarer Beiträge,* 7 (1961), 290–315

Herrmann, E. M., *Zur Theorie und Praxis der Presse in der Sowjetischen Besatzungszone Deutschlands. Berichte und Dokumente*, [West] Berlin, 1963

Hildebrandt, Dieter, *Die Mauer ist keine Grenze. Menschen in Ostberlin*, Düsseldorf, Köln, 1964

Hinckel, Erika, 'Zwei deutsche Staaten und die Perspektive der deutschen Nationalliteratur', *Einheit*, 21 (1966), 915–25

Hochmuth, Arno (ed.), *Literatur im Blickpunkt. Zum Menschenbild in der Literatur der beiden deutschen Staaten*, 2nd revised edition, Berlin, 1967

Hölsken, Hans Georg, *Jüngere Romane aus der DDR im Deutschunterricht. Ein Beitrag zur politischen Bildung*, Hannover, 1969

Hutchinson, Peter, ' "Conditioned against us. . ." ' The East German View of the Federal Republic', *Forum for Modern Language Studies*, 8 (1972), 40–51

'Franz Fühmann's "Böhmen am Meer": A Socialist Version of "The Winter's Tale" ', *Modern Language Review*, 67 (1972), 579–89

Institut für Marxismus-Leninismus beim Zentralkomitee der SED, *Geschichte der deutschen Arbeiterbewegung von 1945 bis 1963*, 3 vols., Berlin, 1967–8

Jacobs, Wilhelm, 'Das zweigeteilte Deutschland', *Moderne deutsche Literatur*, Gütersloh, n.d., pp. 162–70

Jäger, Manfred, *Sozialliteraten. Funktion und Selbstverständnis der Schriftsteller in der DDR*, Düsseldorf, 1973

Jarmatz, Klaus, 'Variationen über das Glück', *Kritik in der Zeit. Der Sozialismus – seine Literatur – ihre Entwicklung*, Halle, 1970, pp. 887–91

Jens, Walter, 'Uwe Johnson auf der Schwelle der Meisterschaft', *Die Zeit*, 6 October 1961, p. 18

Joho, Wolfgang, 'Die Aufgabe des Schriftstellers in dieser Zeit', *NDL*, 2, No. 6 (June 1954), pp. 147–50

Zwischen Bonn und Bodensee, Berlin, 1954

'Blickpunkt Westen', *NDL*, 7, No. 5 (May 1959), 133–5

'Unsere nationale Aufgabe' *NDL*, 9, No. 1 (January 1961) 10–14

'Der Schriftsteller in der neuen Literaturgesellschaft', *Sonntag*, 22 June 1969, *Sonderbeilage*, pp. 20–1

Jokostra, Peter, 'Außenseiter hüben wie drüben', *Die Welt der Literatur*, 8 May 1969, p. 6

Kant, Hermann, 'Darmstädter Dilemma', *NDL*, 8, No. 8 (August 1960), 161–3

'Vielfaches Unbehagen und ein Modell', *NDL*, 9, No. 3 (March 1961), 114–29

'Macht und Ohnmacht einer Literatur', *NDL*, 9, No. 8 (August 1961), 62–80

'Verschiedenes zum Gemeinsamen', *NDL*, 14, No. 6 (June 1966), 3–6

Kloehn, Ekkerhard, 'Christa Wolf: *Der geteilte Himmel*. Roman zwischen sozialistischem Realismus und kritischem Sozialismus', *Der Deutschunterricht*, 20, No. 1 (January 1968), 43–56

Koch, Hans, *Unsere Literaturgesellschaft – Kritik und Polemik*, Berlin, 1965

'Stichworte zum sozialistischen Realismus', *Weimarer Beiträge*, 16, No. 1 (January 1970), 10–38

Korall, Harald, 'Einmal dies schreiben–Zur Genesis eines Romans', *NDL*, 17, No. 1 (January 1969), 145–8

Kraft, Hans Jürgen, 'La politique culturelle [de la RDA] de 1945 à 1959', *Allemagne d'Aujourdhui*, Nouvelle Série Nos 37–38 (March–June, 1973) 105–25

Krispyn, Egbert, 'The Radioplay in the German Democratic Republic', *German Life & Letters*, 21 (1967–8), 45–58

Krömer, Tilman, 'Wertung in marxistischer deutscher Literaturbetrachtung', *Der Deutschunterricht*, 9, No. 5 (September 1963), 75–89

Krumholz, Walter (ed.), *Berlin - ABC*, 2nd, revised edition, [West] Berlin, 1968

Leier, Manfred, 'Die deutsche Teilung – literarisch', *moderne welt*, 8 (1967), 166–82

Leistner, Bernd, 'Die Reise in das andere Deutschland. Zu Wolfgang Johos Buch "Das Klassentreffen" ', *Deutsch als Fremdsprache*, 6 (1969), 451–4

Leonhardt, Rudolf Walter, 'Die deutsche Teilung in Literatur und Kunst', *Neue Zürcher Zeitung*, 18 September 1966, pp. 7–8

Liersch, Werner, 'Roman der Restauration', *NDL*, 8, No. 8 (August 1960), 145–9

Lilge, Herbert, *Deutschland 1945–1963*, 4th, revised edition, Hannover, 1972

Lingenberg, Jörg, *Das Fernsehspiel in der DDR. Ein Beitrag zur Erforschung künstlerischer Formen marxistisch-leninistischer Publizistik*, München–Pullach, 1963

Lücke, P. R., *Das Schulbuch in der Sowjetzone. Lehrbücher im Dienst totalitärer Propaganda*, Bonn und [West] Berlin, 1961

Ludz, Peter C., *Parteielite im Wandel*, Köln und Opladen, 1968. Abbreviated and revised as *The Changing Party Elite in East Germany*, Cambridge, Mass. and London, 1972

  The German Democratic Republic from the Sixties to the Seventies. A Socio-Political Analysis, Cambridge, Mass., 1970

  DDR Handbuch, Köln, 1975

Mayer, Hans, *Zur deutschen Literatur der Zeit. Zusammenhänge, Schriftsteller, Bücher*, Reinbek, 1967

Merritt, Richard L., 'Politics, Theater, and the East-West Struggle. The Theater as a Cultural Bridge in West Berlin', *Political Science Quarterly*, 80 (1965), 186–215

Meyer-Erlach, W., 'The Cultural Scene in Germany Today', *Germany Today. Introductory Studies*, edited by J. P. Payne, London, 1971, pp. 153–78

Meyn, Hermann, *Massenmedien in der Bundesrepublik*, [West] Berlin, 1966

Milger, Peter, 'Wildwest an der Zonengrenze', *Pardon*, 3, No. 2 (February 1964), 16–17

Mohr, Heinrich, 'Gerechtes Erinnern. Untersuchungen zu Thema und Struktur von Hermann Kants Roman "Die Aula" und einige Anmerkungen zu bundesrepublikanischen Rezensionen', *Germanisch-Romanische Monatsschrift*, 21 (1971), 225–45

Nalewski, Horst, '*Sprachkünstlerische Gestaltung.*' *Stilkritische Anmerkungen zur jüngeren Epik*, Halle, 1968

Neubert, Werner, 'Komisches und Satirisches in Hermann Kants "Aula"', *Weimarer Beiträge*, 12 (1966), 15–26

Neue Deutsche Literatur [Redaktion], 'Der Jahreskonferenz entgegen. Der Stand der Literatur und die Aufgaben der Schriftsteller in der DDR', *NDL*, 14, No. 7 (July 1966), 186–200

Nolte, Jost, 'Anderenorts', *Grenzgänge*, Wien, 1972, 141–99

Orlow, Peter, *Die Bitterfelder Sackgasse. Literaturpolitik der SED zwischen 1965 und 1969*, *Die Orientierung*, Erstes Beiheft, 1970

Plavius, Heinz, 'Tendenzen und Probleme der Prosa', *NDL*, 24, No. 1 (January 1976), 28–37

Pongs, Hermann, *Dichtung im gespaltenen Deutschland*, Stuttgart, 1966

Popper, Hans, 'Uwe Johnson', *Twentieth Century German Literature*, edited by A. Closs, London, 1969, pp. 289–90

Prévost, Claude, 'Romans à l'Ouest et à l'Est, mais romans allemands', *alternative*, 38–39 (October 1964), 101–6

Raddatz, Fritz J., 'Tradition und Traditionsbruch in der Literatur der DDR', *Merkur*, 19 (1965), 666–81

'DDR-Literatur und marxistische Ästhetik', *Germanic Review*, 43 (1969), 40–60

'Zur Entwicklung der Literatur in der DDR', *Die deutsche Literatur der Gegenwart. Aspekte und Tendenzen*, edited by Manfred Durzak, Stuttgart, 1971, 337–65

Traditionen und Tendenzen. Materialien zur Literatur der DDR, Frankfurt am Main, 1971

Reich, Hans H., *Sprache und Politik. Untersuchungen zu Wortschatz und Wortwahl des offiziellen Sprachgebrauchs in der DDR*, München, 1968

Reichelt, Paul, *Deutsche Chronik 1945 bis 1970. Daten und Fakten aus beiden Teilen Deutschlands*, 2 vols., Bonn, 1970

Reich-Ranicki, Marcel, *Deutsche Literatur in West und Ost. Prosa seit 1945*, München, 1963

'The Writer in East Germany', *Survey*, 61 (October 1966), 188–95

Wer schreibt, provoziert. Kommentare und Pamphlete, München, 1966

Literarisches Leben in Deutschland. Kommentare und Pamphlete, München, 1965

Literatur der kleinen Schritte. Deutsche Schriftsteller heute, München, 1967

'Bankrott einer Erzählerin. Anna Seghers' Roman "Das Vertrauen"', *Die Zeit*, 14 March 1969, p. 28

Zur Literatur der DDR, München, 1974

Reso, Martin (ed.), '*Der geteilte Himmel' und seine Kritiker*, Halle, 1965

Richert, Ernst, *Das zweite Deutschland. Ein Staat, der nicht sein darf*, 2nd, revised edition, Frankfurt am Main und Hamburg, 1966

Richter, Hans Werner, *Die Mauer oder Der 13. August*, Reinbek, 1961

Rothe, Friedrich, 'Sozialistischer Realismus in der DDR-Literatur', *Poesie und Politik. Zur Situation der Literatur in Deutschland*, edited by Wolfgang Kuttenkeuler, Stuttgart, 1973, pp. 184–205

Rothmund, A., *Der englische und französische Unterricht in den Schulen der SBZ*, Bonn, 1965

Rouse, Helen Ritchie, *The Image of the 'New Society' in East German Novels of the 1960s*, unpublished M.A. dissertation, Sheffield, 1973

Rudolph, Hermann, *Die Gesellschaft der DDR – eine deutsche Möglichkeit?*, München, 1972

Rühle, Jürgen, 'Schwierigkeiten der Verständigung. Die Interpretation der ostzonalen Wirklichkeit', *Der Monat*, 12, No. 136 (January 1960), 70–7

Literatur und Revolution. Die Schriftsteller und der Kommunismus, 2nd, revised edition, München und Zürich, 1963

Sander, Hans-Dietrich, *Geschichte der Schönen Literatur in der DDR*, Freiburg im Br., 1972

Sauter, Josef-Hermann, 'Interview mit Franz Fühmann', *Weimarer Beiträge*, 17, No. 1 (January 1971), 33–53

Schimanski, Hans, *Leitgedanken und Methoden der kommunistischen Indoktrination. Parteischulung, Agitation und Propaganda in der Sowjetischen Besatzungszone Deutschlands*, Bonn und [West] Berlin, 1965

Schlenstedt, Dieter, 'Motive und Symbole in Christa Wolfs Erzählung "Der geteilte Himmel" ', *Weimarer Beiträge*, 10 (1964), 77–104

Schnurre, Wolfdietrich, *Berlin – Eine Stadt wird geteilt. Bilddokumentation*, Olten und Freiburg im Br., 1962

Die Mauer des 13. August. Bilddokumentation, [West] Berlin, 1962

Schubbe, Elimar (ed.), *Dokumente zur Kunst-, Literatur- und Kulturpolitik der SED, 1945–1971*, Stuttgart, 1972

Seghers, Anna, 'Anna Seghers über ihre Schaffensmethode. Ein Gespräch', *NDL*, 7, No. 8 (August 1959), 52–7

Siebert, Horst, *Der andere Teil Deutschlands in Schulbüchern der BRD und der DDR. Ein Beitrag zur politischen Bildung in Deutschland*, Hamburg, 1970

Smith, Jean Edward, *Germany beyond the Wall. People, Politics and Prosperity*, Boston and Toronto, 1969

Sontheimer, Kurt, and Wilhelm Bleek, *Die DDR. Politik, Gesellschaft, Wirtschaft*, Hamburg, 1972. Also available in English translation as *The Government and Politics of East Germany*, London, 1975

Steinhaußen, Ursula, Dieter Faulseit, and Jürgen Bonk (eds.), *Handbuch für schreibende Arbeiter*, Berlin, 1969

Stern, Guy, 'Prolegomena zu einer Studie der deutschen Nachkriegsliteratur', *Colloquia Germanica*, 1 (1967), 233–52

Stroh, Franz, and Gören Löfdahl (eds.), *Zweimal Deutschland?*, Stockholm, 1966

Tailleur, Jean, 'Entretien avec Fritz Rudolf Fries', *Lettres Françaises*, 2 December 1970, pp. 7–8

Tank, Kurt Lothar, and Wilhelm Jacobs, 'Die literarische Entwicklung von der Befreiung Deutschlands vom Faschismus bis zur Bildung der beiden deutschen Staaten', *Geschichte der deutschen Literatur aus Methoden. Westdeutsche Literatur von 1945–71*, edited by Heinz Ludwig Arnold, 3 vols., Frankfurt am Main, 1973, vol. 1, pp. 53–96

Thalheim, Hans G., and Dieter Schiller, 'Diskussion zu aktuellen Aufgaben der Literaturwissenschaft', *Weimarer Beiträge*, 12 (1966), 3–9

Thomas, Rüdiger, *Modell DDR*. *Die kalkulierte Emanzipation*, München, 1972

Trommler, Frank, 'Der zögernde Nachwuchs. Entwicklungsprobleme der Nachkriegsliteratur in Ost und West', *Tendenzen der deutschen Literatur seit 1945*, edited by Thomas Koebner, Stuttgart, 1971, pp. 1–116

'Von Stalin zu Hölderlin. Über den Entwicklungsroman in der DDR', *Basis. Jahrbuch für deutsche Gegenwartsliteratur*, 2 (1971), 141–90

'DDR-Erzählung und Bitterfelder Weg', *Basis. Jahrbuch für deutsche Gegenwartsliteratur*, 3 (1972), 61–97

Tulasiewicz, Witold F., introduction to Anna Seghers, *Die Hochzeit von Haiti*, London, 1970

Ulbricht, Walter, 'Fragen der deutschen Nationalliteratur', *Neues Deutschland*, 17 January 1956, reprinted in *Dokumente zur Kunst-, Literatur- und Kulturpolitik der SED*, edited by Elimar Schubbe, Stuttgart, 1972, pp. 421–6

'Zu einigen Fragen der Literatur und Kunst', *NDL*, 14, No. 2 (February 1966), 3–10

Voßkamp, Wilhelm, *Deutsche Zeitgeschichte in der Gegenwartsliteratur*, Flensburg, 1968

Wehr, Marianne, 'Griff in westdeutsche Gegenwart', *NDL*, 18, No. 12 (December 1970), 165–8

Weimarer Beiträge [Redaktion], 'Die literarische Entwicklung in der Deutschen Demokratischen Republik', *Abschnitt VIII* of 'Skizze zur Geschichte der deutschen Nationalliteratur von den Anfängen der deutschen Arbeiterbewegung bis zur Gegenwart' *Weimarer Beiträge*, 10 (1964), 644–812 (783–812)

Wiegenstein, Roland H., 'Zur Situation der Schriftsteller in der DDR', *Neue Rundschau*, 77 (1966), 330–4

Winter, Helmut, 'East German Literature', *Essays on Contemporary German Literature*, edited by Brian Keith-Smith, London, 1968, pp. 261–80

Wolf, Christa, 'Land, in dem wir leben. Die deutsche Frage in dem Roman "Die Entscheidung" von Anna Seghers', *NDL*, 9, No. 5 (May 1961), 49–65

'Notwendiges Streitgespräch', *NDL*, 14, No. 3 (March 1966), 97–104

'Deutsch sprechen', *Lesen und Schreiben. Aufsätze und Prosastücke*, Darmstadt und Neuwied, 1972, pp. 9–18

Zentralkomitee der SED, 'Entschließung des Zentralkomitees der Sozialistischen Einheitspartei Deutschlands, angenommen auf der V. Tagung vom 15. bis 17. März 1951', reprinted in *Dokumente zur Kunst-, Literatur- und Kulturpolitik der SED*, edited by Elimar Schubbe, Stuttgart, 1972, pp. 178–86

Ziermann, Klaus, 'Einbruch der Barbaren. Anmerkungen zur Taschenbuchproduktion in Westdeutschland', *Sinn und Form*, 20 (1968), 1254–64

Romane vom Fließband. Die imperialistische Massenliteratur in Westdeutschland, Berlin, 1969

BIBLIOGRAPHY

Zwerenz, Gerhard, 'Das gespaltene Wort', *Der Monat*, 12, No. 143 (August 1960), 76–88

II(b) *Other works mentioned*

Bieler, Manfred, 'Das verschluckte Herzogtum', *Sinn und Form*, 16 (1964), 831–57

Biermann, Wolf, *Deutschland. Ein Wintermärchen*, [West] Berlin, 1972

Bock, Claus Victor (ed.), *Deutsche erfahren Holland, 1725–1925. Eine Sammlung von hundert Berichten*, Den Haag, 1956

Böll, Heinrich, *Billard um halb zehn*, Köln, [West] Berlin, 1959

Ansichten eines Clowns, Köln, [West] Berlin, 1963

Ende einer Dienstfahrt, Köln, [West] Berlin, 1966

Booth, Wayne C., *The Rhetoric of Fiction*, Chicago, 1961

Brecht, Bertolt, 'Der anachronistische Zug oder Freiheit und Democracy', *Gesammelte Werke*, Vol. 4, Frankfurt am Main, 1967, pp. 943–49

Bredel, Willi, *Ein neues Kapitel. Erstes Buch. Chronik einer Wandlung* 'Erweiterte und bearbeitete Ausgabe', Berlin und Weimar, 1966

Campos, Christopher, *The View of France*, London, 1965

Curtin, Philipp D., *The Image of Africa. British Ideas and Action, 1780–1850*, London, 1965

Daiches, David, *Critical Approaches to Literature*, London, 1956

Dalnekoff, Donna Isaacs, 'A Familiar Stranger: The Outsider of Eighteenth Century Satire', *Neophilologus*, 57 (1973), pp. 121–34

Demetz, Peter, 'Notes on Figurative Names in Theodor Fontane's Novels', *Germanic Review*, 37 (1962), 96–105

Esser, Manfred, *Duell*, Olten und Freiburg im Br., 1961

Frisch, Max, *Homo Faber*, Frankfurt am Main, 1957

Mein Name sei Gantenbein, Frankfurt am Main, 1964

Fühmann, Franz, *Kameraden*, Berlin, 1955

Der Jongleur im Kino. Studien zur bürgerlichen Gesellschaft, Berlin, 1970

Gaiser, Gerd, *Am Paß Nascondo*, München, 1960

Geißler, Christian, *Anfrage*, Hamburg, 1960

Gerlach, Jens, 'Ich weiß nicht, was soll es bedeuten', '*Wie sie uns sehen.*' *Schriftsteller der DDR über die Bundesrepublik*, edited by K. H. Brokerhoff, pp. 21–2

Gombrich, Ernst H., *Art und Illusion*, 4th, revised edition, London, 1972

Grass, Günter, *Die Blechtrommel*, Darmstadt, [West] Berlin, Neuwied, 1959

Hundejahre, Neuwied und [West] Berlin, 1963

Die Plebejer proben den Aufstand. Ein deutsches Trauerspiel, Neuwied und [West] Berlin, 1966

örtlich betäubt, Neuwied und [West] Berlin, 1969

Gregor-Dellin, Manfred, *Der Nullpunkt*, Wien, München, Basel, 1959

Greenberger, Allen J., *The British Image of India. A Study in the Literature of Imperialism 1880–1960*, London, 1969

Hermlin, Stephan, 'Die Kommandeuse', *Erzählungen*, Berlin und Weimar, 1966, pp. 221–36

BIBLIOGRAPHY

Johannsen, Christa, *Flug nach Zypern*, Berlin, 1969
Kruschel, Heinz, *Jeder Abschied ist ein kleines Sterben*, Berlin, 1958
Künert, Günter, 'Wo Deutschland lag...', *Tagwerke. Gedichte, Lieder, Balladen*, Halle, 1961
Lütkens, Charlotte, and Walther Karle, *Das Bild vom Ausland. Fremdsprachliche Lektüre an höheren Schulen in Deutschland, England und Frankreich*, München, 1959
Meyer, Herman, *The Poetics of Quotation in the European Novel*, translated from the German *Das Zitat in der Erzählkunst* by Theodore and Yetta Ziolkowski, Princeton, N. J., 1968
Morawietz, Kurt (ed.), *Deutsche Teilung. Ein Lyrik-Lesebuch*, Wiesbaden, 1966
Nachbar, Herbert, *Oben fährt der große Wagen*, Rostock, 1963
Opitz, Karlludwig, *Im Tornister: Ein Marschallstab! Die jähe Karriere eines braven Soldaten. Aus seinem brieflichen Nachlass geordnet*, Berlin, 1959
Palmer, Roy E., *French Travellers in England (1600–1900)*, London, 1960
Peacock, Ronald, *Criticism and Personal Taste*, Oxford, 1972
Possin, Hans-Joachim, *Reisen und Literatur. Das Thema des Reisens in der englischen Literatur des 18. Jahrhunderts*, Tübingen, 1972
Robson-Scott, William Douglas, *German Travellers in England, 1600–1800*, Oxford, 1953
Sallmon, Heinz, Liesel Rumland, and Wilfried Bütow, 'Grundpositionen des Literaturunterrichts bei der Verwirklichung der Forderungen des neuen Lehrplans und der Aufgabenstellung für die staatsbürgerliche Erziehung', *Deutschunterricht*, 23, No. 1 (January 1970), 2–9
Schallück, Paul, *Engelbert Reinecke*, Frankfurt am Main und Hamburg, 1959
Schneider, Rolf, 'Die Unbewältigten', first published in *Hörspiele*, 4, edited by the 'Staatliche Rundfunkkomitee der Deutschen Demokratischen Republik'; reprinted in '*Wie sie uns sehen*'. *Schriftsteller der DDR über die Bundesrepublik*, edited by K. H. Brokerhoff, Bonn–Bad Godesberg, 1972, pp. 120–49
Der Tod des Nibelungen. Aufzeichnungen des deutschen Bildschöpfers Siegfried Amadeus Wruck ediert von Freunden, Rostock, 1970
'Krankenbesuch', *Stimmen danach*, Rostock, 1970, pp. 287–321
Schwachhofer, René, 'Westdeutscher Tatbestand', *NDL*, 8, No. 2 (February 1960), 37
Seghers, Anna, *Die Toten bleiben jung*, Berlin und Weimar, 1949
Seidel, Ina, *Michaela. Aufzeichnungen des Jürgen Brook*, Stuttgart, 1959
Spiller, Robert E., 'The magic mirror of American fiction. A study of the novel of national self-inquiry as an instrument of international (mis)understanding', *Problems of International Literary Understanding*, edited by Karl Ragnar Gierow, Stockholm, 1968
Stanzel, Franz, *Typische Formen des Romans*, Göttingen, 1964
Steinberg, Werner, *Wechsel auf die Zukunft*, Halle, 1958
Stern, Joseph Peter, introduction to Arthur Schnitzler, *Liebelei, Leutnant Gustl, Die letzten Masken*, Cambridge, 1966
'War and the Comic Muse', *Comparative Literature*, 20 (1968), 193–216

Stopp, Frederick J., *The Art of Exposition in Lessing's Prose Works*, unpublished Ph.D. dissertation, London, 1948

Sucksmith, Harvey Peter, *The Narrative Art of Charles Dickens*, Oxford, 1970

Trauberg, Ursula, *Vorleben*, Frankfurt am Main, 1968

Wallraff, Hans-Günther, 'Hier und Dort', *Deutsche Teilung. Ein Lyrik-Lesebuch*, edited by Kurt Morawietz, Wiesbaden, 1966, p. 105

Walser, Martin, *Halbzeit*, Frankfurt am Main, 1963
Das Einhorn, Frankfurt am Main, 1966

Weinert, Erich, 'Genauso hat es damals angefangen', *Die Weltbühne*, 1 (1946), 357–8

Wellek, René, and Austin Warren, *Theory of Literature*, New York, 1956

Weyrauch, Wolfgang, *Ich lebe in der Bundesrepublik*, München, 1960

Wolf, Christa, *Nachdenken über Christa T.*, Halle, 1968 [1969]

Wondratschek, Wolf, *Früher begann der Tag mit einer Schußwunde*, München, 1969

INDEX